Additional

"A biography with the verve and pace of a delicious novel . . . a polemic and a pleasure. Showalter deploys her prodigious research and narrative skills, acerbic wit, and feminist commitments to reveal the entwining of Howe's public and private lives, as she righteously battled her husband and society, and finally saw the glory she always believed she deserved."

—*The Boston Globe*

"Fascinating are the personal tribulations that the feminist critic Elaine Showalter probes in her unfailingly vivid—and fair-minded—biography."

—*The Atlantic*

"In a riveting and frankly distressing new biography, the distinguished critic Elaine Showalter insists that Howe, who was born in the same year as Walt Whitman, had 'the subversive intellect of an Emily Dickinson, the political and philosophical interests of an Elizabeth Barrett Browning, and the passionate emotions of a Sylvia Plath.' The problem was her world and, more particularly, her husband."

—*The New York Times Book Review*

"This lively biography of the author of the 'Battle Hymn of the Republic' focuses on what her marriage expresses about the position of women in the nineteenth century."

—*The New Yorker*

"[An] invigorating feminist biography."

—*O: The Oprah Magazine*

"[An] excellent new biography."

—*Harper's Magazine*

"Howe becomes far more than a woman who happened to author a landmark anthem. She emerges as a woman readers will know intimately, and admire for her resoluteness as an early feminist. . . . Showalter masterfully fits it all together . . . Settle in for an absorbing story. . . . [a] powerful biography."

—*Christian Science Monitor*

"Showalter has bravely taken on the task of examining the inner workings of a marriage that ended nearly a century and a half ago. That she succeeds as well as she does is a tribute not only to her scholarly diligence, but also to her proven historical curiosity and her fluent prose. . . . a model of fairness."

—*The New York Review of Books*

"An energetic new look at the author of the lyrics for 'The Battle Hymn of the Republic' finds a modern feminist thread in the heroine's frustrated marriage. . . . A rich life, well deserving of reconsideration."

—*Kirkus Reviews*

"Fresh, delightfully rendered and revealing . . . [an] engaging portrait of a marriage, a society and one woman's struggle for emancipation."

—*Austin American Statesman*

"A robust and enlightening feminist portrait of a national icon."

—*Booklist* (starred review)

"[A] finely rendered biography."

—*The Wall Street Journal*

"Showalter proves there is much more to be known about Howe's achievements, political activism, and feminist commitment. . . . Showalter presents a new, multifaceted interpretation of Howe, the first woman to be inducted into the American Academy of Arts and Letters. . . highly readable and absorbing."

—*Library Journal*

"Showalter skillfully reveals the depths of Howe's pain and talent."

—*Publishers Weekly*

"Elaine Showalter is that rarity: a scholar, feminist historian, sharp-eyed cultural critic, with a knack for choosing subjects that are both entertaining and brilliantly illuminating. *The Civil Wars of Julia Ward Howe* is written with Showalter's usual witty, sparkling, and erudite style. This zestfully narrated life of an early, pioneering feminist, a tireless crusader for social reform and women's rights, would make an ideal PBS series—indeed, all the parts are in place for a felicitous adaptation of Showalter's gem of a biography of a truly remarkable American woman."

—Joyce Carol Oates

"Famous as the author of 'Battle Hymn of the Republic,' Julia Ward Howe had a memorable career beyond this single momentous achievement, as a poet, abolitionist, mother, lecturer, and feminist. This splendid biography shows how Julia emerged from her private tribulations as a stronger and more complete person."

—James McPherson, author of *The War that Forged a Nation: Why the Civil War Still Matters*

"In this gracefully presented biography of the woman we remember as the author of the nation's signature hymn, we find ourselves fighting along with Julia Ward Howe as she wages her long struggle for independence as a nineteenth-century daughter, wife, and mother."

—Cokie Roberts, author of *Capital Dames, The Civil War and the Women of Washington*

"Glory! Glory! Hallelujah! At last a full, fine, modern biography of the independent woman whose words reanimated the American Civil War and crowned Lincoln, its greatest hero, with a worthy anthem."

—Harold Holzer, author of *Lincoln and the Power of the Press*, winner of the Lincoln Prize

"An accomplished literary critic, Elaine Showalter draws on journals and letters to give us a true story worthy of fiction. This finely rendered portrait of the oppressive marriage and inner turmoil that fueled Julia Ward Howe's writing and her later activism on behalf of women's suffrage compels a feminist reinterpretation of the iconic 'Battle Hymn of the Republic.'"

—Ellen Chesler, author of *Woman of Valor: Margaret Sanger and the Birth Control Movement in America*

"Showalter brings Julia Ward Howe alive as a fascinating and powerful woman rather than a legend on a postage stamp—a feminist pioneer who was as witty, engaging, and intrepid as she was scholarly, literary, and enlightened."

—Wendy Martin, Professor of American Literature and American Studies, Claremont Graduate University

"Elaine Showalter has brilliantly narrated the life of Julia Ward Howe, with her unhappy marriage to the famed Samuel Gridley Howe, her dislike of motherhood, and the unpublished novel she wrote about a transgender man. This historical biography is timely, as it shows us the underside of a famed Victorian marriage and how patriarchal attitudes could trap even a powerful woman. The story of how she released herself form the emotional captivity of that marriage through becoming a leader in the woman's movement is inspiring in our own day of considerable backlash against woman's rights. The book is beautifully written—and a delight to read."

—Lois W. Banner, Professor Emeritus,
History and Gender Studies

"Elaine Showalter has produced a compelling portrait of an American literary luminary whose extraordinary career deserves just the kind of exacting reappraisal this biography offers. From a marriage marked by private domestic turmoil, Julia Ward Howe moved onto the public stage with the assertion that 'A comet dire and strange am I,' but by the time she died, at ninety, the poet of 'The Battle Hymn of the Republic' had become an impassioned feminist, a national celebrity, and—in the words of a 1940s admirer—one of the 'Wonder Women of History.' Showalter's introduction to the civil wars and triumphs of her life is utterly absorbing."

—Sandra M. Gilbert, Distinguished Professor Emerita,
University of California, Davis

"Fascinating, readable and beautifully done, Elaine Showalter offers us a deeply studied portrait of a nineteenth-century woman poet, Julia Ward Howe, who found herself imprisoned, her gifts stifled, in her marriage to an autocrat resistant to a wife's right to publish her work. This biography, at once profoundly feminist and balanced, and rounded out with the full range of Howe's achievements as a mother, visionary suffragist and reformer, fulfills Virginia Woolf's ideal: to select for the facts that 'suggest and engender.'"

—Lyndall Gordon, author of *Lives Like Loaded Guns:*
Emily Dickinson and Her Family's Feuds

ALSO BY ELAINE SHOWALTER

A Jury of Her Peers: American Women Writers from Anne Bradstreet to Annie Proulx

Faculty Towers: The Academic Novel and Its Discontents

Teaching Literature

Inventing Herself: Claiming a Feminist Intellectual Heritage

Hystories: Hysterical Epidemics and Modern Culture

Sister's Choice: Tradition and Change in American Women's Writing

Sexual Anarchy: Gender and Creativity in the Fin-de-siècle

The Female Malady: Women, Madness and Culture

A Literature of Their Own: British Women Novelists from Brontë to Lessing

The CIVIL WARS *of* JULIA WARD HOWE

A Biography

Elaine Showalter

SIMON & SCHUSTER PAPERBACKS
New York London Toronto Sydney New Delhi

For Jack and Evan Catherine LaFleur
Emmy and Rose Showalter

Simon & Schuster Paperbacks
An Imprint of Simon & Schuster, Inc.
1230 Avenue of the Americas
New York, NY 10020

First Simon & Schuster paperback edition February 2017

SIMON & SCHUSTER PAPERBACKS and colophon are registered trademarks of Simon & Schuster, Inc.

For information about special discounts for bulk purchases, please contact Simon & Schuster Special Sales at 1-866-506-1949 or business@simonandschuster.com.

The Simon & Schuster Speakers Bureau can bring authors to your live event. For more information or to book an event contact the Simon & Schuster Speakers Bureau at 1-866-248-3049 or visit our website at www.simonspeakers.com.

Interior design by Lewelin Polanco

Manufactured in the United States of America

10 9 8 7 6 5 4 3 2 1

The Library of Congress has cataloged the hardcover edition as follows:

Showalter, Elaine.
The civil wars of Julia Ward Howe : a biography / Elaine Showalter.—First Simon & Schuster hardcover edition.
pages cm
Includes bibliographical references and index.
1. Howe, Julia Ward, 1819–1910. 2. Authors, American—19th century—Biography. 3. Feminists—United States—Biography. 4. United States—History—Civil War, 1861–1865—Women. I. Title.
PS2018.S55 2016
818'.409—dc23
[B] 2015027331

ISBN 978-1-4516-4590-3
ISBN 978-1-4516-4591-0 (pbk)
ISBN 978-1-4516-4592-7 (ebook)

CONTENTS

BATTLE HYMN OF THE REPUBLIC

Mine eyes have seen the glory of the coming of the Lord:
He is trampling out the vintage where the grapes of wrath are stored;
He hath loosed the fateful lightning of his terrible swift sword:
    His truth is marching on.

(Chorus)
Glory, glory, hallelujah! (x3)
His truth is marching on.

I have seen Him in the watch-fires of a hundred circling camps;
They have builded Him an altar in the evening dews and damps;
I can read his righteous sentence by the dim and flaring lamps.
    His day is marching on.

(Chorus)
Glory, glory, hallelujah! (x3)
His day is marching on.

I have read a fiery gospel, writ in burnished rows of steel:
"As ye deal with my contemners, so with you my grace shall deal;
Let the Hero, born of woman, crush the serpent with his heel,
    Since God is marching on."

(Chorus)
Glory, glory, hallelujah! (x3)
Since God is marching on.

He has sounded forth the trumpet that shall never call retreat;
He is sifting out the hearts of men before his judgment-seat:
Oh! be swift, my soul, to answer Him! Be jubilant, my feet!
    Our God is marching on.

(Chorus)
Glory, glory, hallelujah! (x3)
Our God is marching on.

In the beauty of the lilies Christ was born across the sea,
With a glory in his bosom that transfigures you and me:
As he died to make men holy, let us die to make men free,
While God is marching on.

(Chorus)
Glory, glory, hallelujah! (x3)
While God is marching on.

—Julia Ward Howe, *From Sunset Ridge: Poems Old and New* (Boston and New York: Houghton, Mifflin and Company; The Riverside Press, Cambridge, 1899), page 1-2.

[Punctuation and capitalization as in this edition, although the edition does not include the chorus.]

INTRODUCTION

In November 1861, while she was staying at Willard's Hotel in embattled Washington, DC, Julia Ward Howe wrote the lyrics to the most famous patriotic anthem of the Civil War. "It would be impossible for me to say," she wrote in her *Reminiscences* (1899), "how many times I have been called upon to rehearse the circumstances under which I wrote the 'Battle Hymn of the Republic.'"[1] Indeed, until she died in 1910 at the age of ninety-one, Howe endlessly told and retold the story of how she had come to write the lines that made her famous. Everywhere she traveled or spoke—at a school in St. Paul, a Unitarian church in Chicago, a gathering of black women in New Orleans, or a flower-bedecked Memorial Day celebration in San Francisco—she was expected to read the words of the song, or sing them in her trained contralto; and choruses and soloists around the world enthusiastically honored her by performing it as well. This "oft-told tale," she noted, had become for many Americans the story of her life.

A century ago, the first biography of Howe, written by three of her daughters, and published in March 1916, just six years after her death, won the Pulitzer Prize. Awarded for the first time in 1917, in the midst of another war, the Pulitzer Prize had a strong moral and nationalistic purpose. Nicholas Butler, the president of Columbia University and the administrator of the awards, called *Julia Ward Howe* the "best American biography teaching patriotic and unselfish services to the people, illustrated by an eminent example."[2]

Despite this sanctimonious encomium, the two-volume biography was not as didactic as Butler's tribute makes it sound. The daughters drew on the Howe family correspondence, plus Julia's essays, poems, memoir, and journals, to tell a lively story of a woman as charming and funny as she was learned and thoughtful, as devoted to her large family as to public service.[3] Howe was certainly eminent, unselfish, and patriotic. She had six children, learned six languages, published six books; she was a prominent figure in the churches and intellectual societies of Boston; she joined ardently with her husband in the abolitionist struggle; she traveled all over the United States, the Caribbean, and Cuba, and abroad to England, France, Italy, Switzerland, Germany, Holland, Belgium, Greece, Cyprus, Palestine, and Egypt; she founded and led the Association of American Women, served as president for the New England Woman's Club, the New England Suffrage Association, and the American Woman's Suffrage Association. Howe was the first woman to be inducted into the American Academy of Arts and Letters. Born three days after Queen Victoria, she was sometimes called the Queen of America.

The daughters also wrote an inspiring story of their parents' marriage. When she married Dr. Samuel Gridley Howe, Julia Ward was an aspiring poet, a beautiful, accomplished, studious heiress known in New York social circles as "the Diva." Samuel G. Howe, eighteen years her senior, was a hero of the Greek Revolution of the 1820s and a world-famous doctor who had developed a method for educating blind children; his name, the critic John Jay Chapman noted, "was known to everyone in the civilized world."[4] Together the Howes were one of the leading power couples of nineteenth-century America, uniting exceptional intelligence, moral fervor, worldly ambition, immense energy, and public commitment. Living in Boston, they knew many of the key literary, political, intellectual, and scientific figures in the Civil War era, including Charles Sumner, Henry Wadsworth Longfellow, Margaret Fuller, and John Brown. They traveled to Europe on steamers as often as modern jet-setters would amass frequent-flyer miles and made friends there as well; Florence Nightingale was the godmother of one of their daughters; Dickens, their guide in London. They were devoted and imaginative parents, and their marriage, in the title of another memoir by their daughter Laura E. Richards, was the fusion of "two noble lives."[5]

But that first biography hid as much as it revealed. In reality, the marriage was turbulent and unstable—a prolonged domestic battle over sex, money, independence, politics, and power. The Howes disagreed, quarreled, separated, often lived and worked apart. Despite his inexhaustible compassion for the suffering, helpless, and deprived, and regardless of his dedication to the abolition of slavery, Howe held obstinate and conservative views on women's roles in public life. He expected his wife to be completely fulfilled in her domestic and maternal role, and to accept with gratitude his right to make all the decisions about their lives together. A towering figure in the field of philanthropy and social reform, at home he was dictatorial, restless, and touchy about his own authority, "an ordinary man," as Chapman wrote, "a man of headaches and irritability, a man of doubts and errors."[6]

Julia Ward expected to have a partner who would introduce her to his more consequential world of ideas and social reform, and allow her to act in it. She assumed that she would be an equal partner in their decisions and free to develop and pursue her own literary aspirations. She hoped to "write the novel or play of the age."[7] Her husband, however, tried to stop her writing after she published an anonymous book of confessional poems that enraged and humiliated him. He took control of her large fortune, and lost most of it. Throughout most of their marriage, famous and beloved though Julia became, his expectations dominated hers. She had to exercise her power obliquely with the soft feminine weapons of tears, self-sacrifice, unselfishness, domesticity, and maternity. For personal self-expression and public communication, she had to use the conventional medium of lyric poetry, and then even that was eventually denied to her. Nevertheless, in the course of their marriage, she learned how to resist his dictatorship, respect her own needs, and develop, defend, and act upon her convictions—in sum, how to think about the manifold ways that the politics of inequality entered the household.

Writing the "Battle Hymn" was the turning point in her life, and its renown gave her the power and the incentive to emancipate herself. The Civil War challenged nineteenth-century ideals of separate spheres for men and women, changed assumptions about gender, and propelled women out of domestic confinement into public lives and careers. In Howe's case, this transformation was also a rebellion against her marriage. She fought a second civil war at home, battling with her husband over her rights to independence, equality, and a public voice.

After her husband's death in 1876, Julia was free to forge a new identity. For the second half of her life, she was a leader of the fight for women's suffrage. She traveled alone or with other suffragists all over the United States campaigning for women's rights. She became an advocate for the emancipation of the silenced and subjected. Although her children, and then her grandchildren, continued to complain about her extra-domestic activities and attempt to thwart them, Julia insisted on doing what she believed necessary and right. The glorious final decades of her life were a result of the limitations of her marriage and a refutation of its confining bonds. There have been a few excellent biographies since 1916, but there is none that looks at Julia Ward Howe as a major American heroine and sees the marriage of the Howes as a paradigmatic clash of nineteenth-century male and female ambitions. *The Civil Wars of Julia Ward Howe* tells the story of her battle in that other civil war of emancipation.

Chapter One

THE PRINCESS IN THE CASTLE

Julia Ward grew up living like a princess in a fairy tale. The daughter of a wealthy New York banker, the oldest of three devoted sisters, and the pet of three energetic brothers, she spent her childhood in a splendid Manhattan mansion where the finest tutors instructed her in music and languages, and her summers with her grandmother and cousins in Newport. She was cherished, indulged, and praised; but, she confessed in her memoir, she also felt like "a young damsel of olden time, shut up within an enchanted castle. And I must say that my dear father, with all his noble generosity and overweening affection, sometimes appeared to me as my jailer."[1] The combination was paradoxical and prophetic. As she grew up, Julia would often relive the experience of the princess in the castle—loved and admired, but also restricted and confined.

An avid reader, she dreamed from an early age of becoming a great writer herself and tried to prepare herself intellectually for the role: "A vision of some important literary work which I should accomplish was present with me in my early life, and had much to do with habits of study acquired by me in youth, and never wholly relinquished."[2] Her family tolerated her literary dreams, and supported her habits of study, but expected her to become a belle first and a housewife after. Her brothers were educated to be successful professionals; the sisters were trained to have all the feminine accomplishments. At the height of their youth and beauty, they were known as the Three Graces. Julia, the most beautiful and accomplished of all, was called the Diva.

Julia's father, Samuel Ward, had made his own way to riches. He went to work at fourteen as a clerk in the investment banking firm Prime and King, which had handled loans for the construction of the Erie Canal. Even then he knew that he wanted to become "one of the first bankers in the United States."[3] By the age of twenty-two, he became a partner in the renamed Prime, Ward, and King. Ward was a disciplined, purposeful, serious young man, but his marriage in 1812 to sixteen-year-old Julia Cutler was a passionate love match. First to please her, and then to make up for the hard work and long self-deprivation of his apprenticeship, he set up an expensive household. Despite his pious Low Church upbringing, and his wife's even stricter Calvinist beliefs in hellfire, sin, and damnation, Ward had no guilt about his wealth. Spending money on the family was not sinful, he believed, but proper and spiritually sanctioned. Banking was a "lofty and ennobling" profession, valued "for the power it confers, of promoting liberal and beneficent enterprises."[4]

Within a decade of their marriage, the Wards had six children: Samuel, born in 1814; Henry in 1817; Julia on May 27, 1819; Francis Marion in 1821; Louisa in 1823; and Annie in 1824. (Another daughter, also named Julia for her mother, had been born in 1816 and died of whooping cough at the age of three.) Somehow, in the intervals of repeated pregnancy, childbirth, and nursing, Julia Cutler Ward did fund-raising for the Society for Promotion of Industry among the Poor, which helped to train impoverished mothers as seamstresses. She also wrote poems and published them anonymously in the newspapers. Although she joked that her husband was indifferent to her "effusions," he expressed some pride when her poem on General Lafayette's arrival in New York was published. In 1849, her poem "Si Je Te Perds, Je Suis Perdu" was included in Rufus Griswold's anthology *The Female Poets of America*.[5]

By 1820, the Ward family was living in a big house at number 5 Bowling Green, at the tip of Manhattan, fast becoming the chicest address in the city and known as Nob's Row. Ward enjoyed buying splendid furniture, gold cornices, and the grand pianoforte without which no society home was complete. He gave his wife extravagant gifts, most spectacularly a lemon-yellow carriage, which had bright blue cushions and a blue interior, and was pulled by a pair of bay horses with black manes. This luxurious vehicle, the Cadillac of coaches, cost $1,000 and was driven by a black coachman named Johnstone.

The young Wards had an active social life. In the winter, they went sleighing and entertained their friends at "caudle parties," where steaming-hot whiskey punch was served and the guests got "red as roosters."[6] Samuel threw himself into the efforts to find husbands for his wife's two unmarried sisters, Eliza and Louisa, hiring tutors and professors to train them in ladylike accomplishments and social graces, and buying them stylish gowns for their debuts. To inaugurate their Bowling Green home and introduce Louisa to eligible young men, the Wards invited seventy of the most fashionable people in New York, including Mrs. John Jacob Astor, wife of the richest man in the United States, to a lavish dinner dance. There Louisa met a suitable lawyer from Savannah named Matthew Hall McAllister and later married him. As Samuel Ward became richer and richer, he also worked harder and harder, and gave generously to New York universities and charities.

Bowling Green was a good place to raise small children. In 1823, the fort in New York Harbor protecting the city from invasion in the War of 1812 had been converted into a resort named Castle Garden, a popular destination for fireworks, picnics, and ice cream, with a big auditorium for celebrations and concerts. (It is now Castle Clinton National Monument, which gets three million visitors a year as the ticket office for the Statue of Liberty.) Every day, Julia's Irish nurse took her for a walk to nearby Battery Park to watch other little girls playing, and every afternoon at three, Johnstone came to take the Ward children and their nurses for a sedate ride. Julia Cutler Ward tried to teach her little daughter to sew. Reflecting on the failure of her early indoctrination in needlework, especially her struggles with the use of a thimble, Julia Ward Howe blamed her own clumsiness; but she did not have memories of her mother as seamstress. She remembered her parents instead as a glamorous couple whose entertainments she was sometimes allowed to watch as a special treat, especially a night when they took her out of bed and dressed her in an embroidered cambric slip with a pink rosebud on the waist. Four-year-old Julia was taken down to the drawing rooms, "which had undergone a surprising transformation. The floors were bare, and from the ceiling of either room was suspended a circle of wax lights and artificial flowers. The orchestra included a double bass. I surveyed the company of the dancers, but soon curled myself up on a sofa, where one of the dowagers fed me with ice-cream."[7] This dreamlike party, with its illuminations, decorations, music, dancing, beautiful dresses, and sweet foods, was to remain her image of enchantment throughout her life.

The days of wine and roses were short. Julia Cutler Ward endured several bouts of inflammation of the lungs, or tuberculosis, was bled by leeches and blistered with poultices, and became so slender and pale that she drew attention as a fashionable beauty. As her sister Eliza observed, since her illnesses began, Mrs. Ward had "grown wondrous handsome." Her complexion was clear and glowing, "her figure extremely slim and genteel, and the expression of her countenance . . . peculiarly interesting."[8] Genteel slenderness, however, gave way to sunken cheeks and persistent headaches and coughs. Faced with an early death, Mrs. Ward reverted to the Calvinist beliefs of her family, repented for her sins, and prayed for forgiveness.

On November 11, 1824, giving birth to her seventh child, Annie, she died of puerperal fever at the age of twenty-seven. Her relatives had gathered around her sickbed to pray for her salvation; as her granddaughters would write, "she was almost literally prayed to death."[9] In the middle of the night, the family woke the children to tell them their mother was dead and took them to the bedroom to kiss her cold cheek. Julia remembered very little of these early years, but she dreamed of her mother until the end of her life, and each of her own pregnancies was accompanied by depression and fear of death.

Samuel Ward was so devastated that he refused to see his infant daughter for weeks. In his grief, he became a convert to his wife's Calvinist beliefs and a model of evangelical piety and sobriety. He never remarried. Soon after her death, he sold the Bowling Green house and most of its furnishings, and moved the family uptown to a house at number 16 Bond Street, then at the northern edge of Manhattan, just above Houston Street. In 1825, Bond Street was a remote, isolated, and risky neighborhood, but Samuel saw its potential, and he persuaded his family to buy property on the same street—his father at number 7, and two unmarried brothers, his brother John next door at number 8, and his brother Henry at number 14. By the 1830s, Bond Street had become a flourishing and exclusive neighborhood of more than sixty houses. The six motherless children were surrounded in the Ward compound by an enclave of affectionate aunts and uncles. Aunt Eliza, who had not yet succeeded in finding a husband, despite her brother-in-law's best efforts, moved in to take care of them. She was used to being the family caregiver; after her own father's death, when she was fifteen, she had taken over the management of the household and raised four younger siblings. Tall and awkward, with large uneven teeth and hairy moles on her face, she had good-naturedly put up with being the designated spinster and enduring the humiliating customs that went with the role; at the weddings of her younger sisters, she had to dance in her stocking feet. When her youngest sister died, she was available to supervise the upbringing of her nieces and nephews.

As Julia described her childhood, her father's religious views ruled the household, and "the early years of my youth were passed in seclusion not only of home life, but of a home life most carefully and jealously guarded from all that might be represented in the orthodox trinity of evil, the world, the flesh, and the devil." [10] There would be no more parties or balls; Samuel Ward forbade dancing parties, the theatre, and concerts, and gave up his favorite pastimes of smoking and playing cards. To his worldly brothers' dismay, he even became the president of the Temperance Society and threw away the bottles of fine Madeira in his cellar.

To protect his children, especially his daughters, from the "dissipations of fashionable society, and even the risks of general intercourse with the unsanctimonious," Ward restricted socializing to the family circle.[11] Their family routines were unvarying, austere, and strictly observed: simple meals, water to drink, and prayers twice a day. He also took a Puritanical view of Saturday evening, regarding it as the proper time to prepare for the marathon religious observances of Sunday, which started with the luxury of coffee and muffins, but then devolved into two church services plus two Sunday-school meetings. Julia got some pleasure from looking at the showy bonnets, all flowers and feathers, at the Grace Church, known as "the Church of the Holy Milliner." In the intervals between sermons, the children were permitted to read pious books, and Julia was grateful for the didactic stories of Mrs. Sherwood, which passed Sabbath muster. Mr. Ward was a stern disciplinarian, whose displeasure cast a chill over the children, although he never spanked or whipped them. "My little acts of rebellion were met with some severity," Julia recalled.[12] She adored him but feared him as well.

For the Ward daughters especially, life was spent indoors, like the little girls of Victorian genre painting, who are often represented looking wistfully out the barred window. The older boys had a riding ring where they could ride their ponies, but the girls were discouraged from outdoor pursuits. When they were allowed to take walks, they were clothed in thin cambric dresses, white cotton stockings, and Moroccan kid slippers, even in the coldest weather, and often came down with colds, "proving conclusively to the minds of their elders how much better off they were within doors."[13] Much later, with daughters and sons of her own, Julia reflected on the fashions, activities, and health of boys and girls. "Boys are much in the open air. Girls are much in the house. Boys wear a dress which follows and allows their natural movements. Girls wear clothes which almost impede their limbs. Boys have, moreover, the healthful hope held out to them of being able to pursue their own objects, and to choose and follow the profession of their choice. Girls have the dispiriting prospect of a secondary and decorative existence, with only so much room allowed them as may not cramp the full sweep of the other sex."[14]

Still, Mr. Ward, whose own education had been cut short, and who had never been to Europe, wanted his children to have the educational opportunities he had missed, to learn to speak foreign languages, and to be taught by the "best and most expensive masters."[15] The boys were sent to board at the progressive Round Hill School in Northampton, Massachusetts, directed by Joseph Cogswell and George Bancroft. Cogswell was a literary sophisticate who had spent years in Europe, where he became a friend of Goethe, got to know Sir Walter Scott, and even visited the celebrated lesbian couple the Ladies of Llangollen. Bancroft rose to become a distinguished historian and minister to Great Britain and Berlin.

The girls were mostly educated at home, but Julia had a group of extraordinarily gifted and accomplished teachers. Indeed, her private education may have been better than the rote learning her brothers received at boarding school, and was certainly more intense and tailored to her talents and interests. While her brothers often complained of the dullness of their studies, she considered the hours with her books the brightest of her day. As a little girl, she studied French six to eight hours a day for conversation, and read the fables of La Fontaine. A French dancing master came to teach the girls steps they were not permitted to practice outside their home. As Julia grew older, she studied piano and the works of Beethoven, Handel, and Mozart with a London-trained instructor.

Professor Lorenzo L. Da Ponte, the son of the man who had written the librettos for Mozart's *Don Giovanni* and *Le Nozze di Figaro*, taught her Italian, and Giovanni Cardini, who was affiliated with the Italian opera company in New York, worked with her on singing and voice training. She also studied mathematics, philosophy, and history.

Her reading, however, depended on which books her father would allow and buy for her. She dreamed of writing a great novel or play, but she knew very little about either genre. Low Church evangelicals like Samuel Ward suspected fiction of dangerous frivolity, and Julia mentions only a few novels—*Paul et Virginie*, Dickens, Sir Walter Scott, and Anna Jameson's *Diary of an Ennuyée.* She always loved the theatre, or rather the idea of the theatre. At the age of seven she had been taken to the opera to see *La Cenerentola* and *The Barber of Seville*, but then her father cracked down, seeing the drama as "distinctly of the devil."[16] After that, she "knew of theatrical matters only by hearsay."[17] As a little girl, she dramatized and performed a sensational story called "The Iroquois Bride" from a literary annual, which ended with Julia and her brother Marion, playing lovers, stabbing each other. Her shocked father quickly put an end to nursery theatricals. Later she tried to write a dramatic adaptation of Scott's *Kenilworth*, and then undertook an even more ambitious and preposterous subject, a play "suggested by Gibbon's account of the fall of Constantinople."[18] These efforts do not survive.

While her brothers were widening their horizons, Julia's life in the house of girls was increasingly conventional. Her ninth birthday marked the end of her childhood and the beginning of feminine propriety as the oldest daughter of the family. Her dolls were taken away, and she entered a neighborhood school, Miss Catherine Roberts's Day School for Young Ladies, where she learned to parrot the stiff religious language of Calvinist sermons. When her ten-year-old cousin Henry was sick, she wrote him a formal letter notable for its total want of sympathy, affection, or concern: "I hear with regret that you are sick, and it is necessary as ever that you should trust in God, love him, dear Henry, and you will see Death approaching with joy."[19] Luckily, Henry recovered despite her helpful advice. In other respects, though, Julia was still a child, happily writing to her brother Sam in 1828 about her Christmas presents: a skipping rope, a sewing box, Indian moccasins, sugar plums, Heber's *Hymns*, and a copy of the ladies' sentimental annual *The Keepsake*.

On November 16, 1829, Aunt Eliza married Dr. John Francis, the Ward family's physician. Dr. Francis was exuberant and gregarious; Edgar Allan Poe, one of his patients, described him as a man of "prodigious vitality" and a raconteur of rich humor, "a compound of Swift, Rabelais, and the clown in the pantomime."[20] Dr. Francis brought his friends, including musicians, actors, and Edgar Allan Poe, to Bond Street. Samuel Ward gave Eliza a white cashmere shawl and pearl earrings as a wedding present, and she looked almost handsome; the dentist had made her a set of false teeth, and a doctor had removed the hairy moles. After their honeymoon, for which Ward loaned them the blue-and-yellow carriage, the Francises lived at number 16 Bond Street, with their growing family of four sons. "Auntie Francis" became more playful, and even fashionable. She had the idea of dressing the Ward girls to match the family coach, and outfitted them "in bright blue pelisses . . . and yellow satin bonnets. This costume was becoming to Louisa and Annie, who had dark hair and eyes, but Julia thought it did not suit her as well."[21]

When she turned twelve, Julia was sent to a more advanced female academy, Miss Angelina Gilbert's School, which cost two hundred dollars a term. But it, too, was a disappointment; she had been promised that she could study chemistry, but having given her a textbook, Miss Gilbert forbade experiments. Julia started to feel the difference from her brothers, and if not to resent it, at least to long for more freedom: "I made rhymes and even dreamed of speeches and orations, often wishing that I had been a boy in view of the limitations on a girl's aspirations."[22]

Writing was the one amusement she was allowed, and since poetry was considered respectable and ladylike, she began to write poems. She had read a very limited and carefully censored amount of Shakespeare,

Wordsworth, Shelley, and Byron, as well as hymns. At thirteen she presented her first gloomy little book of poems to her father, with a note solemnly explaining that "my object in presenting you with these (original) poems has been to give you a little memorial of my early life." With titles like "All things shall pass away," and "My heavenly home," they were calculated to win Samuel Ward's approval. She urged her sisters to take up poetry too; Louisa resisted, but Annie cheerfully produced a couplet:

He feeds the ravens when they call,
And stands them in a pleasant hall.[23]

Clearly Julia was the only daughter with poetic talent.

In 1832 a cholera epidemic struck New York, and the Ward children were sent to Newport to stay with their grandmother Cutler. The beach town was a respite from the supervision, surveillance, and solemnity of New York. But even on the beach, Julia faced special restrictions as a fair-skinned redhead. While her sisters and brothers played happily in the sand, she had to protect her complexion from the sun under a thick green worsted veil. When the children returned from the beach to their grandmother's house, she would notice if "little Julia has another freckle today," and the nurse would be reprimanded for forgetting to put on her charge's veil.[24]

That fall, Sammy persuaded his father that he needed more advanced training in mathematics and departed for four years in Heidelberg, Berlin, and Paris. From the time he was fourteen, it was said, Samuel Ward Sr. had devoted himself to making a fortune, and from the same age, Sammy Jr. devoted himself to squandering it.[25] In Paris alone, he managed to spend $16,000 on books, theatre, opera, ballet, restaurants, music masters, and gifts for flirtatious young women named Josephine, Florentine, Jeannette, and Rosalie. Sam's alleged agenda in Europe was to write a history of mathematics, and for research purposes, he purchased and shipped home the entire library of Adrien-Marie Legendre, professor of mathematics at the École Militaire. Returning to Boston via Heidelberg again, he met the recently widowed Harvard professor Henry Wadsworth Longfellow, with whom he immediately bonded; "it was a case of love at first sight."[26] "Longo" became a lifelong friend and Sam's connection to a circle of literary companions in Boston.

In 1835, the family moved to Samuel Ward's final and finest enchanted castle, a large brick house at the corner of Bond Street and Broadway, which he designed and had built in the fashionable Greek revival style. Here Ward was free to experiment with his concept of a home that was secluded, protected, and a private sanctuary for family, but also offered the educational pleasures of art, literature, and science, and a community of lively and stimulating relatives and friends. The exterior of The Corner, as it became known, was austere, but the interior was decorated in bright primary colors. In the "house of my young ladyhood," Julia recalled, there were three large drawing rooms called Red, Blue, and Yellow for their walls and draperies. The yellow and blue rooms featured marble mantelpieces designed and built by young Thomas Crawford, who would later become a distinguished and commercially successful sculptor. In the attic cupola, Ward installed a telescope, and in a thunderstorm he would take Julia there to show her the beauties of the skies. In the basement he built a medical office for Dr. Francis. He also built a magnificent private art gallery, the first in New York. His friend John Prescott Hall, the American consul in Madrid, shopped in Europe for Old Master paintings, buying a Frans Snyders and a Poussin as well as canvases reputedly by Rembrandt, Titian, Velázquez, and Vandyke, which turned out to be fakes.

Ward also paid $2,500 to the up-and-coming artist Thomas Cole, now regarded as the founder of the Hudson River School, for four large paintings. "I have received a noble commission from Mr. Samuel Ward," Cole wrote, "to paint a series of pictures, the plan of which I conceived several years since, entitled The Voyage of Life . . . The subject is an allegorical one, but perfectly intelligible, and, I think, capable of making a strong moral and religious impression."[27] The paintings, titled *Childhood*, *Youth*, *Manhood*, and *Old Age*, showed the journey through life of a sensitive young man.[28] In art as well as literature, the voyage of life was represented as male.

Julia's personal study space in the house was the Yellow Room, where her desk and piano had been installed. At sixteen, her school days had ended, and she "began to feel the necessity of more strenuous application, and at once arranged for myself hours of study, relieved by the practice of vocal and instrumental music."[29] Joseph Cogswell from Round Hill, which had closed, was hired to tutor Julia in German. She found it more difficult than French and Italian; nevertheless, she ordered Louisa and Annie to tie her to the chair in the Yellow Room until she had completed her daily assignment, and soon was able to read Goethe and Schiller with ease. When she had opportunities to hear music performed, she felt intensely depressed afterwards; and when she performed in trios and quartets herself, singing or playing the piano or guitar, the aftermath was "a visitation of morbid melancholy which threatened to affect my health."[30] As she wrote to a family friend, "my mind seems to me to be a perfect chaos of different elements confusedly blended together."[31]

Her depression and mood swings may well have been the result of puberty. She had reached her full height of five feet and a quarter inch, and was at the average age of menarche in 1830s America. Of course there is no mention of menstruation in Julia's memoir or her official biography, nor in the diaries and letters of other nineteenth-century American women. How did they learn about it, how did they manage it, how did they feel about it? We can only speculate, because it was held in such secrecy; any public mention, even by a doctor, was considered shocking and indelicate. It must have been Auntie Francis who explained "the periodical function" to Julia. She would have had plenty of experience of all its phases, and Dr. Francis had written a well-regarded textbook on obstetrics.

After puberty, young women were even more restricted in their activities, and yet Julia wanted to go out and make friends: "After my school-days, I greatly coveted an enlargement of intercourse with the world. I did not desire to be counted among 'fashionables,' but I did aspire to much greater freedom of association than was allowed me."[32] Mr. Ward claimed he kept her sequestered because he wanted to protect her from her own sensitivity and vulnerability to social influences. Unconsciously, however, he may have wanted to keep her close to him as a companion and substitute for her mother. At the dinner table, he insisted on having her beside him, where he held her right hand with his left, eating his own meal while seeming not to notice that Julia was unable to eat hers.

In the fall of 1836, Sam came home, a liberator bringing into "the Puritanic limits of our family circle," Julia remembered, "a flavor of European life and culture which greatly delighted me."[33] Sam's friends came often to the house. A frequent guest was Charles Sumner, a brilliant and eccentric Boston lawyer who was extremely tall, thin, humorless, didactic, rude, and so absentminded that he was frequently targeted by pickpockets. He loved music, however, and Sam hosted musical parties with family members performing Beethoven, Mozart, and Schubert trios. Julia also had free access to Sam's large library—his scientific and mathematical collection, which eventually became part of the New York Public Library, and his French novels, including Balzac, Hugo, and Sand. Julia knew of George Sand as "the evil woman, who wrote such somnabulic books," and she had scarcely dared to imagine "the wicked delight of reading them."[34] But when Sam came back, she spent hours every day in his library. As she remembered, many young women read Sand in secret. "We knew our parents would not have us read her, *if they knew*. Yet we read her at stolen hours, with waning and still entreated light; and as we read, in a dreary wintry room, with the flickering candle warning us of late hours and confounding expectations, the atmosphere grew warm and glorious about us,—a true human company, a living sympathy crept near us—the very world seemed not the same world after as before."[35]

Julia did not attempt to write fiction herself, but with the tacit approval of her father, she was writing reviews of European literature. At seventeen, with Cogswell's help, she wrote a review of Lamartine's poem *Jocelyn*, and published it anonymously in the *Literary and Theological Review*, edited by her father's friend Leonard Woods. Her criticism was astonishingly confident for a young novice. "De Lamartine," she admonished, "should study conciseness, and cultivate more concentration of thought." Her uncle John Ward teased her about her superior scholarly tone: "This is my little girl who knows about books, and writes an article and has it printed, but I wish that she knew more about housekeeping."[36] Julia's second review, of John Sullivan Dwight's translation, *Select Minor Poems of Goethe and Schiller*, was more erudite and assured. Longfellow, who was the professor of modern languages at Harvard, was impressed. "Is it true," he wrote to Sam, "that yr Sister Julia wrote the rev. of Gothe [*sic*] and Schiller? It is very good."[37] As she later recalled, "My earliest efforts in prose, two review articles, were probably more remarked at the time of their publication than their merit would have warranted. But women writers were by no means as numerous sixty years ago as they are to-day. Neither was it possible for a girl student in those days to find that help and guidance toward a literary career which may easily be commanded to-day."[38]

There were few role models, female or male, for an aspiring adolescent. The biggest literary lion of New York was Washington Irving, then a pathologically shy and elderly bachelor who went to dinner parties but generally dozed off at the table for a ten-minute nap, like a highly esteemed Dormouse. When the travel writer and art critic Anna Jameson visited New York in 1835, Julia met her, relished her bold wit, and hopefully noted that she was a redhead, too, although her daring taste in fashion scandalized New York society matrons. Julia recalled: "I actually heard one of them say, 'How like the devil she looks!' "[39] Women writers seemed either dull and devout like Mrs. Sherwood, or spirited and disreputable like Jameson and Sand.

In Newport in the summer of 1837, Julia at last made her first real female friend. Mary Gray Ward was a Bostonian and unrelated to the New York Wards, but she too was the daughter of a prosperous banker, who represented the London bank Baring Brothers. The young women had much in common intellectually and emotionally. Like Julia, Mary was literary and lonely, and in their friendship and correspondence each found a confidante she could trust with her deepest feelings of aspiration, frustration, and isolation. As Mary wrote in October 1839, "Before I knew you, Jules, I had no friend . . . I said to myself, 'my life so far has been completely isolated and alone' . . . Do you wonder that I love you as I do? No I think not, for you too know what it is to live *alone.*"[40] They shared descriptions of their depressions, or "blue devils," and Mary gave her very modern self-help advice about living for the moment and "investing it with as much of the golden light as it is capable of receiving."[41]

Mary had studied foreign languages with Margaret Fuller and knew the transcendentalist intellectuals, to whom she introduced Julia: Ralph Waldo Emerson, William Channing, and Fuller. Boston, Julia wrote to Mary, was "an oasis in the desert, a place where the larger proportion of people are loving, rational, and happy."[42] People in Boston, she told Louisa and Annie, were "warm-hearted, intelligent, . . . not cold, carping critics."[43] She described herself to the sisters as "having the least dash of transcendentalism, and that of the very best description."[44] But the Bostonians were judging her too, and not as indulgently as she imagined. Margaret Fuller met her at Washington Allston's art studio and found the "well known Julie" much less impressive intellectually than her own younger sister Ellen, and "as affected as she could be."[45]

Meanwhile, Sammy had gone to work at Prime, Ward and King and became engaged to sixteen-year-old Emily Astor, granddaughter of John Jacob Astor. Chaperoned by Sam and Emily, Julia began to go to parties and to try out ways of being a woman. Emily, pretty and fashionable, was one role model, but Julia's father still exerted considerable control over her appearance and behavior. When she was the first bridesmaid at Sam's wedding in January 1838, he gave her a diamond ring and a jeweled headband called a ferronnière, the most stylish accessory of the year. The society hairdresser, Martel, "a dainty half Spanish or French octoroon," who was "endowed with exquisite taste, a ready wit, and a saucy tongue," came to arrange her hair in braids twisted into a low chignon at the back of the head and darkened with French pomade; red hair was still being treated as a flaw. But after all the anticipation, the ball was a disappointment. The ferronnière, she later realized, "was very ill suited to the contours of my face. At the time, however, I had the comfort of supposing that I looked uncommonly well."[46] The wedding ball was lavish, reminding her of entertainments in the Arabian Nights, but Samuel Ward ordered her to leave, like Cinderella, just as the party was at its height. He escorted her to a few other parties that season but always insisted they leave early.

After her brother's wedding, Julia alternated between independent attempts at a social life and submission to her father's demands. At nineteen, she made up her mind to have her own party at home, consulted with her brothers to decide on a guest list, and told her father only that she wanted to invite a few people to The Corner. Instead, she re-created the ball of her childhood, hiring the best caterer in New York, the most sought-after musicians, and a cut-glass chandelier. When Mr. Ward came down to greet the guests, he saw the *jeunesse dorée* of New York eating and dancing in a blaze of light. After the guests had departed, Julia went to apologize, but he was surprisingly kind and forgiving, and never mentioned it again. She had won the right to choose her own guests. Visiting Mary in Boston, she was invited to three parties in one week and wrote home asking for her mitts, her apron, and the sleeves of her lilac dress.

That summer, though, she was back in the old routine again, staying home in New York to keep her father company while her brothers and sisters frolicked in Newport. She tried to bake a gooseberry pie to please him, but it was a disaster. She joked that at least he was the one who had to eat it. In any case, the pie was a diversion from the dreary monotony of her days in New York: "One day is just like another, tomorrow will be as yesterday and the day before were. The same solitary morning, the same afternoon drive on the same road, the same dull evening and sleepless night."[47]

Sam, in New York working at the bank, wrote to his father to protest that Julia was working too hard, following a vegetarian diet, and "destroying herself by eating vegetables," and "writing all day and half the night . . . She is murdering herself."[48] Alarmed, Mr. Ward sent her to Newport, but even there she kept up her solitary pursuits. "Julia has locked herself up in her room this morning," Marion wrote to Sam, "to write, for how long, I know not . . . Much does she seem revolving over some plan for literary distinction, but this, I hope, as she grows older and wiser, she will lay aside."[49] Both brothers were concerned that Julia was indulging her eccentric tastes rather than acting as a surrogate mother to her sisters.

In summer 1838, the Ward brothers decided to take control of their family lives. Aunt Eliza, Dr. Francis, and their four children left The Corner that fall for their own house at number 1 Bond Street, and Julia and Louisa took over the housekeeping. Their social flowering was cut off when Samuel Ward Sr. died on November 17, 1839, at the age of fifty-five. Like her father after her mother's death, Julia took up severe Calvinism, maybe out of guilt. She had not been a religious girl, but Calvinist doctrines "now came home to me with terrible force, and a season of depression and melancholy followed."[50] Her depression lasted for the two years of prescribed mourning, during which she distributed religious tracts and intensified the sober regime of the household, insisting on cold meals on Sunday so that the Sabbath would not be profaned by cooking. To the family suffering under this spartan diet, she became "Old Bird" rather than "Jolie Julie." She was also writing a series of devout poems and elegies about her father's death.

In the spring of 1840, Mary Ward became engaged to Julia's older brother Henry, and perhaps feeling the pressure to get married herself,

Julia tentatively accepted the proposal from a minister named Kirk, which she had been pondering for six months. Henry strongly disapproved of her choice. Consider, Henry wrote to her, "the want of sufficient acquaintance, the disparity of years, the arduous duties of the wife of any clergyman & the want of a permanent settlement."[51] Mary disapproved as well, and Julia broke it off.

Then Henry died suddenly of typhoid fever in October, and both Mary and Julia were plunged into grief and depression. Mary recovered first, and lovingly questioned Julia's religious extremism and urged her to look at the liberal faith of the Unitarians: "I want you to step out of the religious atmosphere in which so much of your life has been passed and for a moment, at least, to look abroad upon the Church Universal towards which the spirit of the age and of the best and most enlightened men of the age, is so strongly tending."[52] And then, prepared by Mary's encouragement, and ready to shed the burdens of Calvinism, Julia read in an essay by the German poet Matthias Claudius a question that electrified her: "And is he not also the God of the Japanese?" It was an epiphany and "a great emancipation . . . I soon welcomed with joy every evidence in literature to show that religion has never been confined to the experience of a particular race or nation, but has shown itself at all times, and under every variety of form, as a seeking for the divine and a reverence for the things unseen."[53] Her insight freed her from the dark hold of Calvinist doctrine: "It seemed a great relief, afterwards, to have escaped from their dreary phraseology, their set patterns of conviction, their stereotyped way of salvation."[54] As she later summarized the experience, she had "studied my way out of the mental agonies which Calvinism can engender and became a Unitarian."[55] For the first time, and decisively, Julia's studies had led her to action and autonomy.

Free of her religious chains, and free therefore to enjoy society with her sisters, Julia entered a period of pleasure. Her daughters wrote that "her red-gold hair was no longer regarded as a misfortune; her gray eyes were large and well opened; her complexion of dazzling purity. Her finely-chiseled features and the beauty of her hands and arms made an ensemble which could not fail to impress all who saw her."[56] Julia, Louisa, and Annie formed a trio of sisters named by Harvard professor Cornelius Felton as "The Three Graces of Bond Street." Louisa was handsome and flirtatious. Annie, the prettiest, was elfin and demure. But Julia was acknowledged to be the most attractive to men. "From the first," her daughters wrote, "she seems to have stirred the hearts of men. Her masters, old and young, fell in love with her almost as a matter of course. Gilded youth and sober middle-age fared no better; her girlhood passed to the sound of sighing. 'My dear,' said an intimate friend of the three, speaking of these days, 'Louisa had her admirers, and Annie had hers; but when the men saw your mother, they just flopped!' "[57]

At twenty-two, Julia was a bluestocking beginning to make a modest intellectual reputation as a reviewer. As the Diva, her operatic singing voice, musical abilities, beauty, and personality made her popular and admired. And she was a great heiress. Samuel Ward's estate, divided among the six children, with Uncle John and Sam Ward Jr., as trustees, has been estimated at $6 million.[58] Julia inherited stocks and bonds and other securities, plus significant real estate holdings: her own property on Pearl Street, Exchange Street, Beaver Street, Sixtieth Street, Third Avenue and Fifty-Eighth Street, Second Avenue and Seventy-Sixth Street, and, with her sisters and brothers, the entire block between Thirty-Fourth and Thirty-Fifth Streets and Eighth and Ninth Avenues.[59]

None of these assets was completely negotiable, however, without a husband and a home of her own, and none of her smitten suitors seems to have been serious contenders for Julia's hand. Whether too old, like her tutor Joseph Cogswell; or comically unsuitable, like the elderly sea captain who walked out with her in Newport and handed her his card inscribed "Russell E. Glover's heart is yours!"; or young and foolish, like Christy Leonidas Miltiades Evangeles, a Greek boy whose education at Columbia her father had subsidized, no man she had encountered was a remotely suitable partner or an appealing romantic conquest. Perhaps in secret Julia wondered if she would soon be the spinster dancing in her stocking feet at a younger sister's wedding. Yet the death of her brother Sam's wife, Emily, in childbirth in February 1841 was a frightening reminder of the fate that could await married women, and a memory, alongside the death of her mother, that would haunt her.

In the summer of 1841, Julia, Louisa, and Annie went to visit Mary Ward in Dorchester. Sumner and Longfellow came out from Cambridge to see them and suggested that they should all rent a carriage and drive over to nearby South Boston to visit the Perkins Institution for the Blind and meet their friend Dr. Samuel Gridley Howe and his famous deaf-blind student Laura Bridgman. When they arrived, Dr. Howe was away, but they toured the asylum and met Laura and another pupil. Then Sumner looked out of a window, and announced, "Oh! Here comes Howe on his black horse." As Julia told the story in her old age, "I looked out also, and beheld a noble rider on a noble steed."[60] He "dismounted, and presently came to make our acquaintance. One of our party proposed to give Laura some trinket which she wore, but Dr. Howe forbade this rather sternly. He made upon us an impression of unusual force and reserve."[61] Sternness, force, reserve, command—these were qualities Julia had respected and loved in her father. She was swept away.

Chapter Two

THE KNIGHT-ERRANT

When he galloped up to Perkins on his black stallion, Samuel Gridley Howe seemed like the perfect knight, come to rescue Julia Ward from her enchanted castle. Eighteen years her senior, almost a foot taller, educated at Brown and Harvard Medical School, he was acclaimed as a national hero for his exploits in the Greek Revolution and his pioneering work in the education of the blind. He was internationally admired as a philanthropist, humanitarian, and friend of the unfortunate or oppressed. Always celebrated in chivalric images—Coeur de Lion, the Red Cross Knight, Bayard, Paladin—Howe seemed almost too heroic to be true.

He was also a very handsome man. Both men and women commented on his good looks. In college, in medical school, in war, and as a veteran, Samuel Howe attracted admiring attention. A Brown classmate recalled him as "erect, agile, and elastic in movement. With fine features, a fresh, pink complexion, a keen blue eye, . . . with open, frank, and genial manners, he could not fail to win the kind regard of his youthful contemporaries."[1] His customary black horse, always named Breeze or Blast, and wearing a crimson saddle-cloth, added to his romantic image. His friend

Franklin Sanborn called Howe "an Arab in figure and in horsemanship" with "a manner that bespoke energy."[2] A Boston matron confided to his daughter Laura Richards many years later that "your father was the handsomest man I ever saw. When he rode down Beacon Street on his black horse . . . the girls ran to the window to look after him."[3]

Drawing upon such comments, her own memories, and paintings of her father as a young man, Richards described him with veiled phallic suggestiveness; he had "the lithe, erect figure, the noble head with its profusion of black hair, the eyes of blue fire which were yet the tenderest in the world, the whole presence like the flash of a sword."[4] Everything about him signaled masculine power. As Dr. Henry I. Bowditch, a distinguished medical colleague, summed it up, "I have always considered Samuel G. Howe the manliest man it was my fortune to meet in this world."[5]

But for Bostonians, noticing Sam Howe's attractiveness and calling him "manly" did not imply that he was virile or seductive. In mid-nineteenth-century America, manliness implied honorable self-restraint rather than sexual enterprise, as well as daring, hardiness, and self-confidence.[6] Despite his flashing eyes and erect bearing, Samuel Howe was no womanizer; the girls of Boston might hang out their windows seven days a week, and he would scarcely notice them. A tireless workaholic, he was unaware of the dramatic impression he created. He was fortunate to keep his thick dark hair and his youthful looks for most of his life, but he did not trade on his physical assets, vain as he might sometimes appear.

Howe was the breakout star of a respectable and unadventurous Boston family. His father, Joseph Neal Howe, was a prosperous rope and cordage maker; his two brothers chose careers in business and seamanship; his four sisters were good domestic women. He adored his sympathetic mother, who died when he was a young man, and based his ideas of the devoted wife and tender mother on her example. But from his youth until his death, Sam was a rebel, a risk taker, and a romantic, a "black swan" among the "steady, intelligent, plodding" Howes.[7]

Joseph Howe hoped that at least one of his sons would enter a profession, and as the most academically gifted, Sam was sent to Brown University, where he ungratefully distinguished himself only for undergraduate pranks, such as taking the president's horse onto the top floor of the main building. In the spring and summer of 1819, he was "rusticated"—suspended and sent away from the college to study with a worthy Protestant minister in rural Massachusetts. He read some books and attended some lectures but had no strong intellectual, philosophical, or political interests, although he loved poetry and especially Byron, whose poems he could still recite to his children decades later. Nonetheless, while young Julia was confined to home and restricted to the companionship of her relatives, young Sam had the opportunity to form close friendships with his classmates. Among the lifelong friends he made at Brown was Horace Mann, two years ahead of him, who grew up to become a pioneer in education and an ally in Howe's reformist projects.[8]

By the time he went to Harvard Medical School in 1821, he had matured academically. Like many bright young men, he could be a diligent and driven student when he was interested in the subject matter. Nevertheless, when he graduated as an MD in 1824, he did not want to settle into the profitable monotony of a humdrum medical practice. In a letter to his friend William Sampson, he explained himself: "Shall I toil away my best days in amassing a fortune? And are the lists worth entering, when the only goal is gold? I know I shall never be rich, for I do not set sufficient value upon money."[9] At the time when he should have been starting his medical career, he announced, to the horror of his family and friends, that he was going to Greece to offer his services as a surgeon to the Greek army in their fight for independence from the Turks. Although he did not know a word of Greek, and had never had any military training, he had no doubts about his decision or his ability to cope with the rigors of life in a foreign war. In the year that Julia Ward lost her mother and entered her long years of confinement in The Corner, Sam Howe boldly broke free from his home, his country, and his culture, and took a heroic journey to the other side of the world.

Why did he make such a reckless decision? Initially, Howe was swept up in the international humanitarian movement called "philhellenism," the fervor to save Greece for the world. The Greek war for independence from the Turks and the Ottoman Empire, a long and bloody battle with many casualties and atrocities on both sides, had a base in the efforts of various Greek leaders to establish a unified government in a fragmented, impoverished tribal society. It was sometimes portrayed as a crusade of Christians against Muslims, and often heralded as a war of liberal Western values against barbaric Eastern oppression. Although the rhetoric of the war had parallels to today's "conflict of civilizations" in the Middle East, it was not a religious war or an uprising that came solely out of the people's grievances against the Turks, who had ruled them for four centuries. Indeed, the populations were so mixed that many Turks living in Greece could no longer speak Turkish, and many Greeks had converted to Islam.

Nonetheless, a generation of young men in the United States and Europe who had been imprinted by a classical education became obsessed with the liberation of Greece. This generation of romantic revolutionaries were ardent believers in pagan Greece as the Cradle of Civilization, the source of democracy, art, philosophy, science, and all that was noble in human history. The Greece they imagined and lauded, a country few of them had ever seen, was a fictional patchwork of mythology and epic, of remembered school days and proudly declaimed lines of verse, where Odysseus and Plato, Socrates and Hercules, Demosthenes and Homer gathered still in groves of olive and laurel. With such anachronistic and heady sentiments to guide them, and a youthful passion to change and repair the world, philhellenes wrote the kind of stirring slogans that future generations would repeat in other places and other times, from Spain and Berlin to Rwanda and Kosovo. The British Romantic poets were especially identified with the cause. "We are all Greeks," proclaimed Shelley in the preface to "Hellas," while Byron's Don Juan stands on the plain of Marathon and dreams "that Greece might still be free."

The media too played a key role in stirring up the emotions of idealistic young men. In London, Madrid, Leipzig, Paris, and St. Petersburg, small groups of Greek expatriates described the sufferings of their people and created a powerful image of a desperate Hellenic nation crying out for freedom. The Greek Committees they founded with local philhellenes were skillful pressure groups; they deluged the press with stories of Turkish atrocities and massacres of the innocent and raised funds from public subscription, private donation, and all kinds of fairs, bazaars, and charitable events. With visions of tearing down the walls, driving away the oppressors, and winning glory for themselves, young men set off, ill prepared, unequipped, and often outlandishly dressed, in search of Aegean glory.

Byron was among the first, and by far the most famous, of these pilgrims. Bearing gifts to the Greek army from the London Greek Committee, and also prepared to spend thousands of pounds of his own on weapons, ships, supplies, and Albanian mercenaries, Byron was on the scene by 1821. Despite his reputation for hyperbolic ecstasy and poetic rhapsody, he was a practical, clear-sighted witness of the revolution on the ground. He was quickly disillusioned by the greed and infighting of the different factions of Greek leadership, and he realized that fundamental change would have to come before they were ready for democracy and self-government. Still, he stayed on. On April 19, 1824, reports of his tawdry death in Missolonghi from a fever exacerbated by the primitive bleedings and leechings of his doctors made him a martyr to the Greek cause throughout the world. After his death, Byron was refused burial at St. Paul's or Westminster Abbey by English clerics scandalized by gossip about his sexual behavior and radical politics; but he was sanctified and eulogized by his friends and companions. He was also honored by a statue in the garden of war heroes in Missolonghi, where he stands out by virtue of his youth and absence of a mustache.[10] In his lonely and inglorious death, Byron became the international symbol of philhellenism as a courageous sacrifice for liberty.

In the United States, classical scholars, politicians, statesmen, and poets joined the chorus of philhellenism and argued for humanitarian intervention in the fighting. At a fund-raising dinner in Cincinnati, an American general opined that "the Star-Spangled Banner must wave in the Aegean."[11] President James Monroe, in the pompous and bloodless rhetoric with which American presidents endorse faraway wars, said, "the emancipation of Greece fills the mind with the most exalted sentiments, and arouses in our bosoms the best feelings of which our nature is susceptible."[12] Boston, which had long styled itself the Athens of America and had been the center of a Greek revival in architecture, was especially drawn to philhellenism, although there were groups in cities as un-Athenian as Cincinnati, Charleston, South Carolina, and Louisville. In 1823, Edward Everett, the twenty-nine-year-old Eliot Professor of Greek at Harvard, appealed in the *North American Review* for young American men to enlist in the war of the cross against the crescent. At the beginning of a brilliant career that would take him to Congress, the governorship of Massachusetts, and the Court of St. James, Everett became the official voice of the Greek cause in the United States. Nevertheless, Everett's call did not find passionate classicists eager to volunteer. Even at Harvard, James Freeman Clarke remembered, "We were expected to wade through Homer as though the *Iliad* were a bog, and it was our duty to get along at such a rate per diem."[13] In the end, only a handful of Americans went to wave the flag in the Aegean, and Samuel Howe, no classicist, no patriot, and not especially religious ("I pray with my hands and feet," he said) became the most celebrated among them.[14] In the summer of 1824, he met the other New England recruit, Jonathan Peckham Miller, a farmer from Vermont, who was astonished to hear that this city boy who "looked more like a doll than a soldier" was going to fight in Greece. Sam told him that he been taking fencing lessons and invited him home for a duel with sword, masks, and gloves.[15] Miller won, but he was impressed by Sam's grit and guts.

Even Howe struggled to explain why instead of earning a comfortable living as a doctor in Boston, he embarked on such a reckless odyssey. In 1857, reflecting (in a letter to Horace Mann) on his reasons for going to Greece, Howe brushed away political or religious conviction and gave an explanation that both emphasized his lack of financial ambition and blamed his youthful impulsiveness. "Thoughtless indifference, perhaps ignorance of what course would have been profitable to me. Lacking prudence & calculation, I followed an adventurous spirit."[16] Elsewhere he hinted sentimentally at a broken romance. But Howe stayed in Greece for six years, under conditions of extreme hardship and continual danger. It is obvious that something in the experience was deeply profitable to him in discovering where his talents and inclinations lay. Certainly these six years changed and formed him forever. He would come back as a different man, with a different destiny, even a different name.

In November 1824, Sam boarded the *Triton* for Malta and Greece, carrying *Childe Harold's Pilgrimage* among his few belongings. When he arrived in Navarino, on the Peloponnesian coast, he met up with Miller, who had gone native—shaved his head, put on Greek costume, and stuck a dagger in his belt—and a much more experienced American philhellene, George Jarvis, who spoke fluent Greek and helped him get oriented. He quickly realized that there was no Greek army as such, but guerrilla warfare, brigands, and tribal insurgencies, with a few strong leaders who had to be sought out and convinced of the volunteer's seriousness and capability.

The chaos and uncertainty suited his idealism, dislike of routine, and penchant for "frenetic activity."[17] Initially, he improvised, traveling with guerrilla fighters, sleeping on the ground and in caves, supporting himself by practicing medicine, amputating a hand one day, removing a facial tumor the next. He found the Greek insurgents tough and brave but completely undisciplined and individualistic. They had no esprit de corps, no sense of military authority, no high-minded motives, no willingness to obey orders or take risks. By March 1825, he was beginning to speak some Greek; the first words he understood came overhearing a Greek comrade describe him: "What a handsome youth!" It says a lot about Howe's sexual innocence that he was not alarmed to overhear the compliment.

He lost his naïveté as he witnessed the atrocities of Turkish raids and attacks, and saw perversity unimaginable in Boston. In the village of Palio Kormis in July 1827, he saw a ten-year-old girl vaginally mutilated with a knife and raped; and described the "unnatural crimes" the Turks carried out against "women, men & beasts." "Not content with serving women in the way God meant, they search for men & boys and even the jackasses and sheep do not escape. Nor is this a matter of concealment with them: as soon as they take any Greeks prisoners they abuse the men in this way and then kill them or keep them as slaves; unless someone is very young and beautiful, then he is kept for the embraces of some high officer." [18] The Greeks were equally capable of brutality in massacres and torture of Turkish soldiers. "The Greeks," Howe concluded in 1825, "are most abominably selfish and most cruelly unfeeling," and "the women are if anything worse." [19] He scorned Greek doctors as conceited, unprincipled, superstitious, and stubbornly reluctant to try modern methods of treatment. Often he had to overrule them in caring for patients.

Throughout his years in Greece, Howe participated in virtually every aspect of the fighting, on land and on sea, in every kind of terrain, in every season, often under the worst imaginable physical conditions. While he was never wounded, he had a long bout of "swamp fever," or malaria, the effects of which may have permanently weakened his system. Despite plagues of fleas and lice, he sometimes went for two months without changing his clothes; only a "smoke bath," he wrote, would kill the bugs. At least once, at the siege of Athens, he shot a Turkish soldier and found the reality of killing a man more disturbing than he expected: "I hardly know whether pleasure or pain predominated in my mind as I witnessed his fall."[20] Throughout these ordeals, he never lost confidence in his own capacity to make the right decisions and form the correct judgments. As the scattered Greek leadership realized the extent of his surgical skills, they gave him paid positions of responsibility, as physician to the Greek fleet at Crete, director of the military hospital at Nauplion, and finally surgeon on the military ship *Karteria*.

Howe's vivid, colloquial, and graphic letters about the Greek campaign were also his first chance to try his hand as a writer. With a sense for the ridiculous as well as the shocking aspects of war, and an unquenchable optimism about the justice of the cause, he found an eager audience for his eyewitness accounts of the campaign. Like his journal, they displayed his gifts for narrative and exposition, along with imagery and suspense. The Boston critic John Jay Chapman was among those who understood and appreciated the almost novelistic quality of Howe's literary style. "Before I had read this journal," he wrote in 1910, "I did not know that the United States had ever produced a man of this type, the seventeenth-century navigator, whose daily life is made up of hair-breadth escapes and who writes in the style of Robinson Crusoe." He quoted Howe's zest for battle when passing a pirate ship: "If vessels only knew what cowards these pirates are, they would never be robbed, for the least resistance will keep them off. Give me a vessel with moderately high sides, two light guns, and twelve resolute men, and I would pledge my all on sailing about every port of the archipelago and beating off every vessel which approaches."[21] Sam's father and Edward Everett saw to it that these exciting missives were published in Boston newspapers, from which they were picked up by papers around the country.

Although he was repelled by the Greek tribal women, whom he found coarse, illiterate, and ugly (moreover, he wrote primly, they did not wear stays), Howe probably had his first sexual experiences in Greece. He occasionally admitted in his journal that he had been aroused by seeing the body of a young camp follower, "a most elegant young creature," and even confessed to getting involved with a woman while he was doing relief work in Corinth, although the Greek government, unsurprisingly, "treated the matter liberally."[22] Despite many opportunities, however, Howe was not looking for sexual adventures. He was much more enthusiastic about the adventures of foraging for food—a huge boiled beet, sorrel, snails, wasps "roasted to a crisp and strung on a straw like dried cherries," donkeys or goats hacked into small pieces and eaten half-raw.[23]

In 1828, he published his hastily written *Historical Sketch of the Greek Revolution* and returned home to raise funds for Greek relief. Tanned, handsome, passionate, he was a charismatic speaker, collecting $60,000 plus clothes and toys. Returning with the loot to Corinth, he found a village of fifty families and built them a wheelbarrow, the first wheeled vehicle they had ever seen. Welcomed like a divinity bearing gifts from the heavens, he led his villagers in constructing a harbor. These were the months he recalled as the happiest time of his life. "I was alone among my colonists, who were all Greeks. They knew I wanted to help them, and they let me have my own way . . . I labored here day and night, in season and out, and was governor, legislator, clerk, constable, and everything but *patriarch.*"[24] Naming the little village Washingtonia, he also set up a school, where the children could be heard "repeating 'Alpha, beta, gamma, delta,' as they run about, and when out of school they play at making letters in the sand." The school became his sanctuary, the center of his reformist dreams and "when any petty Greek trick, or any attempt to impose upon me, has ruffled my temper, I retire there, and immediately all my disgust is gone, and all my hopes and anticipations are revived."[25]

He delighted in giving orders and following his own intuitions about how to get things done, and he came away convinced that his plan was the best one and should be obeyed. His dictatorship was benign; he harbored no secret desires to rule over Corinth forever or to exterminate the Greek brutes, but his benevolence would always have a darker side. Not yet thirty years old, he was already very sure that his way was the right way. In the future, his missionary convictions of saving the oppressed could easily turn to frustration and rage when his schemes failed, and he would always blame other people for the failure, rather than admit the weaknesses of his own plans.

At last in 1831, Howe packed up his baggage and headed slowly home. Among the treasures he was carrying was Byron's helmet, which he had bought at an auction in Poros. The helmet says much about Byron's epic concept of the revolution, and the glorious role he expected to play in it, and much about Howe's investment in that myth. Byron himself had designed the helmet before he left for Greece, following descriptions of Hector's armor in the *Iliad*, with his own family coat of arms and motto, "Crede Biron," on the front. He designed equally elaborate and heavy helmets for his friends Edward John Trelawney and Count Pietro Gamba, and had them made by a craftsman in Genoa. With a huge curved appendage, edged with blue plumes, bending over the face, Byron's helmet was an absurd object, as unsuitable for guerrilla fighting in Crete as a top hat.

Not for another six months, after yet more bloodshed among the tribes, did British, French, and Russian diplomats convene in London in May 1832 and decide that a monarchy was the best option for the Greeks. In an unheroic conclusion to the years of freedom fighting, they selected Prince Otto of Bavaria as the new king. One of his first acts as monarch was to establish an order of merit for Greek citizens who had fought in the War of Independence, and foreigners and heads of state who had rendered outstanding service to the cause. The first head of state to be thus honored was Otto's father, King Ludwig I of Bavaria.

Despite the numerous opportunities he had had to perfect his surgical skills in the field in Greece, Howe knew when he went back to Boston that he still did not want to practice medicine as a profession. He had discovered how much he liked being in charge, creating a colony out of nothing and ruling it wisely. Moreover, he was a restless man, always on the lookout for new causes, experiences, and responsibilities. No sooner did he win acclaim for mastering a difficult task than he was looking for a harder one, or at least a different one, as much an "errant"—a wanderer—as a knight. In letters to his Boston friend William Sampson, he admitted his fears that he might be sacrificing his own domestic happiness by giving up a lucrative medical career, since "I cannot marry a poor girl, and will not marry to be supported by a wife."[26] On the other hand, such a quandary meant that he could postpone marriage indefinitely.

Back in Boston, he started writing for the *New England Magazine*. He met with the American Polish Committee, which was raising money for Polish revolutionaries against Russian rule—a possible repeat of his Greek triumphs. He applied for positions as a newspaper editor and as the director of a Liberian colony of repatriated slaves. He got himself in trouble in New York when he demanded to examine Chang and Eng, the "Siamese twins" then being exhibited as freaks by their agent, James W. Hale. Hale refused, Howe insinuated that the twins were a fraud, and Hale sued him for slander. Howe won the case eventually, but his self-importance and bumptiousness had increased. When he was unemployed, he was a loose cannon. Fortunately, fate intervened. The Massachusetts legislature had voted to establish a school for the blind, the first in the United States, and the trustees were looking for a director. As the family legend told it, in July 1831, three of the trustees encountered the doctor walking on Boylston Street and realized on the spot that their search was over. "Here is Howe!" said Dr. John Fisher. "The very man we have been looking for all this time."[27] Less dramatically, Fisher, his Brown classmate, offered him the job.

Howe knew nothing about educating the blind or running an asylum school, but the job mightily appealed to his humanitarian interests, and he immediately negotiated funding from his employers for a lengthy sojourn in Europe to study existing schools in England, France, and Prussia. Before he departed, he met with the American Polish Committee, which gave him funds to deliver to the revolutionaries in Paris.

For five months there, he studied the methods at the Institut National des Jeunes Aveugles and visited other asylums. Meanwhile, the Polish fighters had surrendered to the Russians and sought refuge in Prussia. Making his way to Berlin to visit their school for the blind, Howe was arrested in his hotel by Prussian police and held without charges in solitary confinement for almost a month. Released by the intervention of friends in Paris and Washington, he returned to his studies, although he would never recover from the claustrophobia and fear of imprisonment the experience produced.[28]

While he dismissed European methods of education for the handicapped as outdated, obtuse, and inhumane, the time abroad gave him broad familiarity with asylums and their principles. He returned to Boston after a year away, convinced that the perils of total institutionalization, especially helplessness and passivity, had to be eliminated, and that blind boys especially must be encouraged to be hardy and self-sufficient. Parents needed to be tough with their blind sons in order to prepare them for adulthood; it was essential not to protect them by "excessive indulgence" and "undeserved preference over others," but to allow them to stumble and fail in order to develop "courage, self-reliance, generosity, and manliness."[29]

John Jay Chapman saw this phase of Howe's career as a continuation of his knightly quest. "The early history of the Boston Blind Asylum is like a great medieval romance—voluminous, glowing, many-sided. That history is recorded in multitudinous documents and papers, letters, arguments, reports, anecdotes—the whole mass of them being illumined by the central figure of Howe, who looms through the story like Launcelot or Parsifal."[30] In one sense, it was a quest for romance, like the search for the Grail. Howe believed that the blind should be educated to take their place alongside other citizens and were fully capable of work, love, and independence. These beliefs, along with many others, would be tested and undermined by his experience, but his ardor, energy, determination, and dedication were permanent.

The beginnings of the project, however, were slow and thorny. He had spent all the money allotted for the school on his year in Europe and had to scramble to persuade Massachusetts legislators and philanthropists to support the enterprise, to find a building, identify suitable pupils, and convince their families to entrust their children to him. Since his father and stepmother had moved to Milton, he took over their house in Boston as a site for the asylum, with his sisters Lizzie and Jennette as matrons. The educator Elizabeth Peabody saw him in 1833, making maps, schoolbooks, and mathematical diagrams. "He had gummed twine, I think, upon cardboard, an enormous labour, to form the letters of the alphabet. I shall not, in all time, forget the impression made upon me by seeing the hero of the Greek Revolution . . . wholly absorbed and applying all the energies of his genius to this apparently humble work."[31] In France, Louis Braille was experimenting with an alphabet of dots for blind readers, but the news had not reached Howe, who formed the standard letters. His first blind pupils were little girls—the sisters Abby and Sophia Carter of Andover, whom he taught the alphabet, numbers, punctuation, and map reading, using raised letters and shapes. To formalize the opening of the Institution, Howe had his portrait painted by Gilbert Stuart's daughter Jane. He was thirty years old.

The shipping magnate Colonel Thomas Perkins donated his house and garden on Pearl Street as a school, and having lobbied the Boston legislature for funding, and raised $61,000 through contributions and bazaars in Boston and Salem, Howe moved into the house on August 18, 1833, with seven children and two blind male teachers from Europe. He found a printing press he could adapt to use raised type, and started to print books, beginning with a hymnal and the New Testament. Davy Crockett stopped by in 1834 to hear a blind girl read from the books.

In 1835, Howe was at last officially recognized as one of the foreign heroes of the liberation and awarded the title of Chevalier of the Order of St. Saviour from the King of Greece. He never wore the silver star-shaped medal—it would have looked ridiculous on Beacon Street. He kept it with his Turkish pipes and other souvenirs in a place his children called the "picknickle and bucknicle" drawer, and he allowed them to play with it, just as they played dress-up with his fancy uniform. But the award marked a significant moment in his life. From then on, he was known to his family and friends as "Chev," an affectionate American abbreviation of his knightly title, and a tribute to his gallant image. He always signed his personal letters with this new name.

An ardent believer in the pseudoscience of phrenology, Chev was thrilled to meet the preeminent Edinburgh phrenologist George Combe, who was in residence in Boston from 1838 to 1841. He revered Combe as one of the leading thinkers of the century and believed his writings were among the great works of the ages. Combe would become one of his trusted friends. For his leisure time in Boston, Chev also turned to the company of the Five of Clubs, a group of ambitious, intellectual, and convivial young professional men, the lawyers Charles Sumner and George Stillman Hillard; the poet and Harvard professor Henry Wadsworth Longfellow; the teacher Henry Russell Cleveland; and the Harvard professor of Greek Cornelius Conway Felton. They were so close that Bostonians called them "the Mutual Admiration Society." Chev liked them all, but his closest tie was with Summer, who soon became his "alter ego, the brother of his heart."[32]

Chev and Charlie Sumner had much in common. Ten years younger, Sumner had found his calling at Harvard Law School, where he was an outstanding student and a tireless researcher. He launched his practice in Boston in partnership with Hillard. But like Chev rejecting a medical career, Sumner discovered that he did not actually like the practice of law. In December 1837, despite the disapproval of his Harvard professors, mentors, and friends, he decided to spend some time in Europe, allegedly to expand his legal expertise. Like Chev, Sumner had a strong Puritanical streak and resistance to pleasure, especially sexual pleasure. When he arrived in Paris, he was shocked by the gambling halls and roulette, and alarmed by the whores wandering among the tables. "It is a perfect Sodom," he wrote to Hillard, "without religion and without any morality between the sexes."[33] Although he went to the opera, theatre, and art museums, he spent his days mastering French and studying Continental law.

After six professionally profitable months, Sumner moved on to London, where he found himself unexpectedly popular. He was given a seat at the Court of Common Pleas and the Queen's Bench and was admitted to both the House of Commons and the House of Lords. Socially, he became an honorary member of several exclusive male city clubs, including the Garrick, the Travellers', and the Athenaeum, where he met aristocrats and authors from Carlyle to Macaulay. "My acquaintance is most extensive—extensive beyond my most sanguine anticipations," he boasted to a friend in the US.[34]

When he returned to Boston in the spring of 1840, with an elegant London wardrobe and a much more sophisticated aptitude for conversation, Sumner was in demand. But under the European polish, he was still eccentric and raw. Six feet two inches tall, and weighing only 120 pounds, he was an awkward giant, uninterested in games, art, poetry, or sports, and without a sense of humor. His friends in the Five of Clubs loved to tease him to hear his literal-mindedness. According to Sumner's biographer, "Oliver Wendell Holmes exaggerated only a little when he declared that if one told Sumner that the moon was made of green cheese, he would say: 'No! it cannot be so,' and proceed to give weighty reasons to the contrary."[35]

Chev, however, liked Sumner's seriousness and especially his high-mindedness about women. Sumner too was uncomfortable with women and cherished romantic ideals of marriage. Marriage might work, he lectured his fourteen-year-old sister Jane, if the wife knew "a female's place is at home"; her finest quality should be "to listen intelligently."[36] Nothing could jibe better with Chev's prudery, idealism, and love of an admiring audience. In an emotional letter to Horace Mann, he explained his adoration of innocent virginity and his horror of a woman with sexual feelings: "As there is nothing in nature so beautiful as the fresh young heart of the guileless girl, so there is nothing as hideous as the passions of a depraved woman."[37] Chev and Charlie had many opportunities to reinforce each other's ideas about ideal marriage and the exemplary wife. As Sumner wrote to a college friend, "Both have been wanderers, and both are bachelors, so we are together a good deal; we drive fast and hard, and talk—looking at the blossoms in the fields, or those fairer in the streets."[38] They looked at women, and did not pursue them.

All of Chev's energy was channeled into his work. By the late 1830s, he had formed the idea that a gifted deaf-blind child would be the best advertisement for his methods. Moreover, he wanted to find a pretty girl: "When the supposed sufferer is a child—a girl—and of pleasing appearance, the sympathy and interest are naturally increased."[39] In the summer of 1837, Chev found the perfect pupil: eight-year-old Laura Bridgman. The daughter of a farming family in Hanover, New Hampshire, Laura had been a bright, active toddler, but a month after her second birthday, she and her two sisters caught scarlet fever. The sisters died, but Laura survived, although with shriveled eyes and progressive loss of hearing resulting in total deafness. She had begun to speak at eighteen months, but when she lost her hearing, she also lost her speech. For a time she repeated "dark, dark," but after a year's convalescence, that stopped too. Her very last word, her mother reported, was "book."[40]

Chev heard about her through a professor at Dartmouth Medical School, and in July he rode out to see her. Despite her severe handicaps, Laura was a pretty child. Chev persuaded her parents that she should be sent to his school, and in October 1837, she arrived in Boston. In her first few weeks at Perkins, she was frightened and wild, but she was calmed by the warm affection of the house-matron, Lydia Drew. Even more, she was tamed and disciplined by Chev's firm authority. He took her hand and led her around the rooms, tightening his grip when she resisted. Through a combination of force and determination, Chev asserted control. Soon, one visitor observed, she "was very much under the command of the Doctor," and she quickly came to depend on his approval and attention.[41] Under his new title, "the Doctor" became the dominant presence in her life, more important than mother or father or teachers. She proved an even more gifted student than he had anticipated, quickly mastering raised letters, and then the manual alphabet, at which she became very adept. In Chev's words, "her little hands were continually stretched out and her tiny fingers in constant motion, like the feelers of an insect."[42] From the start he saw her as not quite human.

As Laura learned to express herself, she bombarded her teachers with questions, spelling them rapidly into their hands: "Why don't fish have legs? Is the worm afraid when the hen eats him? Why do cows have two horns?" Once she had learned to write, she kept a daily journal, composed letters, a memoir, and even some poems of her own. Thinking of words quite literally, unaware of rhyme, or elevated poetic language, or traditional forms, Laura's poems are startlingly modern, a kind of poetry of the future:

Light is sweet as honey, but
Darkness is bitter as salt, and more than vinegar . . .
Darkness is frosty.
A good sleep is a white curtain.
A bad sleep is a black curtain.[43]

Chev did not admire her poetry, but her attachment to him was passionate and absolute; he was her father, her teacher, her beloved. When he left the school on trips, she became frantic; during the summers, when she went back to Hanover to be with her family, she longed for him: "I think much about Doctor. I want to see him. I cannot wait until he comes. I am in hurry until Doctor come. Why did he go? Does he know I want to see him very much? I think Doctor does not love me, to go away."[44]

Laura's eagerness to learn encouraged Chev to develop new techniques and hypotheses about the blind-deaf in general. Like Charcot's Augustine or Freud's Dora—the great female psychiatric patients and hysterics of the nineteenth century—Laura entered her doctor's life at an intellectually formative time in his career, and she served as the founding case of his theoretical work. She needed the Doctor to teach her language; he needed her to galvanize and compress his thinking, to give him a cause and a philosophy, a theory of learning and perception. Like Charcot with his theatrical demonstrations of the contortions of hysterical young women at the *leçons du mardi* at the Salpêtrière in Paris (which Chev had visited), he exhibited Laura to visitors on Saturday afternoons and publicized her to the world at large. Through Laura, Doctor Samuel G. Howe was celebrated worldwide as the great teacher and emancipator of the blind and deaf.

By May 1839, the school had more than sixty students and had outgrown its original building; they moved into a newly built hotel in South Boston, which was also called the Perkins Institute in honor of the founding donor. Chev was proud of the generous space that allowed separate dormitories, classrooms, and dining rooms for boys and girls, and separate living quarters for staff, plus a bowling alley, gymnasium, and large interior courtyard. The building was close enough to Boston Harbor that the students could bathe in cold saltwater, which he felt was the most healthful of all therapies. Among the blind boys, there was always a risk of public masturbation, and frequent cold baths were remedies for such behavior. Chev also spoke to the boys about "the wickedness and mischief of masturbation," and a few guilt-ridden boys came to his office afterwards to confess.[45] Chev's office had room for his large collections of skulls, plaster heads, and busts for phrenological study.

Three years after Laura had come to the school, Chev felt confident enough in her progress to write about her achievements in his widely read annual reports. By the 1840s, the case of Laura Bridgman was internationally known. One recent scholar called her "the most famous female in the entire world,"[46] no small claim during the reign of Queen Victoria. It is obvious why the first deaf-blind person who had ever been taught the fundamental means of human communication would interest medical experts and pedagogical theorists, even philosophers. Howe succeeded in more than that; he made her a celebrity. Using his talents for narrative, he wrote about her in the language of sentimental fiction, stressing epiphanies of comprehension rather than the halting, imperfect steps by which she acquired language.

In order to make her life an appealing story, the Doctor also had to conceal her many oddities and misbehaviors from his readers. The other blind children did not like Laura; she was nasty to them; she hit her teachers; she bit Sumner. A budding feminist, she complained when Chev read her mail: "Doctor was wrong to open little girl's letters. Little girls open theirself."[47] Even after learning the manual alphabet, Laura laughed, shrieked, growled, howled, and made special noises to "name" and greet each person at Perkins. Chev found her loud noises ugly and animalistic. Having tried unsuccessfully to get her to soften her voice, or control her outbursts, he added to her daily routine periods when she could go into a closet and make sounds. In the annual reports, however, he described her noises as charming cooings and hummings.

He was also pleased that Laura, unlike many of the blind girls, was always immaculately dressed and groomed, of her own will. She had been trained to cover her eyes. In his *Eighth Annual Report*, he wrote: "It has become as much of a habit for her to put a clean green ribbon over her eyes when she dresses herself, as it is to put on her gown. When thus dressed, and her eyes shaded, her features are comely and pleasing; and the regular oval of her face, surmounted by her fine, glossy hair, makes her quite handsome."[48] The implication is that Laura's eye sockets were unsightly or frightening or disfigured. Some scholars say that all the children at Perkins wore these ribbons, but pictures of Bridgman with a deaf-blind boy, Oliver Caswell, show him without one. Perhaps only girls were required to cover their eyes in order to present a more pleasing appearance and protect visitors from the unpleasant sight of their disfigurements. The green blindfold sashes that Laura wore have been preserved in the Perkins archives. After adolescence, though, she wore a close-fitting black blindfold cut like sunglasses, and as an adult, after 1870, she habitually wore opaque spectacles. Yet there is one late photograph of Laura without her blindfold, allegedly taken in Hanover after 1870, and she looks perfectly normal; her eye sockets are not scarred, her eyeballs not shrunken. Could the blindfold have been unnecessary all along, and something of a badge of strangeness and ghettoization, like the yellow star?[49]

Howe also claimed that he had never seen Laura in a position or an action "at which the most fastidious would revolt," and that she was "remarkable for neatness, order, and propriety." In other words, she was never seen blowing her nose, scratching herself, sitting with her knees spread or her skirts carelessly raised. He also believed that she was entirely unaware of sex and sexual feelings: "Laura is still so young, and her physical development is still so imperfect—she is so childlike in appearance and action, that it is impossible to suppose she has yet any idea of sex."[50] She would not even allow a man to touch her, he declared, would not sit on most men's knees—except of course for those of Howe—and, in short, was "as pure and spotless as the petals of a rose."[51]

In February 1841, Laura moved in with Chev and his sister Jennette. Chev's own daughters would write that before they were born, she "was like a daughter to him, the pet of all the friends who visited him."[52] Late that summer, at the suggestion of Horace Mann, Chev commissioned Sophia Peabody—Elizabeth's sister and the fiancée of Nathaniel Hawthorne—to sculpt a bust of Laura, which he could take on his journeys to display to the crowds of people eager to see her. Mann thought "it would do not a little towards keeping up, and indeed extending, the interest which the public now take in her."[53] Elizabeth even suggested that he might make extra money by selling plaster casts of the statue to visitors at Perkins. Sophia sculpted Laura with a blindfold, rather than a ribbon, over her eyes, her shoulders bare and draped with a marble scarf. Laura enjoyed the sittings, and called the ethereal and childlike statue her "white baby."[54] The marble bust was later copied for distribution to the leading American schools for the blind and deaf.

By the end of the summer, Chev had established a chaste pseudo-household, with an adoring surrogate family—Jennette as an undemanding housewife and Laura as a worshipful silent daughter. But he was beginning to be bored and impatient with the exhausting routine and mundane demands of life at Perkins. He analyzed his restlessness to Mann: "If I am good for anything it is as a pioneer in a rough, untrodden path. I want the stimulus of *difficulty.*"[55] When he heard of an opening as ambassador to Spain, he applied for it. The fact that he couldn't speak Spanish and knew nothing about the country made the prospect even more enticing; it was Greece again in the land of Don Quixote, another chance at his chivalric ideal. But he was turned down by President Jackson. Mann tried to comfort him by reminding him that the age of chivalry was over, and professional achievement entailed routine: "The nineteenth century is too late for your military knight-errantry. . . . You must tame your war-horse to work in common harness."[56]

He was also uncomfortably reminded that he had not taken on the adult responsibilities of marriage and fatherhood, and that time was going by. Longfellow had noticed that Chev was "painfully conscious of the passing of time, as if life itself were slipping from under his feet. At the asylum, a bell rings every quarter of an hour—a constant *memento mori*; and wherever he goes he hears this melancholy bell."[57] George Combe advised Chev to tame his war-horse by marrying a sedate middle-aged woman and thereby establish domestic tranquillity, and the "inexpressible charm . . . which relieves and cherishes the better faculties of the mind . . . and makes them wear longer."[58] A plain older woman was certainly the last kind of spouse Chev desired. Even his servants knew that "a plain woman was one of the things he liked least in life."[59] And Combe himself had married a pretty heiress six years younger than himself. Chev was also indignant in May 1840 when John P. Bigelow, the secretary of the Commonwealth of Massachusetts, spread rumors that he was having an affair with a married woman, an accusation both false and at odds with his horror of female sexual desire. At the age of forty, circumstances were forcing Chev to begin thinking of wedding bells.

Chapter Three

THE HERO AND THE BELLE

After their dramatic meeting in July 1841, Julia did not see Chev for almost a year. In November, he left Boston for a four-month fund-raising trip in the South, taking three of his pupils along on the principle that blind children attracted the highest charitable donations. In New York, the Wards were presiding over the sale of their Newport and Manhattan properties. They sold The Corner for $60,000, disposed of the furniture, and sold or gave away many of the paintings, including the Cole series of *The Voyage of Life*. The mansion itself survived until 1873, when it was razed to house the first showroom of Brooks Brothers. It was always a gentleman's abode.

The Three Graces moved in with their widowed brother, Sam, at 32 Bond Street, and soon Julia was visiting Mary in Boston again. The surveillance team of Five of Clubs men in Boston avidly observed and logged her social activities in letters to Chev. "Julia is enjoying herself very much in Boston, and making many friends and admirers," Longfellow reported. "Felton is in love with her; and in speaking of her uses the superlative degree only."[1]

That winter, Boston was obsessed by the first American visit of

Charles Dickens, who arrived in Boston on January 29 with his wife, Catherine; they left their four children behind in England. The finest minds and eldest statesmen of Boston vied to honor the great Boz. Confronted with a sunny young Englishman instead of a white-bearded Concord sage (Dickens had just turned thirty), young Bostonians also hosted a rowdy banquet with seriocomic speeches in the spirit of *The Pickwick Papers.* Women were not invited to the banquet, but Julia did attend a huge party "given to *Boz and me* . . . At least I was invited before he came here, so think that I will only give him an equal share of the honor," she wrote playfully to Louisa and Annie. She danced with Sumner, Hillard, and Longo, and admired Dickens's "bright and most sparkling countenance . . . He circulates as universally as small change, and understands the art of gratifying others without troubling himself."[2] Along with receiving honors, going to parties, and being mobbed by adoring American fans, Dickens was keen to see American social institutions, and Perkins was at the top of his list. In Chev's absence, Sumner and the mayor of Boston, Jonathan Chapman, escorted him to the Institute, where the teachers and staff had been frantically scrubbing and dusting the rooms in preparation.

Dickens was polite about the beauties of the building but captivated by Laura Bridgman. In the journal of his tour, *American Notes for General Circulation*, which came out the following fall, he quoted extensively from Chev's *Ninth Annual Report*, "a very beautiful and touching narrative"; but his description of Laura became the most celebrated account of her appearance and affect. In language very much like his portrait of Little Nell in *The Old Curiosity Shop*, he described Laura as a heartbreaking heroine, rescued from her tragic confinement by the valiant doctor. "There she was, before me; built up, as it were, in a marble cell, impervious to any ray of light, or particle of sound; with her poor white hand peeping through a chink in the wall, beckoning to some good man for help, that an Immortal soul might be awakened." Dickens added a poignant detail to the standard description of Laura's green blindfold: "Like other inmates of that institution, she had a green ribbon bound round her eyelids. A doll she had dressed lay near upon the ground. I took it up, and saw that she had made a green fillet such as she wore herself, and fastened it about its mimic eyes." No one else had noticed the doll with the green blindfold. I suspect that Dickens had made it up.

Chev intensely regretted missing his chance to appear before Dickens as Laura's knight. He had much in common with Dickens; they were both dashing, confident, energetic, extroverted, restless men, committed to social reforms of all kinds. On June 6, Chev got a second opportunity for a meeting, and he, Felton, and Mayor Chapman traveled down to New York to see Dickens at a farewell breakfast the day before he sailed back to London. It was a perfect summer day, and at the country estate of the host, James Gore King, in New Jersey, there were mountains of strawberries and champagne. Since King had been Samuel Ward Senior's partner in the bank, Julia was also invited; and that evening Chev and Felton unexpectedly showed up at a party at Sam Ward's house, claiming they had missed their boat back to Boston.

Julia sang at the party, living up to her reputation as the New York Diva; and after the music the guests all played blind man's bluff with the children—a rather tactless choice, considering Chev's profession. When the Doctor's turn came to be blindfolded, he forcefully caught hold of Julia, tore off his shade, and looked commandingly into her eyes. She stared straight back and flirtatiously asked him, "Did you ever kill a man—Doctor—*do* tell me." Women seldom dared to tease the Doctor, and Chev was intrigued. The next morning, he and Felton paid an unprecedented four-hour morning call on the Wards.

Once they got home, they composed an elaborate joint thank-you note, with Chev's words in the center of a sheet of blue paper, and Felton's message around it like a frame. Chev scolded Julia for her levity: "Laugh less at others now, and you will look back more complacently upon the past," he lectured her. But he ended on a sweeter note: "I will not allow anyone but you to be amused at my expense; but you, you may laugh at me, scold at me, do anything, so you forget not that I am truly your 'Gentle Doctor.'"[3] Felton explained to Sam Ward that "the Chevalier" was not at all offended by Julia's teasing, but flirting too after his fashion. "He thinks as I do that your incomparable sister writes extraordinarily natural poems with high intellectual culture, and that all this is lighted up with a play of fancy and wit which makes her conversation the most brilliant and delightful entertainment a man of sense can ever hope to enjoy."[4] Soon all the Club men were buzzing about the Doctor's obvious interest in Julia Ward. "I think Howe very much touched by the Fraulein Julia's various charms," wrote Sumner to Longfellow.[5] In September, Hillard reported to Longfellow that although Chev seemed "much captivated," it was hard to tell whether Julia was responding or just "indulging her love of mischief."[6]

In the fall, Chev wrote Julia two long letters in an elaborate language unlike his warm, chatty letters to the Club members. Half criticizing, half courting her, Chev expressed his fascination, but also addressed her as someone to be guided and controlled by his wisdom and experience. Undeterred, Julia came back to Boston for a repeat visit to the Institution, along with her sisters and George Hillard, and Chev escorted her to be reintroduced to Laura Bridgman. Now thirteen, Laura had grown taller and was no longer a little girl. When they arrived, she felt Chev's hand, and her face "was irradiated with joy," Julia told Louisa and Annie. Laura was not so pleased to feel the hand of a strange woman. "Where does she come from? New York. Whose friend is she? The Dr—do he go to see her. . . . Indeed, replied Hillard with a quizzical laugh." Julia never says it straight out, but it must have been clear that Laura was besotted, jealous, and very possessive. The Doctor had begged Julia to wear her snake bracelet to show Laura "what a snake was like."

The Dr put her hand upon my snake, and made her feel it. She started back, making a quick impassioned noise, half-laughing, half-afraid—at last she took hold of it, tried to clasp and unclasp

> *it on my wrist, and laughed a great deal—she liked my muff very much and played with the little tails on it—the Dr went away and staid some time. When he came back, she took his hand, and said at once, "I do not want a snake." She had been laughing in a very painful manner, distorting her features very much—the Dr told her she did not look pretty when she laughed so, whereupon she immediately stopped and forced her mouth into a pleasanter expression.*[7]

To post-Freudian readers, Laura's play with the snake, the muff, and its fur tails is almost parodically sexual. Of course, touch was her only sense, and she liked the feel of fur. Still, her "painful" laughter and her rejection of the snake bracelet, as well as the Doctor disciplining her by warning that she did not look pretty when she laughed, alerted Julia to the dangers of female dependence. Laura's silencing and submission to the Doctor's orders were a hint of what might be expected in the bonds of matrimony. "The Dr. calls me child," Julia noted succinctly at the end of her letter to her sisters. The relationship they were establishing was uncomfortably like Julia's with her father, and Chev's with Laura Bridgman.

But by winter 1843, Chev seemed to have backed off from the edgy flirtation. Julia went to Boston for a long visit, but Chev stayed away from her, and she then took off for New York to see her sisters. Playing power games to the last, he gave Julia the impression that he was going to propose to Louisa. Julia pretended not to care, but wrote to Sam: "Howe left early this morning for Hartford without having seen me, and goes to New York. The object of his visit is not to be mistaken. . . . I do not think the position he has to offer is one suited to Wevie, who does depend very much on the atmosphere in which she lives. South Boston will not be Bond Street."[8]

Thus everyone in their circle was surprised and relieved on February 21, when Chev and Julia announced their engagement. That day both of them wrote to Sam Ward, communicating the news, and revealing their emotions and expectations. The two voices of these letters were very different in language, style, and imagery. Chev's letter was confident and triumphant:

> *My Dear Ward,*
>
> *Since Julia considers you to be to her in loco parentis, she insists that I shall inform you I have had the boldness openly to offer her (what both you & she knew very well she possessed) my heart; and moreover, that she, unwilling to hold me in suspense, has accepted it, in the hope that you will ratify the compact.*
>
> *I am too happy, too much ém　u, to be able to find any words at all fitted to express my feelings; so I trust I need not, for you will do me the justice to believe I can somewhat appreciate the rare charms & gifts of your Sister; & your own warm heart will tell you that, for such an one, mine cannot fail to bear a life long harvest of affection.*
>
> *In a day or two, or as soon as I hear from you, I shall write you (if I do not see you) to say to you many things you will be desirous of knowing; until then, Dear Ward,*
>
> *believe me very truly yrs*[9]

Julia's letter was one of constraint, sacrifice, and surrender: "The Chevalier says truly—I am the captive of his bow and spear. His true devotion has won me from the world and from myself. The past is already fading from my sight; already I begin to live with him in the future, which shall be as calmly bright as love can make it. I am perfectly happy to sacrifice to one so noble and so earnest, the daydreams of my youth. He will make life more beautiful to me than any dream."[10] Imagining herself as a trophy and captive, she was already planning to give up her daydreams and her worldly frivolities, in the interests of a calm life of service in which she would be "perfectly happy." Perhaps she was echoing a famous line in Austen's *Pride and Prejudice*, when Mr. Darcy tells Elizabeth Bennett she will be "completely and perfectly and incandescently happy" as his wife. In any case, her version was submissive and muted. To her sisters she confessed that she had made Chev extravagant vows of obedience. "Yesterday I sat with the Ch. and said to him, among other things: I shall try to please you in everything. 'What?' said he, 'even to the paring of a nail?' My dear children, you know the general state of my unfortunate nails. Of course I ran instantly upstairs and cut them very short, at which he was most pleased."[11]

Chev wrote more emotionally to his friends, stressing his own joy. To Longfellow, he exclaimed about his luck and his requited love. "I need say but one word—Julia loves me! & you know all the rest; for such is your sensibility, & so carefully have you studied the passions, that you can perhaps form some faint idea of the rapture with which I pour out my long pent up affections for her. That she is a pure, & noble, & gifted creature, we all knew, & so this is much,—but oh! how little compared to what I alone have found her—gushing over with tenderness & love."[12]

Julia's family and Chev's Club brothers expressed satisfaction about the engagement. "I approve most cordially of your decision," Sam Ward wrote to Julia. "He is of all my acquaintances the *man* whom I should have chosen for you."[13] Sumner, who had become Chev's dearest friend, wrote warmly to Sam, endorsing the "strength and beauty" of the Doctor's character and emphasizing Chev's mixture of womanly "gentleness and delicacy" with manly energy, "perseverance, constancy, [and] devotion."[14] Longfellow too assured Sam that "everybody seems delighted with Julia's engagement."[15] Hillard reported on the consensus of the Club. "The piece of news which interests us most is Dr. Howe's engagement to Julia Ward—the Diva, as she is generally called among the club. Howe is very happy—his whole heaven being painted with purple streaks of love and hope. I hardly know the lady myself well enough to know how wisely and well he has chosen, but her intimate friends all value and admire her very much, and that she has had the good sense to choose a true and good man, and give up all hope of a brilliant establishment . . . is in itself an excellent trait in her nature."[16] All in all, crowed Henry Cleveland, "When a hero and a belle—and *such* a hero, and *such* a belle—are thus connected, the sound of rejoicing should be spread far and wide over the land."[17]

More privately, though, not everyone was rejoicing. Julia's brother Francis Marion called Chev that "confounded bit of Boston granite."[18] And behind the scenes, the Club members had their own doubts about Julia. Hillard admitted that "I have not been altogether pleased with what I have seen of her, though there is certainly much to admire and doubtless to love."[19] Longfellow thought Julia was too high-maintenance and demanded too much attention from Chev. She is "a fine, young, buxom damsel of force and beauty, who is full of talent, indeed carrying almost too many guns for any man who does not want to be firing salutes all the time."[20] Julia's two rivals for Chev's affection and attention, Laura Bridgman and Charles Sumner, were especially upset and agitated by the news. Bridgman asked her teacher Mary Swift whether the Doctor loved her as he did Julia. "No," Swift bluntly replied. Sumner too realized that he would never be Chev's soul mate again. Both were forced to accept the new reality.

There were signs of trouble, or at least of a power differential, from the beginning. Julia had wanted a long engagement of two or three years; Chev insisted on two or three months. Of course, the wedding would be held in New York, at the home of Uncle John Ward at 8 Bond Street. Chev felt strongly, however, that they should not linger at Bond Street with her relatives after the ceremony. "I think you would like the privacy of a crowd," he wrote to her, "on steam boat, car or hotel, to being the observed of all observed at home."[21] He was also determined to sail to Europe from New York for an extended honeymoon—to please and educate her, to be sure, but also to get her away from her family as fast as possible. Julia capitulated, since her prospective husband seemed "determined to have things his own way." She found his eagerness to begin their marriage romantic and endearing. "The Chevalier's way will be a very charming way, and is, henceforth, to be mine." Still, in a letter to her sisters, she admitted to some worries of her own: "The thought of what I have undertaken weighs upon me . . . but the wind is tempered to the shorn lamb, and the Chevalier is an angel of light—so all will be well."[22]

Only a few weeks after the engagement, however, Chev's alleged angelic temper was tested even more by the discovery that Julia was an heiress as well as a diva. He would have preferred, he said, a "penniless bride." Sam, the trustee of her estate, also wrote to Julia urging that for safety, the couple should take a steamer to Europe from Boston, rather than a sailing ship from New York—indeed, the steamer he recommended was the *Britannia*, the Cunard ship Dickens had traveled on. He offered to lend Chev money to cover the extra expenses. The Doctor was offended and shot off a testy reply:

> *I did not press her to a decision respecting the European expedition because I wished her to be with you, & uninfluenced by my views, to decide as you & she should think it best. I must say however that when I proposed to take her to Europe I did so in the full expectation, of course, of bearing the expenses myself, nor can I conceive how you should supposed (as you seem to do by your letter) that it would be otherwise. And this leads me, my brave Ward, to say a word to you on my own circumstances. I am a poor devil of a Chevalier, it is true, but when I asked Julia to share my lot in life I did so in the full belief & conviction that I could support her decently during my life, to leave her above actual want at my death, for I was led to believe that she would bring nothing with her to my humble roof but her own precious self to by my my* [sic] *household deity. My salary is 2000$ besides my quarters which are good enough for a bachelor; my pen occasionally might bring me more coppers than Riches, & I have some property well invested, which, at simple interest, gives me 1000$ per annum; so that while I can work, I can count upon 3000$.*[23]

Chev was touchy about his authority, manly prerogatives, and earning capacity, and his insistence on the husband's rights would only intensify over the succeeding years. Julia tried to see both sides. Chev, she wrote, is "very sensitive, and accustomed to an independent course of action. Sam, on the other hand, is fussy, has a great love of power, and is fond both of finding fault and of giving advice, things to which Dr. Howe is not accustomed."[24] In the end, they agreed on a compromise, which pleased nobody. Julia would have a trust fund of $3,000 a year; her property would be handled by her brothers and Uncle John Ward; and Chev would have $10,000 to draw upon when they came to buying a house. Counseled by Sumner, he signed an "antenuptial agreement," which listed all her considerable assets. Having spent his entire adult life disdaining money and property, Chev was not an expert on investments and real estate. But he saw no reason why he should not easily become one, and as his ironic joke about being "a poor devil of a Chevalier" implied, he was irritated by Sam's giving advice to an older man of fame and honor.

Julia, Chev, and Sam also clashed over her insistence on continuing to write poetry, and Chev's expectations that a wife and mother should find her sole fulfillment in her family. Again, Sam tried to persuade him not to antagonize Julia by insisting on her obedience, but to trust love and time in figuring out a mutually satisfying arrangement. He reminded Chev that poetry was as much a part of the Diva's nature and attraction as her music: "As for a woman's poetical aspirations, I should cherish them as I would the melody of her voice."[25]

Chev was unconvinced, but also deeply in love. In the two months between the engagement and the wedding, he wrote passionate, if still highly abstract, love letters to Julia. "I have no longer any *me*," he rhapsodized; "what formerly was *me* is taken away, & you hold its place."[26] He even accepted her unusual wish to call herself Mrs. Julia Ward Howe, instead of Mrs. Samuel Gridley Howe. "My family wish me to retain my maiden name, and I am myself attached to it," she wrote to Auntie

Francis.[27] It was not a great victory. The marriage began with Chev holding most of the power, and Julia trying to please him by giving up what little power she retained.

The wedding took place as scheduled on the evening of April 26, 1843. Julia's uncle, Reverend Benjamin C. Cutler, performed the ceremony, and Sumner was the best man. Compared to the glamour of Sam's Arabian Nights celebration, the wedding was modest and subdued. In fact, Julia was making such an effort to control her love of parties and fashion for Chev's sake that she turned over all the planning and shopping to Louisa and Annie. They picked out the wedding gown, fine white muslin with lace inserts, and she wore square-toed white satin shoes. Chev was rather more splendid in a bright blue broadcloth suit with gold buttons, and a waistcoat of white satin with white velvet brocade. Engraved on the gold wedding ring were their names and Chev's watchword, "Truth." Nobody noticed what Sumner was wearing—no doubt his black suit—but at the reception Julia playfully planted some silver spoons in his pocket and accused him of nicking them. Already depressed at losing his beloved friend, Sumner could not have been amused.

Laura Bridgman, the other competitor for Chev's attention and affection, was not at the wedding. She had pleaded to attend, but the Doctor refused, on the grounds that the trip to New York would be too tiring. After the wedding, Laura had a nightmare that a pig had come into her bed and was crushing her. To compensate for excluding her, Chev had suggested that Laura and another Perkins pupil, Oliver, be taken on an excursion to Boston Harbor to visit the *Britannia*, a big ship with twelve furnaces and two giant paddle wheels, which carried seventy-three passengers, forty-four crew members, and a cow. On board Laura insisted on touching everything, including the cow. If she could not share their honeymoon cabin, she could at least participate vicariously in the voyage.

On May Day, the Howes boarded the ship for Liverpool, taking Annie along with them. At seventeen, she was shy and graceful, looking, people said, "so like a lily-of-the-valley that one expected to see two long green leaves spring up beside her as she walked."[28] She had been a rather droopy lily for some months, though, and everyone in the family felt that it was good for her to have a long trip abroad and to keep Julia company while Chev was doing the research he planned to carry out in Europe. Horace Mann, and his bride, Mary Peabody, who had been married that very morning, were on board as well. They were older than the Howes, and Julia found them unfashionable and given to embarrassing public displays of affection. "Mr. and Mrs. Mann are very loving;" she wrote home, "she wears a monstrous sunbonnet; he lies down in his overcoat."[29]

The voyage was much smoother than Dickens's stormy winter crossing had been, but Julia and Annie were very sick. Chev was chivalrous and attentive. Julia wrote home:

> *During the first two days of the voyage, I was stupefied with seasickness, and even forgot that my sister was on board the steamer. On the evening of the second day I remembered her, and managed with the help of a very stout stewardess to visit her in her stateroom where she had for her roommate a cousin of the poet Longfellow. We bewailed our common miseries a little, but the next morning brought a different state of things. As soon as I was awake, my husband came to me bringing a small dose of brandy with cracked ice. "Drink this," he said, "and ask Mrs. Bean (the stewardess) to help you get on your clothes, for you must go up on deck; we shall be at Halifax in a few hours." Magnetized by the stronger will, I struggled with my weakness, and was presently clothed and carried up on deck. "Now I am going for Annie," said Dr. Howe, leaving me comfortably propped up in a safe seat. He soon returned with my dear sister, as helpless as myself. The fresh air revived us so much that we were able to take our breakfast, the first meal we ate on board, in the saloon with the other passengers. We went on shore, however, for a walk at Halifax, and from that time forth were quite able-bodied sea-goers.*[30]

The whole trip lasted fourteen days.

On a pitching and plunging ship, Chev's masterful behavior was very welcome. "I cannot tell you," she wrote to Louisa, "how good my husband is, how kind, how devoted—he is all made of pure gold."[31] He was playful, too. One night he came to bed with his hat on, and another night he wore his "hair mittens," or horsehair massage gloves, which made Julia laugh. (A brisk rub with these gloves stood in for exercise aboard ship; Harriet Martineau had taken them along when she sailed to America in the 1830s.) The evening before they landed, the captain hosted a formal banquet with a champagne toast to the Queen. The next morning, Julia assembled all the female passengers in the ladies' lounge, where she led them in singing a tribute to their hardworking stewardess:

God save our Mrs. Bean,
Best woman ever seen,
God save Mrs. Bean!

She followed it up with a toast to the cow, which one Scottish lady declined to drink; "I think she is the poorest *coo* I ever heard of."[32]

On June 2, the Howes arrived in London and moved into lodgings at 31 Upper Baker Street. The culture shock of foreign travel and setting up a household in a new country may have exacerbated Julia's anxieties about married life, and perhaps sharing a bed with Chev was more intimate on land than in a tiny cabin on a tossing ship where he was wearing his hat and hair mittens. At any rate, poems in her diary, dated June 4, suggest that she was already disappointed in marriage and apprehensive about the future. In "The Present Is Dead," she wrote about her fear of merging with a stronger personality and losing her creative gifts:

I feel my varied powers all depart
With scarce a hope they may be born anew,
And nought is left, save one poor, loving heart,
Of what I was—and that may perish too.[33]

Even worse, she wrote that "Hope died as I was led / Unto my marriage bed."[34]

What was wrong? Both Chev and Julia had high expectations of their honeymoon, but with every passing week and month, she felt more strongly that Chev's masterfulness could become domination and that his chivalry was no substitute for tenderness. For his part, he was doing his best to entertain and protect her, although as always he was impatient of socializing and wanted to be working. In London he was a celebrity. They were besieged by callers and deluged with invitations to dinners, balls, musical evenings, late-night suppers, and ten a.m. breakfasts, which were a popular way of fitting even more social occasions into the day. Samuel Rogers served plover's eggs at his, and the first week they had breakfast out four times.[35] She was fascinated by the city and diverted by the social opportunities it presented. In her letters to Louisa, she reported on the astonishing freedom older women had to dress colorfully and seductively. The Duchess of Sutherland, who had grown-up children, dressed girlishly for her ball in "a dress of brown gauze or barége over light blue satin, with a wreath of brown velvet leaves and blue forget-me-nots in her hair."[36] The Duchess of Gloucester wore a low-cut gown and white plumes in her hair; Caroline Norton's dress was "unusually *decolletée*," and Julia hinted that her hair, which was "decidedly black," might be dyed. Harriet Grote, the intellectual wife of the great historian George Grote, struck her as "grotesque . . . very tall and stout"; but even she was decked out in blue silk with a pearl necklace. In New York, married women and women of a certain age were expected to look matronly, to wear plain dresses and neat bonnets.[37]

In London, Julia realized that her husband was a luminary. Edward Everett, the American minister to Britain, said that "none of our countrymen, since I have been here, have excited greater interest,—received more attention,—or left a better impression than the Howes."[38] Julia wrote proudly to Auntie Francis, "Chev receives a great deal of attention, ladies press forward to look at him, roll up their eyes, and exclaim, 'Oh!

he is such a wonner!' I do not like that the pretty women should pay him so many compliments—it will turn his little head!"

Dr. Samuel Gridley Howe was a London lion; but a Bond Street belle, even a diva, Julia quickly realized, had no special claim to distinction. "Annie and I are little people here—we are too young to be noticed," she wrote home. "We are very demure and have learned humility."[39] At one musical evening, she told Louisa, she had shyly "lent my little wee voice."[40] Carlyle invited them for tea and toast, and favored them with a monologue, including a jab at Sumner, "a very dull man, but he did not offend people."[41] Unfortunately, Jane Carlyle had a headache that day or said she did, and so we have lost the benefit of her sharp remarks about the Howes in her diaries. Julia tried to be patient during a side trip to Dublin, when they had lunch with Maria Edgeworth. She greeted them warmly and had an animated conversation with Chev about Irish politics, slavery, Dickens, and other important things, but said to Julia only "what one says to little women in general."[42]

Julia put up with the snubs for a while, but she could not stay meek and little for long. In July, they were invited to tea with the Wordsworths, and went up to the Lake Country by train. The visit was a disaster; the trip was tiring, the weather was chilly and wet, the Wordsworths were stingy and inhospitable, and the much revered Great Poet, she wrote to Louisa, was "a crabbed old sinner, who gave us a very indifferent muffin." His widowed daughter had lost a lot of money by investing in Mississippi lands, and the conversation became increasingly "harassing" as "he was inclined no doubt to cast part of the odium upon us." The Wordsworth ladies, mother and daughter, sat icily at one end of the drawing room, Annie and Julia at the other, balancing their teacups and feeling very miffed not to be seated for a proper tea at a table. Finally the Wordsworths whined one time too many about their losses, and Julia exploded, telling them that it was their own fault for speculating in foreign stocks. "Why did you not keep your money at home?" she cheekily asked.[43] Wordsworth himself came across as narrow, biased, and rude.

Decades later she remembered his obnoxious assertion that "the misfortune of Ireland is that it is only a partially conquered country."[44] She was glad to get away.

On their side, the Wordsworths were just as pleased to see her go. "The Husband is an intelligent man," the poet opined in stately prose, "and his Wife passes among Americans as a great specimen of the best they produce in female character." His daughter Dora was much more irate about the tea party in a letter to her cousin. Dr. Howe "came with a horrid, rude, clever, radical woman of a wife. Oh what a dislike I took to that woman."[45]

After a few weeks, Julia recovered some of her American confidence. To her pleasant surprise, the performers at fancy London musicales were no better than trios she and her brothers sang back home. "They have, of course, infinitely better voices," she told Louisa, "but hang me if they sing with half the enthusiasm."[46] She was getting used to life as the silent partner of a sought-after spouse, although she was rethinking what it might be like to be a mother as well. As she confided to Louisa, "I am not good with children—for their sakes, I should almost be willing not to have any."[47]

It was too late to make that choice, if she could have. By August she knew she was pregnant and told the Howes. Sam was annoyed; he thought Chev should have brought her home before starting a family. He married again on September 20, however, so he was too busy to complain. The Howes continued on their Grand Tour, to Switzerland and Vienna, then to Milan, where Julia and Annie spent a month alone while Chev was in Paris getting his teeth fixed. A month seems like a long time for dentistry, and Francis Marion Ward, who came to visit his sisters, thought that Chev was neglectful of Julia's needs for companionship and reassurance. "The good Chev is so taken up with his own ideas and notions of education and reformation that he cares and thinks little about the objects which interest Jule and Annie."[48] Yet from his side, Chev was still ecstatic about married life, and urging Sumner from Paris to take it up. "I have been married six months; I have been by my wife's side nearly twenty-four hours of every day: I thought I knew how much I loved her but, now in my solitude, I find I did not value her enough, and all that Paris or the world could present would not hold me away from her a minute. Charlie, dear, dear Charlie, get married and make my happiness complete by the consciousness of yours."[49]

In November, back in Milan, Chev confided the news of Julia's pregnancy to Sumner, with many moral precepts on women's feelings about childbearing: "No true woman ever considered it a burden to bear her infant within her, to nourish it with her own blood, & to furnish every fibre of its frame from her own flesh. It is not, however, as some suppose, the long gestation, the pain & the suffering, that cause the mother's love for her child, because her love begins long before she feels any pain, or any inconvenience; hardly has she become conscious of the existence of her infant, when an intense and absorbing love for it fills her bosom."[50]

Julia was not quite so selfless. In her diary she recorded her fears that she would not survive childbirth. When they settled in Rome to await the birth of the baby, she found the city dark and medieval: "a great gloom and silence hung over it."[51] Catholicism offended her. The city, she wrote to Uncle John, was populated by "artists, priests, and beggars," and the Catholic Church seemed to value pomp and ceremony far above charity and humility. "They take, I think, the fattest priests to make the Cardinals, and the fattest Cardinal to make the Pope." She actually saw the Pope three times, and he looked like "an old woman dressed up very finely."[52] Chev was even more cynical about the Pope and the Catholic Church. On this at least they agreed.

Louisa's unexpected arrival on December 11, bearing trunks of beautiful clothes, and introductions to Italian society, cheered Julia up considerably. Soon, to Chev's annoyance, they were going to balls. Prince Torlonia's ball, he wrote to Sumner, was "vulgar, stupid, tawdry," ditto the Austrian ambassador's ball. There were also private parties, and Julia sang at one to great acclaim. "Julia sang beautifully, far better than she usually does," he boasted to Sumner; but he was frustrated by the long months in Rome. He whiled away the time by horseback riding with Annie and setting up a small class for blind children in their apartment. At Christmas, he tried to cheer up their chilly apartment by lighting some yule logs, but he managed to set the beams under the floor on fire instead. Annie and Louisa kept the accident a secret from Julia.

Fortunately, George Combe and his wife were in Rome for the winter. Chev and Combe busied themselves by studying the heads of Roman statues from a phrenological point of view. Julia went with them to the sculpture gallery of the Vatican, where they were much taken with the head of Zeus; and she made sly fun of them in her straight-faced account of their approval of the mythic statue by the standards of phrenology. She did get some fashion tips from Cecilia Combe, who always wore black, and told her that "she adopted this dress on account of its convenience, and that English ladies, in traveling, often did so."[53] As the daughter of the great actress Sarah Siddons, Cecilia knew something about dramatic clothes. A painting of Julia in Rome during the winter shows her dressed in black, holding a lace handkerchief, sad and pensive.

Julia herself was going to galleries and museums, particularly the Villa Borghese with its Sala dell'Ermafrodito, exhibiting statues of beautiful hermaphrodites. They fascinated her, and she was trying to write about them. In an 1843 diary, there is a fragment, perhaps a piece of a letter to an unidentified person:

> *My pen has been unusually busy during the last year—it has brought me some happy inspirations, and though the golden tide is now at its ebb, I live in the hope that it may rise again in time to float off the stranded wreck of a novel, or rather story, in the which I have been deeply engaged for three months past. It is not, understand me, a moral and fashionable work, destined to be published in three volumes, but the history of a strange being, written as truly as I knew*

how to write it. Whether it will ever be published, I cannot tell, but I should like to have had you read it, and to talk with you about it.[54]

The Boston Unitarian minister Theodore Parker and his wife, Lydia, arrived in Rome on February 17, 1844, and stayed for two months. Chev knew Parker and invited them to dinner, and a friendship began, which for Julia would be "one of the great opportunities of my life."[55] Parker was a learned clerical radical, more of a transcendentalist than a Unitarian, a linguist who had mastered Latin, Greek, Hebrew, and German. In his studies of German biblical criticism, he had begun to doubt the historical truth of the Bible and the validity of Christ's miracles. His ordination sermon, *A Discourse on the Transient and Permanent in Christianity* (1841), scandalized the Boston Unitarian clergy, and in September 1843 they tried to force him to resign from their association. In an emotional sermon, Parker resigned his pulpit in the Spring Street Church and they set out for a sabbatical year in Europe, to reflect and let things simmer down. Julia had heard reports in Boston of his heretical and sacrilegious views, but she found him delightful company, with a youthful vigor contrasting with his prematurely bald head. From the beginning she regarded him as an inspiring theologian and thinker, although Jane Carlyle had seen only "a little dreary snubnosed American with long hair over his coatneck, . . . who always had a hand like a frog when you touched it."[56]

Julia was impressed by the Parkers' marriage, which seemed much closer and more affectionate than her own. Lydia Parker was quiet, shy, and childlike. "A certain want of physical maturity," Julia wrote mysteriously, "seemed to have prevented her from blossoming into full beauty. It was a great grief both to her and to her husband that their union was childless."[57] Nonetheless, Parker made a game of calling "this mild creature 'Bear,' and he delighted to carry out this pleasantry by adorning his étagère with miniature bears, in wood-carving, porcelain, and so on. His gold shirt stud bore the impress of a bear. At one Christmas time he showed me a breakfast cup upon which a bear had been painted, by his express order, as a gift for his wife."[58] Chev did not have teasing pet names for Julia or collect little nightingales to please her.

Yet behind this illusion of conjugal bliss lay a story even grimmer than the Howes'. Julia could never have suspected how much animosity and even despair Parker had felt in his marriage; he kept his comments in his diary in Latin, or crossed out, or even in code. Lydia was a Cabot—that most elevated of Boston families—and he had worked his way through Harvard as a schoolteacher. In January 1842, they had quarreled violently over his romantic friendship with a young woman named Anna Shaw. Both the marriage and his career were at a low point when they came to Europe. In Berne, Lydia had been entranced by the bears who lived in their own pit in the center of town. There Parker started to call her "Bear" or "Bearsie," and to collect bear artifacts and souvenirs. Parker's biographer, Dean Grodzins, speculates that the pet name had double meanings for Parker, who had pleaded in his journal in the trying, woeful, unhappy days, "Let me *bear bear bear*."[59] While abroad, he and Lydia seem to have reached a deeper understanding, but the reconciliation and second honeymoon of Europe did not last long. Both Lydia and the Unitarian ministry soon made Parker miserable, but he could not leave either one. He accepted his fate. "I cannot be otherwise than hated," he would boast in 1852. "I believe there is no living man in America so widely, abundantly, and deeply hated as I have been, and still continue to be." No one, before or since, has managed to feel quite so put-upon by Unitarians. "Bear & Forebear," he wrote in his journal in 1855.[60]

There was no English-speaking midwife in Rome, and Chev had had no formal training in obstetrics, although he would assist at several of Julia's deliveries. Fortunately, her first labor was relatively short—eight hours—and she delivered a baby girl on March 12, 1844. The Howes decided to name their daughter Julia Romana. The name drew attention; as the only American minister in Rome, Parker was asked to christen the baby, and suggested they should also have a son and name him "Samuel South Boston."

Chev was overjoyed to be a father and wrote to Sumner that witnessing childbirth had given him "further knowledge of the depth & strength of woman's nature." He felt that Julia loved him even more, in her intense love of her baby. "How beautiful, how wonderful is nature," he rhapsodized. "Only a year ago, Julia was a New York belle—apparently an artificial, possibly by some thought a beautiful one. Now she is a wife who lives only for her husband & a mother who would melt her very beauty, were it needed, to give a drop of nourishment to her child."[61] Or so he wished. Thoroughly satisfied that all had gone well, and confident in Julia's ability to manage with the help of Louisa and Annie, he took off by himself for a long-postponed trip to Greece to see at firsthand developments in the fourteen years since the war, to revisit Corinth, and to meet the king in Athens.

Meanwhile in Rome, Louisa, a lighthearted flirt who already had one broken engagement, had begun a serious romance with the expatriate sculptor Thomas Crawford, who had made the fireplaces at The Corner. Sumner had connected him with the Howes, and by the spring he had proposed to Louisa. To the horror of Sam Ward and Uncle John Ward, who regarded him as an impoverished artist at best, and a fortune hunter at worst, they wanted to be married in Rome. Chev took Crawford's side, although Tom had annoyed him by making fun of Combe and phrenology. "He seems to be doing well," he wrote Sumner, and praised Crawford's talent, taste, imagination, and potential as a brother-in-law. In fact, Crawford would have a very successful career as a sculptor and get enough important commissions to make him a rich man. His marriage to Louisa was a happy one.

In June, the Howes and Annie packed up for the slow trip back to Liverpool and the ship home, by way of Naples, Marseilles, Avignon, and then Paris, where they spent a few weeks. Chev was so sure that motherhood was a minor issue for a healthy young woman like Julia that he booked their passage to Marseilles aboard a steamer without sleeping accommodations, and he had to rush ashore to hire mattresses every night when they docked in port. Julia drily chalked up the lack of planning to his "love of the unusual."[62] They stopped in Paris for a few weeks with Crawford tagging along, and Chev persuaded him to put off the marriage until he could go to New York himself to plead his case to the Wards. But Chev could not bring himself to set a date for their departure and nearly drove Crawford crazy with his dithering. Crawford writes from Paris on June 20, "Howe has kept everything and everybody as *usual* topsy-turvy . . . One day the berths would be engaged in the summer and the next day abandoned; the packet would be thought of and talked about and given up . . . God only knows when we shall leave Europe."[63]

At last they headed to London, stopping often for the Doctor to make detours to schools for handicapped children. Making the most of their remaining time, he and Julia went to Embley in August to visit the Nightingales. Florence Nightingale, exactly Julia's age and also an heiress, was then pleading with her family to be allowed to study nursing, and she sought the Doctor's advice in a private consultation. "Dr. Howe, do you think it would be unsuitable and unbecoming for a young Englishwoman to devote herself to works of charity in hospitals and elsewhere as Catholic sisters do? Do you think it would be a dreadful thing?" she asked. He replied, "My dear Miss Florence, it would be unusual, and in England whatever is unusual is apt to be thought unsuitable, but I say to you, go forward if you have a vocation for that way of life; act up to your inspiration, and you will find that there is never anything unbecoming or unladylike in doing your duty for the good of others. Choose, go on with it wherever it may lead you, and God be with you."[64]

It was a pivotal moment for Nightingale, and also for Julia, who corresponded with Nightingale, an astringent and informative letter writer, for several years but increasingly resented Chev's double standards of womanly behavior. He seemed hypocritical in encouraging Nightingale but objecting to any vocational ambitions of her own. When she confronted Chev with the paradox, he "responded by saying that 'if he had been engaged to Florence Nightingale, and had loved her ever so dearly, he would have given her up as soon as she commenced her career as a public woman.'"[65]

In the few days left before they caught the ship back to New York, Chev managed to squeeze in some time to meet the venerable physician Richard Fowler at Salisbury. At the age of eighty, Fowler still walked three miles a day and had become an enthusiast of phrenology. He insisted on palpating Julia's head and annoyed her by pronouncing she had "no music in you by nature."[66] She was not pleased either when Chev, at Fowler's insistence, rushed down to visit a blind, deaf, and crippled old woman in the Portsmouth workhouse.

In her parting shot at Fowler, phrenology, and Chev's obsession with the disabled, Julia wrote "a humorous travesty" of his report on the visit:

Dear Sir, I went south:
As far as Portsmouth,
And found a most charming old woman,
Delightfully void
Of all that's enjoyed
By the animal vaguely called human.
She has but one jaw,
Has teeth like a saw,
Her ears and her eyes I delight in:
The one could not hear
Tho' a cannon were near,
The others are holes with no sight in.
Her sinciput lies
Just over her eyes,
Not far from the bone parietal;
The crown of her head,

Be it vulgarly said,
Is shaped like the back of a beetle. . . .[67]

When she showed the verses to Chev, he was not amused. As Julia admitted in her old age, at this time in her life she was "a person of antipathies rather than sympathies."[68] At last they sailed from Liverpool on August 17. Despite Chev's rebuke, Julia was still in high spirits on the voyage, composing a comic "Milsiad" for their friend Arthur Mills, a Conservative MP who was on the ship. As they approached Boston Harbor, she wrote an elegiac note of farewell to her poetic harp, her laughter, and her youth.

Harp of the West, through wind and foggy weather
We've sung our passage to our native land,
Now I have reached the terminus of tether,
And I must lay thee, trembling, from my hand.
That hand must ply the ignominious needle,
This mind brood o'er the salutary dish,
I must grow sober as a parish beadle,
And having fish to fry, must fry my fish.
Some happier muse than mine shall wake thy spell,
Harp of the West, oh Gemini! farewell.

The belle and the hero were beginning their marriage for real.

Chapter Four

MARRIAGE AND MATERNITY

On September 11, 1844, the Howes arrived in Boston and moved into the Doctor's Wing of the Perkins Institution. Chev had not even unpacked before he wrote ecstatically to Sumner to describe his feelings: "I have at last brought home my noble & beloved bride & her beautiful suckling babe. We have been here but two hours, have taken but one meal, yet in that brief time I have enjoyed a feeling [of] satisfaction & of happiness unequalled by any I have experienced in all my journeying. When my heart is full of joy or sorrow, it turns to you & yearns for your sympathy; in fact as Julia often says, Sumner ought to have been a woman & you to have married her: but I should not agree to this in any monogamic land, for Julia is my love as a wife."[1] It's typical of Chev that he should have written to Sumner only two hours after getting home, emphasizing his new manly status, expressing his affection, but setting out the new terms of their friendship. Sumner was assured of Chev's special affection but explicitly demoted to second place. He would have to adjust to his new position.

The noble and beloved bride did not share Chev's joy at returning to the Institution. South Boston did not feel like home to her at all. Fifty years later, when she wrote her memoir, the shock of her arrival was still vivid: "The change had already been great, from my position as a family idol and 'the superior young lady' of an admiring circle to that of a wife overshadowed for the time by the splendor of her husband's reputation. This I had accepted willingly. But the change from my life of easy circumstances and brilliant surroundings to the mistress of a suite of rooms in the Institution for the Blind at South Boston was much greater."[2]

"A suite of rooms"—Julia had the gift of scornful understatement. At best, Perkins was still more like a hotel than a home, but in contrast to the luxurious hotels of Europe, it was grim. The walls were dark gray and green; the water closets stank. In contrast to the hotels on the humming streets of London, Paris, Rome, or New York, the building stood on a high hill, in a field overlooking the ocean. Getting to Boston meant a two-hour trip by omnibus through some rough parts of town. The Howes' daughter Laura, who loved the Institution herself, imagined it through her mother's eyes as a Gothic castle, a "bleak, lofty house set on a hill, four-square to all the winds that blew; with high-studded rooms, cold halls paved with white and gray marble, echoing galleries; where three fourths of the inmates were blind, and the remaining fourth were devoting their time and energies to the blind."[3] As her comic poem about the old lady of Plymouth had revealed, Julia was physically repelled by the disabled. She had to draw on all her spiritual strength to make herself live among them.

Chev could not have anticipated Julia's feelings about the Institution. In his eyes, Perkins was a handsome building. Moreover, he saw Julia as a wife who lived only for her husband and child. Satisfied that her needs had been met, he plunged back into his usual hectic schedule, leaving Julia to run the household. Although Chev's sister Jennette had stayed on to supervise the Doctor's Wing, she was a "silent, inarticulate person," decorous and judgmental; Julia did not want to seem incompetent before her.[4] She set herself to learning the craft of housekeeping, dealing with the soap fat merchant and the rag man and all the prosaic details of everyday life. The transition from princess and bride to mother and housekeeper was abrupt and traumatic, as her daughters understood:

> *She had been a flower of the field, taking no thought for food or raiment; her sisters chose and bought her clothes, had her dresses made, and put them on her. Her studies, her music, her dreams, her compositions—and, it must be added, her suitors—made the world in which she lived. Now, life in its most concrete forms pressed upon her. The baby must be fed at regular intervals, and she must feed it; there must be three meals a day, and she must provide them; servants must be engaged, trained, directed, and all this she must do. Her thoughts soared heavenward; but now there was a string attached to them, and they must be pulled down to attend to the leg of mutton and the baby's cloak.*[5]

Cooking was a particular trial. The Ward family had teased her that she could describe every room at The Corner except the kitchen. Now she spent much of her time in the kitchen, struggling with the aid of Catharine Beecher's *Domestic Receipt Book*. Chev also wanted to entertain his male friends for dinner every week, and Jennette, who did not like socializing, stayed away on party night. Moreover, Chev was a health advocate who would not eat fried food, pastry, ham, or coconut cakes. He was also becoming increasingly abstinent about wine, although he expected a fine spread for the Club members. Julia hired cook after cook, but Chev had a tendency to overrule her decisions and fire them, so there was a considerable turnover in the kitchen. Inevitably, she made many mistakes in her first efforts to act as hostess. She ordered ice cream delivered for a dinner party and was embarrassed when it was left in a snowdrift and not discovered until the next morning. She left the pass-through between the kitchen and the dining room open, and one night Annie reported that she could see the cook at work on the venison through the open window. These standard domestic catastrophes, which Louisa May Alcott would play for humor and sentiment in her account of Meg's first year as a bride in *Little Women*, were humiliating failures for Julia.

Learning to care for the baby was another trial. Julia Romana hardly ever napped during the day and wet the bed she shared with her mother every night. Although she felt "weakened by the long nursing," Julia refused to wean her for fifteen months.[6] At least the combination of a breast-feeding wife and a bed-wetting baby kept Chev out of the bedroom, a covert form of birth control that Julia would maintain. Socially, too, Julia found Boston unexpectedly difficult to negotiate. She had been popular as a lively visitor from New York; as a tired housewife in an unfashionable part of the city, however, she was kept at a chilly distance. Those first impressions of snobbery colored her attitudes towards the "frozen ocean of Boston life" for a long time; walking by the Charles Street Charitable Eye and Ear Infirmary, she quipped to a friend, "Oh, I did not know there *was* a charitable eye or ear in Boston!"[7]

One great comfort was attending Theodore Parker's sermons at his new congregation. Challenging Unitarian orthodoxy to focus on social reform and abolitionism, he drew hundreds to his pulpit at the Melodeon Theater. "It was hard to go out from his presence, all aglow with the enthusiasm which he felt and inspired, and to hear him spoken of as a teacher of irreligion, a pest to the community." Boston society was frigid, but she would rather "hear Theodore Parker preach than go to the theater."[8]

Chev was very little help in her efforts to adjust to a new environment and a new set of responsibilities. He got up early and came back late, with "scarcely half an hour in twenty-four to give me."[9] He was opposed to her teaching at the Institution, so that outlet was closed to her. Meanwhile, Chev was brimming over with new causes and new crusades. He got involved in an acrimonious dispute about the education of deaf children, opposing those who argued that the children should be taught to sign, while he was staunchly in favor of teaching them to read lips and to speak. In league with Horace Mann, he criticized the Boston School

Board for its old-fashioned curriculum and outmoded methods of memorization and rote learning. He was elected for a brief term on the Boston School Committee; then he threw himself into a campaign to set up a school for the mentally handicapped, and became the General Superintendent of the first Massachusetts School for Idiotic and Feeble-minded Youth in 1848. He stayed active in the role for the next twenty-five years. As Julia noted affectionately in her letters, he was "intoxicated with benevolence," the very model of a "perfectabilian philanthropist."[10]

Finally, he got into a ferocious argument with the Boston Prison Discipline Society about the abolition of solitary confinement. The argument about the efficacy and psychological costs of this system had been debated for years, but Chev's views came from his feelings that his solitary confinement in Prussia would have been much worse if he had been made to mix with the ribald, sweaty mob of ordinary convicts. Although he was held in a solitary cell, his prudery was threatened by the obscene bantering of the male prisoners and the shameless solicitations of the female prisoners. It was better for the moral development of the convict, he insisted, to be isolated from the bad influence of other prisoners and exposed only to good jailers. How ordinary convicts might feel about being cut off from other prisoners was not his concern. In this shortsighted advocacy of solitary confinement, as in his rejection of signing, Chev was on the wrong side of history.

Nonetheless, he and Sumner, who had no real commitment to prison reform but went along out of friendship, aggressively argued their case for solitary confinement in seven debates before the Society in June 1847. They were soundly defeated, and even some of their friends and colleagues were dismayed by their harsh fanaticism. Among Howe's biographers, Harold Schwartz regards their speeches as a low point for both men, "patronizing when agreed with, but wild with rage, contemptuous, and vituperative when opposed."[11]

Julia loyally went to six of the seven debates and praised Sumner's "masterly" final address: "he held the audience breathless for two hours and a half," she unpersuasively insisted.[12] But even she had to admit that Sumner was "recondite in language and elaborate in style" as a speaker, with an addiction to long quotations.[13] Dinner guests at the Howes', she warned a friend, had best avoid a long list of topics that could goad Chev and his friends into furious arguments and endless monologues, including "all insane hospitals, idiots, educated or otherwise, and madness of every description . . . All prisons, prison disciplines, prison societies, prison reforms, secretaries of prison reform societies, every form of legal imprisonment, . . . philanthropic enterprises, workhouses, relief and vigilance committees, interests of the African race."[14]

While Julia was trying to find her place on the icy slopes of Boston society, her old friendships were shifting too. Mary Ward and her sister Martha paid a formal welcoming call soon after she arrived, but the visit was awkward, since Louisa had broken her engagement to their heartbroken brother John and was about to marry Thomas Crawford. "Martha was very constrained," Julia wrote to her sisters, but "Mary was more like her old self than I expected—the interview was, however, a painful one. It was kind of them to call—I think Mary will love me again, as I will ever love her."[15] Indeed, Mary married the Bostonian Charles Dorr, and stood faithfully by Julia through the years ahead.

Laura Bridgman, now fifteen, was still living in her room in the Doctor's Wing. While the Howes were away, she had written frantically to them both, but Chev rarely replied. Her teachers had told her about the birth of Julia Romana. "I love your baby very much & am your precious," she wrote to Julia. "I should like to live with you and your husband & dear baby. While you were away one year I was in great misery, & had to miss you many times."[16] Laura had been so obsessed with Chev's return that the teachers decided not to tell her the exact date of his arrival, because she would not be able to sleep. In August she dreamed that "his coat was made of velvet in Europe and he did not ask me how I did."[17]

Chev was not wearing velvet when he returned to Perkins, but Laura had accurately sensed that he had been distancing himself from her for many months. Now that he had a real family, he had no more need of a surrogate one. He complained that Laura was much less gifted in language than he expected for the time elapsed, with "a constitutional disposition to irritability and violence of temper" he had not previously observed.[18] Chev was also angry that in his absence, Laura had become a baptized Christian; he had given orders that she should not be taught about religion, so he could investigate her pure and "natural" religious ideas. He did not consider how his disappearance and silence might have contributed to her emotional volatility, or understand how she had been comforted by religious faith. An unacknowledged element in his feelings was that Laura's physical appearance had altered as she entered puberty; when he came home she was an awkward disabled adolescent, rather than a pretty child, and her sexual maturity and developing body made him uncomfortable. He gave orders that she should not be allowed to share a bed with her teachers or any of the other pupils, probably to prevent sexual contact or stimulation; but that prohibition too cut Laura off from the pleasures of touch, her only remaining sense.

Sarah Wight was assigned to take over as Laura's teacher and to help her make the transition to "self-controlled," i.e., sexually disciplined, womanhood.[19] As the Doctor withdrew to spend more time on his work and with his family, Sarah Wight began to take over his place in Laura's life, although never to replace him in her heart. To his great credit, it must be said, Chev never abandoned Laura professionally. He continued to see her once a week at Perkins and made sure she would always be safe and supported. But after his marriage, she was never again his surrogate child, his muse, his partner in reform. While he was minutely observant of her intellectual development, he was thoroughly obtuse about her feelings. In their long relationship, Laura was not the only one who was deaf and blind.

On November 2, 1844, Julia went to New York for Louisa's wedding to Thomas Crawford. The Howes and Wards had again demanded an antenuptial agreement, but unlike Chev, who had encouraged him to resist, Crawford made no fuss when he was presented with the dreaded document. Confident that he could support his family on his earnings as a sculptor, Crawford was happy to leave Louisa's income in her name, with Uncle John Ward having the power of attorney. The Crawfords traveled in the South for almost a year. Then Louisa and Annie came to stay with the Howes for a brief, wonderful reunion in the summer of 1845, in the last months of Julia's second pregnancy. At the end of July, Tom and Louisa moved to Rome, leaving Julia deep in her prepartum depression. "I do not think that I shall ever write poetry again," she wrote to Louisa in August. "But you must not think sadly of me—it looks very dull and cloudy for me, just now, but God has given me a strong and hopeful nature—with patience, I may yet be happy."[20]

On August 25, 1845, she gave birth to a second daughter, Florence Marion Howe. Chev chose the name in honor of Florence Nightingale. Julia wrote to Louisa, "I would much rather have called the child for you, but he was so sadly disappointed about it's [*sic*] sex, that I thought it most politic to have his own way about the name in the hope that it would make him love the little creature."[21] By October, he was pestering her to wean Flossy. But she resisted, although she was nursing on demand every two hours, and Flossy was a restless sleeper, who kicked, scratched, pummeled, and rolled on top of her mother, and regularly drenched the bed. But these pummels and puddles were small prices to pay for keeping Chev out of the bedroom. They hardly saw each other during the days either. "My days and nights are pretty much divided between Julia and Florence," she wrote to Louisa. "I sleep with the baby, nurse her all night, get up, hurry through my breakfast, take care of her while Emily [the maid] gets hers, then wash & dress her, put her to sleep, drag her out in the wagon, amuse Dudie, kiss, love and scold her, etc., etc." Some days she didn't get to brush her teeth until dinnertime. Dependable Louisa sent her a box of beautiful clothes from Paris; in May she wore the new green bonnet to church, and "frightened the sexton, made the minister squint, and the congregation stare. It looked rather like a green clam shell, some folks thought." Her spirits were still high, although listening to Sumner and Chev pontificate about the sorrow of unmarried women was annoying. "Oh, my dear friends, thought I, if you could only have one baby, you would change your tune."[22]

By the New Year, however, she had concluded that Chev's coldness and indifference, rather than the babies' insistent needs, were the cause of her depression and hopelessness; she was losing all confidence in herself as a poet. Metaphors of numbness and freezing appear in her letters. "My voice is still frozen to silence," she wrote mournfully to Louisa in January 1846, "my poetry chained down by an icy band of indifference. I begin at last to believe that I am no poet and never was one, save in my imagination."[23] A month later, for the first time, she admitted to Louisa that her marriage was a failure and wondered whether marriage itself was an emotional trap for women, and maternity a draining of their animation and verve. "Dearest Wevie, what is this problem? Are we meant to change so utterly? Is it selfish, is it egotistical to wish that others may love us, take an interest in us, sympathize with us, in our maturer age, as in our youth? Are our hearts to fade and die out with our early bloom, and, in giving life to others, do we lose our own vitality, and sink into dimness, nothingness, and living death? I have tried this, and found it not good—so methinks, I will not hold it fast. But then again, what shall I do? Where shall I go to beg some scraps and remnants of affection to feed my hungry heart?"

She had tried giving in to Chev's wishes and prejudices, but she could not appease him and could not solve the problems in their marriage by herself. Still, she could not stop blaming herself for the friction between them. "May God teach him to love me, and help me to make him happy," she continued. "For our children's sake, for our own, we must strive to come nearer together, and not live such a life of separation. . . . I have come to him, have left my poetry, my music, my religion, have walked with him in his cold world of actualities. There I have learned much, but there, I can do nothing—he must come to me, must have ears for my music, must have a soul for my faith—if my nature is to sing, to pray, to feel—his is to fight, to teach, to reason; but love and patience may bring us much nearer together than we are . . . We sleep apart and baby lies in my arms."[24]

To Chev she wrote a piteous declaration of reproach and surrender. "I firmly resolved when I married you to admit to no thought, to cultivate no taste, in which you could not sympathize . . . It was long before I realized that you neither desired, nor appreciated this renunciation on my part . . . I will not expect too much from you. I will enjoy the moments of sunshine which we can enjoy together. I will treasure up every word, every look of yours that is kind and genial, to comfort me in those long, cold wintry days that I feel you do not love me."[25] There is no record of how Chev replied to this damning summary, or whether he felt any surprise, guilt, or remorse.

By this time in their young marriage, the Howes had established the terms by which they would live for the next thirty years. Julia had hoped for a progressive partnership of loving equals; Chev for a traditional union of the dominant protective husband and the submissive protected wife. He wanted her attention, appreciation, and admiration, and expected her to share his political interests and support his philanthropic endeavors. She wanted his affection, sympathy, companionship, and cooperation with her literary aspirations. They had never had the opportunity to discuss their very different expectations of marriage, and indeed, Julia, as the much younger wife and less experienced spouse, had tacitly consented to sacrificing her dreams for his happiness. But she had expected that his adoration would be increased after the honeymoon, and even more once they had a baby. She had no idea that his working life would so overpower their private life, and she did not anticipate how little he would adapt to her. She felt betrayed by Chev's inability to show his love, neglected by his workaholism, perplexed by his failure to understand her loneliness and her need to have a life as full as his own. With Annie and Louisa to write to, Julia voiced all her resentment, hurt pride, and fear of the future. Chev did not complain to his friends about his disappointments in the marriage, but he had his own resentments and feelings of betrayal, which he expressed in headaches, depression, and increased absence from home.

It is very tempting to see Chev as the heartless villain in the marriage and Julia as the helpless victim; some of Chev's friends and biographers see it the other way around, with Chev much oppressed by his wife's complaints. In a number of significant ways, however, the marriage resembled the British Victorian marriages provocatively analyzed by Phyllis Rose in her book *Parallel Lives.* In the nineteenth century, marriage followed a "patriarchal paradigm" of male power and female dependence. If husband and wife agreed with the paradigm, they could be happy and content. But as Rose persuasively argues, "every marriage was a narrative construct—or two narrative constructs. In unhappy marriages, for example, I see two versions of reality rather than two people in conflict. I see a struggle for imaginative dominance going on." Indeed, for women, marriage was a "primary political experience," an introduction to "power and powerlessness, . . . authority and obedience." Rose is interested in the way men and women negotiated the unspoken terms of dominance and obedience in their marriage. "Whatever the balance," she suggests, "every marriage is based upon some misunderstanding, articulated or not, about the relative importance, the priority of desires, between the two partners."[26] In the beginning, Julia's desires had a lower priority than Chev's. But she was not helpless, and she had sharp weapons of her own, which she would slowly learn how to deploy. As she often told her daughters, she first learned stealth: "If I told no one what I intended to do, I should be enabled to do it."[27]

In May 1846, however, Julia and Chev started sleeping together again, and their sexual reconciliation may have augured other improvements in their relationship. Soon after, using part of the $10,000 agreed upon in the antenuptial, Chev bought an old farmhouse with six acres of land, six miles from the Institution, close enough that he could walk to work, but remote enough that Julia felt independent. They moved in June. Julia was elated. "We removed to this abode on a lovely summer day; and as I entered the grounds I involuntarily exclaimed, 'This is green peace!'" Her friends teased her about her joy in the new home, and asked, "How are you getting on at Green Beans—is that the name?"[28] Green Peace had its own multiple staircases, the cat-stairs and the dog-stairs, the top-stairs and the long-stairs, but they were charming and Dickensian—not the chilly marble stairs of Perkins. Without Jennette to spy on her, or Laura to make her feel uncomfortable and guilty, Julia happily unpacked her household goods and set to decorating her first real home with the primary colors she had loved as a child. She chose turkey-red cushions for the window seat, and put her old bookcase lined with crimson silk in the dining room. Their best furniture from Europe went into the parlor, along with a new Chickering piano (paid for by Uncle John Ward), and Lord Byron's helmet hung atop a green iron hat tree in the hall. The helmet was surprisingly tiny. As their daughter Maud tactfully noted somewhat later, Byron "had a very small though beautiful head." In the tradition of grasping Excalibur or wearing the glass slipper, many visitors to the Howe home would try unsuccessfully to put the helmet on. Eventually the third daughter, Laura, would be able to wear it. "My dear child," Chev congratulated her, "if your head was a very little smaller, you would be an idiot!"[29]

Chev did some renovating and decorating of his own and even began to enjoy gardening. He built a new wing, a greenhouse, and a bowling alley, and set up a kitchen garden with peas, tomatoes, beans, squash, and potatoes. He also laid out strawberry beds, a rose garden, and fruit trees, especially the seven pear trees that "he watched as if they were deficient children," wrapping the pears in cotton wool to ripen in drawers.[30] Forbidding the children to touch a berry or a fallen peach, Chev hired an English gardener, Mr. Arrow, to care for the trees. The laburnums, the two pink hawthorns, and the Balm of Gilead tree, plus phlox, dahlias, jasmines, mignonettes, peonies, lilies, and lilacs made the outside of Green Peace colorful, fragrant, and lush.

In June 1846, Annie married Adolph Mailliard in New York, in a gown of white tulle and lace, which cost two hundred dollars; Julia attended her in a Parisian frock supplied by her personal shopper, Louisa.[31] Adolph was a handsome, bearded Frenchman who had been secretary to Prince Joseph Bonaparte and then the executor of his estate. He was a serious horse breeder, and the Mailliards planned to live in Bordentown, New Jersey, on the Bonaparte estate, and look after their Thoroughbred stables. Annie would face some trials in her marriage, but on the whole she was much more content with Adolph than Julia was with Chev. When Julia visited her, she found Annie happy, "handsomer than ever before," and enjoying her splendid home.[32]

In the middle of July, Chev took off for a vigorous two-week water cure in Brattleboro, Vermont. Longfellow had been there in the spring and recommended it. Chev always found hydrotherapy helpful for his headaches and constipation, and believed the daily regime of bathing, showering, wrapping up in cold sheets, and drinking the mineral water would "astonish your bowels."[33] Back in Boston, he kept up the spa routine, as he wrote to Horace Mann: "A part of each day I have to *fight for life*; if I do not take at least one cold bath I get sick; and if after each bath I do not take smart exercise for at least half an hour, I should turn into an icicle and die. I am up by half-past five, and chilled down and warmed up again by half-past six, for the first exercise at the Institution. I have to work there and to walk some six miles daily and see to my idiots, and worry the rest of the time."[34] Hydrotherapy gave him a manly excuse to be nurtured and cared for.

Decorations and renovations at Green Peace continued throughout the summer. At the end of July, Adolph Mailliard's father had a big sale of the Joseph Bonaparte household furnishings, and Julia bought a blue Gobelin carpet with a central medallion of portraits of Napoleon and

Josephine and a strawberry-colored border of fish, dolphins, birds, and flowers on a soft gold ground. Installed at Green Peace, the carpet became a favorite play space for the children.

Once the summer was over, however, the old problems of loneliness and isolation came back to plague Julia. Chev's work routines started again, and as usual he was "a little grumpy, never fond of kissing."[35] He needed only four or five hours of sleep a night, got up at 5:00 a.m., went to work at 6:30, and "cared nothing for recreation in the ordinary sense of the word."[36] Green Peace was much more comfortable and attractive than the Doctor's Wing, but it was still in remote South Boston. She tried to establish calling hours on Friday afternoons, but only Edward Everett and his wife ventured out, and Sumner was the only unmarried man who came to the house. She was desperate for company and stimulation. "I have nothing but myself to write about—for four months past I have heard only myself, talked with myself, eaten and drunk myself, made a solemn vow to myself every morning, and condoled with myself that I was about to be left to myself for another day."[37]

To make things worse, the Howes were facing financial problems. Ever resentful of the Wards' control of Julia's money, Chev had nagged and strategized to gain control over her estate and managed to get enough to speculate in real estate. In 1845, he had started to buy land in South Boston, with her money but in his own name, expecting a boom that did not come for one hundred fifty years. Julia had no money of her own for clothes or household goods. Once again, her letters to her sisters were dominated by self-pity and impotent complaint. "I live in a place in which I have few social relations, and all too recent to be intimate . . . nobody takes the least interest in what I think, I am forced to make myself an imaginary public, and to tell it the secrets of my poor little ridiculous brain. While I am employed with fictions my husband is dealing with facts . . . At least I know all that is in *his* mind, if he does not occupy himself much with mine."[38] At some level, too, she confided to Louisa, she feared that bitterness and boredom were destroying her abilities to write: "My fingers are becoming less and less familiar with the pen, my thoughts grow daily more insignificant and commonplace."[39]

Since the first few months of her marriage, she wrote mournfully, she had "lived in a state of somnambulism, occupied principally with digestion, sleep, and babies . . . Oh dearest Wevie, God only knows what I have suffered from this stupor—it has been like blindness, like death, like exile from all things beautiful and good." For the first time, she began to formulate opinions about the sanctification of motherhood, and the expectation that all women should welcome and embrace it. "It is a blessed thing to be a mother," she wrote Louisa, "but there are bounds to all things, and no woman is under any obligation to sacrifice the whole of her existence to the mere act of bringing children into the world. I cannot help considering the excess of this as . . . degrading to a woman whose spiritual nature has any strength. Men, on the contrary, think it glorification enough for a woman to be a wife and mother in any way, and upon any terms."[40]

To her relief, Chev decided they should rent a house in Boston for the winter of 1846–47, and Julia saw friends, gave parties, and started writing again. "It has been strange to me," she told Annie, "to return to life and to feel that I have any sympathy with human beings, after the long interval of quiet and indifference which succeeded my marriage. I have been singing and writing poetry, so you may know that I have been happy . . . God forgive me if I do wrong in following with ardor the strongest instincts of my nature."[41] By March she was writing to Louisa breathlessly describing "a devil of a winter, full of pleasure, of excitement, *le tourbillon des passions*!"[42]

And that spring Julia was reveling in a room of her own at Green Peace—a den off the library where she had "fitted up a lovely oratoire, hung with muslin draperies, and my religious engravings—in a recess, lined with red, is Crawford's lovely bas-relief of Apollo—my little brackets are placed on the walls, with statuettes on them—my Prie-Dieu is there, with the crucifix elevated above it on a bracket supported by an angel's head—my old chairs, and a little sofa complete the furniture of the room."[43] Chev bought her a season ticket to the opera, and a carriage with horses to convey her, and she went almost nightly. She was playing the new piano and singing, although she was thinking that her uncle John had been right when he had warned her not to marry. "Everyone else, instead of helping me on in my vocation tried to turn me aside from it, and I was fool enough to believe that the advice of others was better than the instinct of my own heart."[44]

And at least she was not pregnant. In June, she rejoiced that Flossy was twenty-two months old, but there was still "as yet, thank heaven, no prospect of a successor."[45] At the end of June, she hosted a triumphant dinner for the Five of Clubs—from soup to salmon, sweetbreads, spinach, and strawberries. She had mastered the art of entertaining, although "for myself it is easy to find companions more congenial than the Club." To that end, she initiated a club of intelligent women who did not take themselves too seriously, including herself as the "grand universal philosopher," Jane Belknap as the "charitable censor," Mary Ward as the "moderator," and the editor Sarah Hale as the "optimist." Chev even promised to take her abroad in five years to visit Louisa. And she published an anonymous article on Goethe and Schiller in a Boston newspaper, which was praised, albeit condescendingly, in the *North American Review*, as "a charming paper, said to be written by a lady."[46] She seemed to have made it through the trials of childbirth and nursing, mastered the arts of hostessing, found congenial women friends, and made some progress with her writing.

Then on September 20, 1847, Julia learned she was pregnant again, with the baby due in March. She reacted with horror and despair. "At first I cried & raved about it, but now I am more reconciled to the idea. It will be a girl and is already christened Dolores."[47] At the end of the month, they heard that her brother Francis Marion had died in New Orleans of yellow fever. Finally, Sam Ward had lost a lot of money in speculation. Prime, Ward, and Company went bankrupt, his wife left him, and he resigned as the trustee of Julia's estate. Chev was quick to take advantage of the moment. He sold all of her New York real estate—great tracts of land in midtown and downtown—and invested the money in buying land in South Boston. Chev was not the only Ward son-in-law, however, to make a foolish real estate decision. Adolph Mailliard sold Annie's property on Thirty-Fourth Street for $1,500 and they took a belated honeymoon in Europe.

Julia kept active during her pregnancy, if only to spite Chev, who was unsympathetic to her complaints, talking about a fourth child to keep "Dolores" company, or giving her the silent treatment. "I have been alone all day with my husband, who, being out of sorts, has hardly spoken one word to me in twelve hours," she wrote to Auntie Francis.[48] Her pregnancy coincided with a time of major medical debate about the pain of childbirth. In London, in January 1847, the distinguished obstetrician Dr. James Simpson had successfully given ether to a woman in labor. Longfellow read some of the flood of articles in the *Edinburgh Review* and other periodicals about the experiment and decided ether must be used when his second wife, Fanny, delivered their third child. (His adored first wife, Mary Potter, had died slowly after a miscarriage, and he was determined to spare Fanny any pains and risks.) But he had to scramble to find a Boston physician willing to administer the drug. Finally he located a dentist, Nathan Cooley Keep (who later became dean of the Harvard dental school), and on April 7, Fanny "heroically inhaled . . . the great nepenthe," becoming the first American woman to use ether in childbirth. She wrote to her friends praising the drug: "I feel proud to be the pioneer to less suffering for poor weak womankind. This is certainly the greatest blessing of this age and I am glad to have lived in the time of its coming."[49] By 1850, English husbands, from Darwin and Dickens to Prince Albert, were demanding ether for their wives as well. Chev was not among their number, but Julia was determined to have it for her upcoming delivery.

On March 2, 1848, she went into labor while she was having tea with

Sumner in the parlor, and delivered a son. Julia and Chev both wrote to Louisa giving accounts of the birth of their first son. Chev described it as a quick and easy delivery, lasting about twenty minutes, and both "pleasant" and "enjoyable." In his account, he was in charge of the whole procedure: "I went down and dispatched the man servant for the Doctor, sent Sumner for the midwife & the girl for . . . 'chloroform.'" Neither doctor nor midwife nor chloroform was required, however; Chev delivered the infant himself, and could not refrain from lecturing Louisa on the morality of natural childbirth and the evils of ether: "A woman of good constitution, good training, good habits, & good courage need not anticipate & will not have a formidable delivery. Depend upon it, it is all wrong & wicked for women to make such delicate things of themselves & the pains of child birth are meant by a beneficent creator to be the means of leading them back to lives of temperance, exercise, and reason."[50] What Louisa, who had been in labor for fifty-two hours with her first child, Annie, thought of Chev's sermonizing and rhapsodizing, we do not know. He was certainly thrilled with his first son, who he predicted would be another classical military hero, the equal of Julius Caesar, Pericles, and Brutus.[51]

Julia's version was earthier, and contradicted Chev in several respects; "pleasant" and "enjoyable" were not the terms she chose to describe the birth. As she told the story, she was the one who sent Sumner for the doctor and nurse, and sent the maid to the pharmacy for chloroform, while Chev just hung around. He was no use for the delivery either. "The child was born after half an hour's labour, without any assistance. I suffered very little for the head, but as Chev did not know how to assist me, I had to make a tremendous effort for the shoulders, & gave one horrid scream, the only one of which I was guilty. Chev soon gave one himself: 'Oh, Dudie! It's a boy!' I couldn't believe it—we both cried & laughed . . . I had very severe afterpains."[52] They named their first son Henry Marion, although one friend suggested "Sumner Longfellow Parker Wilmot Howe." Harry was a good baby who rarely cried and slept almost all night from the beginning. At seven weeks, Julia thought of him as "the little saint" and hoped he would not feel "the melancholy which oppressed me during the period of his *creation.*"[53]

Within a month, she had recovered and was expressing her aesthetic and spiritual frustrations to a bewildered Fanny Longfellow. "Julia Howe was here *a cheval* yesterday afternoon wishing for the *intense* in life. What more can she desire than the extremes of joy and suffering in domestic life?"[54] There was not much joy for Julia in domestic life. Chev's sexuality was limited to procreation, while Julia wanted more general intimacy, kisses, and cuddling. Having tried to change his ways without success, she became convinced that he found her repulsive. In October, she wrote to her sister Annie, with comic exaggeration, but with a note of desperation: "I only feel as if my death were the one thing desirable for his comfort, but live I must, and I can unhappily be nothing but my poor half crazy self. Don't let this make you sad; it does not me. I am quite jolly as usual, but I should like to know how it feels to be something better than an object of disgust to one's husband."[55] In an effort to reassure herself about her attractiveness to Chev, she weaned Henry after only nine months and then worried about another pregnancy. She was relieved to get her period—"a certain course of nature"—in November.[56]

Some of her poems were published that month in the popular anthologies of American women's writing. The anthologist Rufus Griswold included seven of her poems in his *Female Poets of America.* Among them was a tribute called "Wordsworth," eight stanzas of the weakest poetry Howe ever committed to a page. Considering her cynical view of Wordsworth when they met in England, it is surprising that she wrote such an overwrought address to a poet "to whom we listen / As never to bard before," imploring him to "speak, for our hearts are thirsting / For the light of righteousness." As usual, she employed archaic terms, rather than the language of men speaking to men, or women to women: hark, thee, thy, thou, bard, sitteth. She depended heavily on feminine end-rhymes: winging/bringing/singing, clearer/dearer/nearer, deepest/weepest. Julia was not very proud of the poems, but she was pleased that Chev had to take notice of them; "I find that my name has been advertised in relation to Griswold's book—people come to ask Chev if *that* Mrs. Howe is his wife."[57] They should not have been in doubt, since Griswold's introduction to her contributions identified her by all her male relations: daughter of the "late eminent banker" Samuel Ward, sister of Mr. Samuel Ward Jr., "one of our most accomplished scholars," and wife of Dr. S. G. Howe, "one of the most active and wise of living philanthropists." In the best of the Griswold poems, "Woman," she began with a description of the ideal woman poet as "a vestal priestess," meek, calm, self-sacrificing, and indifferent to fame; but concluded with her witty admission that she was not that kind of woman at all.

It is a sly confession. In fact, between 1846 and 1848, Julia had begun in secret to write an extraordinary novel about her feelings of loneliness, rejection, and uncertainty as a woman and an artist. Unfinished, unpublished, and unread for over a century, the manuscript tells the tragic experience of Laurence, born with both male and female sexual organs but raised as a boy by his parents. Both a metaphor for her own feelings of androgyny and a meditation on her husband's emotional and sexual absence, the story reveals a wildly unconventional side of her imagination, with hidden depths of sexual fantasy, anger, and protest.

The discovery of the novel is among the great sagas of scholarly adventure. In 1951, Julia's granddaughter Rosalind Richards gave the manuscript to the Houghton Library at Harvard along with a huge collection of Howe family papers. Piled among what the curators labeled "10 boxes of unsorted prose manuscripts and speeches," without a title page, beginning on page 2 in the middle of a sentence, and ending midsentence in the final fragment, the narrative escaped notice until 1977, when it was discovered by Mary H. Grant, a historian researching her dissertation on Howe. She was baffled by the fragmentary text, by pages that seemed out of numerical order, and characters who appeared and disappeared as if Julia had forgotten them. "All this," she recalls, "gave the writing a slightly dreamlike quality, vague and inexplicable." She mentioned it in her biography of Howe published in 1982. In 1993, another biographer, Valarie Ziegler, looked at the manuscripts and discussed them briefly in her 2003 study *Diva Julia.* Two years later Gary Williams came upon the manuscript while researching a study of Howe as a poet. In his book *Hungry Heart*, Williams suggested a number of interpretations and lines of inquiry about the text. Finally, in 2004, he completed the huge task of organizing the fragments and published his edition of the manuscripts under the title *The Hermaphrodite.* The marketing division of the publisher, the University of Nebraska Press, had come up with the title.

The Hermaphrodite stunned Americanist scholars with its sophistication and daring.[58] No one would have guessed that the nineteenth-century female author of the conventional and pious verses printed in Griswold's anthology could be capable of producing such a sensational story and creating such lurid images of androgyny, bisexuality, homosexuality, and monstrosity. Influenced partly by her reading of French novels about androgynous creatures, and inspired by a copy of the famous Greek statue *The Sleeping Hermaphrodite*, which she had seen in the Villa Borghese in Rome, Julia foreshadowed the mid-twentieth-century female Gothic in its obsession with freaks, monsters, and especially hermaphrodites, and suggested that the woman artist is not only a divided soul but also a monster doomed to solitude and sorrow.

Laurence narrates the first part of the novel, describing his lonely childhood, baptized by "a masculine name, destined to a masculine profession, and sent to a boarding school for boys, that I might become robust and manly, and haply learn to seem that which I could never be."[59] When his younger brother is born, his father coldly sends him off to college, highly advanced intellectually, and thus presumably masculine; but physically delicate and "endowed with rare beauty" (4), thus presumably feminine. Attractive to women, but indifferent to their charms, Laurence is pursued by Emma, a beautiful widow in her late twenties. He overhears two students commenting on his physical beauty and peculiar effeminate gestures, and comparing him to the "lovely hermaphrodite in the villa Borghese." He is alarmed that his secret may be coming out. Then Emma comes to his room and begs him to make love to her. He pulls away, and she looks directly at him for the first time. "She saw the bearded lip and earnest brow, but she saw also the falling shoulders, slender neck, and rounded bosom—then with a look like that of the Medusa, . . . she murmured 'Monster!' 'I am as God made me, Emma'" Laurence replies (19).

Emma has convulsions and dies, and Laurence, rejected also by his father, flees to a hermitage in the woods, with "an apartment of moderate size, but of beautiful proportions, fitted up as a study. The pointed windows, curiously carved woodwork, and ancient furniture of the room were all in perfect keeping with each other. The walls were adorned with well-filled bookshelves, a massive writing table occupied the centre . . . Beyond it lay a small bedchamber, almost meanly furnished." In an adjoining chapel there is an altar decorated by a "strange monumental conceit," the sculptured bust of a beautiful woman, "with a marble veil covering the face" (37–38). There he stays for years, writing poetry, studying, his hair growing long, until he is discovered and rescued by Ronald, a beautiful lad of sixteen. Ronald too falls instantly in love with him, believing him to be a woman, and after many romantic vicissitudes, they meet in Heidelberg, where Ronald is befriended by fellow students. Laurence is persuaded to play Juliet in a student production, and with his hair falling in loose locks around his neck and a garland around his brow his performance is greeted with rapturous applause. Overcome by passion Ronald breaks into his chamber and attempts to rape him. Laurence drugs his wine and escapes.

Book 2 leaps to Rome, where Laurence is once again a student, but dressing as a woman, giving Howe an opportunity to denounce the confinement of women's roles, in a passionate manifesto:

> Women, the adored of all, but trusted of none; women, the golden treasures too easily lost or stolen, and therefore to be kept under lock and key; women, who cannot stay at home without surveillance, who cannot walk abroad without being interrogated at every turn by the sentinel of public opinion; women, I say, are very naturally glad now and then to throw off their chains with their petticoats, and to assume for a time the right to go where they please, and the power of doing as they please.
>
> What a new world does this open to a woman! What a delightful, dangerous abyss of novelty! It is a world of reality in exchange for a world of dreams—it is dealing with facts instead of forms, with flesh and blood, instead of satins and laces. She can hear the conversations of the camp, the cabinet, the café, the gaming table. She can learn how men talk and act when they are drunk, and angry, and sincere. She will marvel to find so much or so little in them. If she be so minded, she may learn to drink, game, and swear the best of them . . . And this masculine mania may last long, and go far, but it will not last forever. However strong, or depraved, or metaphysical the emancipated woman may be, she will in the end feel the want of someone to bully and protect her, the necessity of being cherished and admired, or kicked and cuffed. And so someday she will ignominiously strike her flag of defiance, and creep back to her woman's trappings, and to her woman's life as best she may, happy . . . [if she can find] someone who though he may outrage her best feelings, laugh at her convictions, and offend her taste, will yet praise her eyebrows, and pay her bills (131).

Howe was unable to organize these powerful fragments into a narrative whole. The manuscript peters out into fragments of poetic dialogue; Laurence never confronts or resolves his sexual ambiguity, or finds a role for himself in the world. He has another tragic parting from Ronald, succumbs to a fever, has visions and hallucinations, and is examined by a physician who is unable to pronounce him "either man or woman" but gravely declares "that he is rather both than neither" (195). In the final paragraph Laurence is in a deathlike trance and about to be buried alive; he hears the step of Ronald, who falls to his knees beside the coffin. But then? Is he rescued? The manuscript ends "he knelt for"—. The rest of the page is blank.

Critics have suggested numerous interpretations of this extraordinary work.[60] What stands out for me are the rewritings and projections of Julia's own experiences and feelings. Laurence is the poet and adventurer she might have been if she had been a boy. He competes in the university poetry competition and wins. He spends some years in an idyllic and perfectly furnished study, the apotheosis of her den at Green Peace. He enjoys the bohemian life of Heidelberg, where Sam had been a student. He speaks for her longing to move freely in the streets, unencumbered, unobserved. Julia was trying to express a sexuality and consciousness forbidden to women, but she also had to invent a fictional form to contain it. The task was formidable; unable to discuss her work with anyone, lacking narrative models and unaware of contemporary women's fiction including *Jane Eyre*, Julia abandoned the book. She was aware that it was too scandalous to be shared. Yet it must have been a comfort to her to have such a document hidden away, and to lose herself in it when the marriage was too turbulent and hurtful. Her writing was starting to come more directly from her own real life and to express her genuine feelings. But she needed a literary community to support her.[61]

In the summer of 1849, Julia sadly realized that she was pregnant again. Louisa and her family came to visit her at Green Peace, but Chev was rude and hostile to the Crawfords and critical of their noisy little girls. He created an awkward situation for Julia, broadcasting the strain in their marriage. "Louisa has had but a humdrum time of it, I fear—you know how gloomy the house is," she confided to Annie. "Chev sits in the library—Crawford and Louisa in the dining room—I flit from one to the other, quite uneasily, having nothing to bestow anywhere but my tediousness. We are all heartily glad when bedtime arrives." She admitted to Annie that she was afraid of Chev, although she insisted that she was also "tenderly attached to him." Annie would have recognized the mixed emotions; they had felt those tensions with their father. Still, Julia clung to the hope that she would feel better after the baby was born. "When the unwelcome little unborn shall have seen the light, my brain will be lightened, and I shall have a clearer mind."[62]

The unwelcome little unborn saw the light on February 27, 1850. Julia told Annie that the delivery had been her easiest, and Chev was more than usually nonchalant about the occasion. When she began to have labor pains at 9:30 p.m., he went to his study to write a letter to Horace Mann, saying he did not see the need to come up to the bedroom until he heard her screaming. Of course Julia resolved not to give him the satisfaction, and she was silent until Laura was born in half an hour, with Chev arriving at the last minute to cut the cord. Julia was cynical in her letter about the birth; the baby, she wrote, "looked like an insect . . . her arms and legs looked as if they had been parboiled."[63] The insect-like baby was first called Anna-Louisa, after Julia's sisters, but a few days later, Chev insisted that she must be named Laura Elizabeth. Laura Bridgman's position as his honorary daughter was supplanted by real daughters, and none of them would ever be named for the Ward family.

Six years had passed since Julia came home to Boston from her honeymoon; and her youthful fantasies about marriage had been shattered. She had her children, her studies, and her secret writing, but her marriage had turned out to be another imprisonment with her husband as the jailer.

Chapter Five

ROME AGAIN, HOME AGAIN

On June 12, 1850, Chev and Julia set off for their long-promised holiday in Europe. Chev had a few months' leave from Perkins; Julia was planning to stay for a longer time with the Crawfords and the Mailliards in Rome. Harry and Laura, the youngest children, came with them, along with their beloved nurse Margaret MacDonald, whom Julia called "Donald," and the children "Dee Dee." Seven-year-old Julia Romana and six-year-old Flossy, however, were left behind with the family of Chev's colleague Dr. Edward Jarvis, who ran a school for retarded children in his Concord home. Julia was more concerned that their nursemaid's daughter, Fanny Jarvis, lived there too than she was about the other inhabitants; but she was so desperate to get away from Boston that she consented to the arrangement. Chev was a reluctant passenger, unhappy to leave his daughters behind and wishing he could disembark and go home when the ship made a stop in Nova Scotia. Leaving one's children behind for long periods was not unusual in the nineteenth century; the Dickenses had done it when they came to America. Leaving some of the children behind and taking others, however, was more problematic, and Julia Romana and Flossy never completely forgave their mother for abandoning them.

They arrived in England in late June. In August, visiting the Nightingales in Derbyshire, they heard about Margaret Fuller's death in a shipwreck off Fire Island on July 19; their ship may have crossed with hers in mid-ocean. Then they went to Paris to meet Thomas Crawford. Chev stuck it out for a while, and then dashed off in September to a spa at Boppard on the Rhine to try a new water cure. While he complained that the waters at Brattleboro were tastier and more effective than those at Bad Salzig, he admitted at the end of his stay that his health was sufficiently improved to allow him to "eat my weight in anything edible, climb the steepest crags, and warm up a wet sheet in a very few minutes."[1]

On October 12, 1850, he went home to Boston aboard the *Asia*. A week later, although he would still have been at sea, Julia wrote anxiously to ask why he hadn't written: "Your silence causes me great uneasiness," she lamented.[2] At last he wrote on October 27 about his arrival and reunion with their daughters, who were overjoyed to see him when he arrived at the Jarvis home and ran out to meet him. He said they were constantly kissing him and hanging on to him, unwilling to let him out of their sight or touch. Julia wrote immediately to tell the girls how much she missed them, and with what sadness she dreamed of them; but an affectionate Papa in their hands was worth much more than an undependable Mama sending guilt-ridden letters from across the ocean. The competition between the parents for their children's loyalty was launched in that year, and Julia Romana and Flossy always felt closer to Chev, while Laura and Harry formed bonds with their mother and each other.

Julia and the rest of the clan had made it to Rome via Heidelberg in October. Thomas Crawford was doing very well financially; he had received a commission for an equestrian statue of George Washington, worth $52,000, and had bought a magnificent apartment in the Villa Negroni, surrounded by gardens of ilex and stone pines, roses, and many fountains. Julia was thrilled by the space, the luxury, the lack of restrictions, the absence of Chev. "After the privations entailed by maternity," she wrote, "the weakness and physical discomfort, the inevitable seclusion, I found myself free and untrammeled . . . I was absolutely intoxicated with the joy of freedom and used to dance across the great salon in my sister's apartment, singing 'Liberty, Liberty!'"[3]

But to the horror of Louisa and Annie, and the shock of the Anglo-American community in Rome, she did not stay at the Villa Negroni for long. This was her first chance to live alone, and she did not want to let it slip away. She quickly found a suitable apartment in the Via Capo le Case close to the Trevi Fountain and the Piazza di Spagna, bought a grand piano, and settled in. As Julia described it to her family and friends back home, her Roman holiday was placid, domestic, respectable, and reassuringly dull. Her days were filled with the children and the company of neighboring American mothers, Mrs. Dudley Field downstairs and Mrs. Augusta Freeman upstairs. To top off this decorous routine, she took lessons in Hebrew from an aged Roman rabbi, who had to be back in the ghetto by six o'clock. Julia found him a wise man and Judaism a serious religion that, unlike the idolatrous Catholic monks around her, understood the "unviolable unity of God." Still, he was no threat to Chev. Theodore Parker, however, regarded her studies as a waste of valuable time she could be devoting to her writing. He scolded her and urged her to devote herself in earnest to her work. "You have not merely talent for literature, but genius . . . and you—do nothing, nothing of much permanent value."[4]

Rome was certainly easier and more pleasant than isolated South Boston and standoffish Old Boston. During the day, she went to the park with the children and met her neighbors for tea. The Crawfords had quickly become centers of the art colony in Rome, and at night Julia went to concerts, dinners, and private theatricals, playing Tilburina in Sheridan's *The Critic* and Juliet (her favorite part) in a reading party. Even in Rome, of course, there were eyes and spies reporting on what she wore and how she behaved. At Christmas, Annie, over for yet another visit, saw Julia crying as she played the piano for the babies, and assumed that she was thinking about her festivities with all the children in Boston a year before, when she had trimmed their holiday tree.

On Christmas night, Louisa had a big party. She introduced Julia to an American traveler from Philadelphia, with the rhyming name of Horace Binney Wallace. Wallace was a graduate of Princeton, two years older than Julia. He had passed the bar in 1840 and practiced law for some years, but he was much more attracted to artistic and literary pursuits. Wallace kept his writing and publications secret, with many pseudonyms, which he frequently changed; his biographer calls him "a man of masks."[5] He was also a disciple of the French philosopher of science Auguste Comte, whose theory of positivism, and science replacing theology, became his creed. Wallace had no romantic history and was conspicuously unattached. For a while he had been a great friend of the sentimental poet Emily Chubbock, who wrote under the pseudonym Fanny Forrester. She described him as "a perfect gentleman; refined, high-bred, delicate, and manly. He is not handsome . . . but he has a very intellectual look, and a peculiarly sweet expression."[6] Julia commented on "the silvery *timbre* of his rather high voice."

Wallace was a welcome addition to the small feminine circle Julia had built up over six months in Rome. He was a writer, and he took Julia's writing seriously. Unlike Chev, he had nothing to do in Rome, no agenda, except to enjoy the city and look at pictures. He was available in a way no man in her life had ever been. Together they went to the Pantheon, the Tarpeian Rock, and the bridge of his namesake, Horatius Cocles. Every morning he bought her a bunch of violets in the plaza. With bright red hair, Wallace playfully advocated the innate superiority of the *rosso*; to Julia's delight, he was always on the lookout for a new and remarkable specimen. As she recalled later, she loved shopping for jewelry and other odds and ends. "I was not then past the poor amusement of spending money for the sake of spending it. The foolish things I brought home moved the laughter of my little Roman public. I appeared in public with some forlorn brooch or dilapidated earring; the giddy laughed outright, and the polite gazed quietly. My rooms were the refuge of all broken-down vases and halting candelabra. I lived on the third floor of a modest lodging, and all the wrecks of art that neither first, second, nor fourth would buy, found their way into my parlor, and stayed there at my expense." Wallace, she said, was amused by her scavengings, and "coming to talk of art and poetry, on my red sofa, sometimes saluted me with a paroxysm of merriment, provoked by the sight of my last purchase."[7]

Julia became infatuated. Convinced that this engaging companion was the soul mate she had dreamed of, she built up a fantasy of their attachment. Wallace was the companion who had come to feed her hungry heart with his attention. Were they lovers? I am certain they were not. Julia would not have taken the risk, and her view of love was a meeting of minds, not a twining of bodies. Wallace was a restless aesthete with a history of depressive episodes; he was not interested in an affair, and he was certainly not as infatuated with her as she was with him. At the end of January, he took off for Naples and Greece, and stayed there until March. He returned to Rome for a few weeks, and then left Rome permanently to visit Comte in Paris. By April he had returned home to Philadelphia. Julia was left in the lurch in a romance that she was mostly imagining.

Her sisters, however, were worried about her behavior, her reputation, her marriage, and her future. On April 29, Annie wrote an extraordinary letter to Chev pleading with him to ask Julia to come home. Explaining that she was writing without Julia's knowledge, she told him that Julia was miserable and lonely, needed his protection, and was on the brink of social catastrophe. If Chev would not act by the end of May to call her home, Annie would feel obliged to take Julia and the babies back to Bordentown, which would create a scandal for all of them. If she didn't hear from Chev, she herself would persuade Julia to go home. Clearly, the Crawfords as well as the Mailliards had been talking about Julia's situation, and Annie, who had become close to him, had been chosen to appeal to Chev. The letter was carefully phrased:

> *Julia is only anxious to do your bidding and I am sure that a little word from you, added to our entreaties, would bring pleasure to you both, dear Chevie—She is living very quietly with Donald, in some small apartments near us, and has devoted the winter to her children and her studies—But we all feel that it would be difficult for her to face another one so entirely alone and unprotected . . . Once on the other side of the ocean I have at least a home to offer her, should you still wish to prolong her absence—but here she must stand alone, and unprotected; save by her own virtue and dignity. Indeed I cannot tell you, dear Chevie, how much it would grieve me to leave her in such a position. I do not write at her request, nor shall I even tell her that I have done so—But I know that you will understand the motive which prompts me to trouble you.*[8]

Annie's supplicating tone suggests that there was reason to believe that Chev was now viewing the Roman stay as a break in the marriage, and wanted to punish Julia by casting her out and disgracing her. Louisa too disapproved of Julia's behavior with Wallace, and her general disregard of Roman social mores. Later, Julia would write to Louisa, apologizing for her "eccentric habits of life" in Rome, and explaining that she had felt "cast adrift, and given up to the caprices of life."[9] Chev may also have heard gossip about Julia and Wallace to add to his anger and mistrust. Later he asked her to burn his letters from that year, and he burned hers. So there is no way to be sure what happened.

At all events, Chev must have come through and done the honorable thing, because Julia packed up and left Rome in August with the Mailliards. She had been away from her husband and oldest children for more than a year, and tasted independence and the pleasures of making her own schedule, making her own friends, cooking her own meals, with no one to complain about her inadequacies as a housewife, and no one to give her the silent treatment. When she left, she felt that Rome, not Boston, was her home, and America was "the place of exile."[10]

Aboard the ship for a month, she passed the time reading, brooding about Wallace, and writing poems. In her memoir she recalled that "when others had retired for the night, I often sat alone in the cabin, meditating upon the events and lessons of the last six months. These lucubrations took the form of a number of poems, which were written with no thought of publication, but which saw the light a year or two later."[11] One was a long recollection of Rome, and of her joy in escaping home, where an unnamed "querulous voice" asked of every independent project "to what good end?" and "punctual duty" waited "with weapon duly poised to slay / Delight ere it across the threshold bound." Now she was heading back to cross that threshold, and preparing herself for the worst.

Chev's querulous voice did not greet her immediately when she returned to Green Peace early on a Saturday evening in September. He had not come to meet her at the pier, and she had made the long, dusty ride back on her own by coach. Dudie and Flossy came running out when she came up the path, hugged her fiercely, and chattered away about their activities, but her sour and critical account of their reunion is very different from Chev's full-bodied emotional one. She barely recognized the pretty little girls she had left behind in these noisy, solid, rambunctious children, who had been allowed to play outside and say what they thought without regard to feminine propriety, and who spoke with Boston accents learned from the servants. She was instantly critical of their appearance and behavior: "They seem to me very petulant and a little coarse-mannered, I mean given to loud and quick talking, contradicting each other, etc. They are in good health but constant exposure to the sun has injured the beauty of their complexions. Julia is freckled and Flossy is badly tanned. I cannot help a feeling of disappointment at finding them so, they were so fair when I left them—their voices too have a harshness of tone most unpleasant to me, who esteems too highly grace of speech in a woman." She instantly made plans to impose restrictions on them and retrain them, "if their father is willing."[12] One might think that she could have stayed home with them if she cared so much about their fair skin. Considering how much she had resented the efforts her grandmother made to keep her from being freckled or tanned, especially the thick scratchy green veil that had hidden her face as a girl, Julia's belated endorsement of pale feminine grace seems unwarranted at best. Of course, she was tired, and disappointed not to be welcomed home by Chev, and primed to blame him by her self-pitying shipboard meditations. Most of all, she had to unload her guilty feelings about leaving the girls for so long, in finding fault with them and with Chev's parenting.

The news of her arrival was printed in the newspapers, and Boston society was watching closely to see what she would do. On September 3, Fanny Longfellow wrote to her sister, "Julia Howe has returned—I hear she was much admired in Rome and her soirees much courted. With her many resources of languages, music, and clever conversation, I can imagine how attractive she must have made them, where people love society for its own sake. How dull she will probably find it in South Boston, for she is not to be satisfied with the society of husband and children, and a social nature like hers really requires more not to consume itself."[13] Superficially complimentary, the letter was packed with barbs and innuendos. With her clever conversation, need for admiration, and un-Bostonian "social nature," Fanny implied that Julia Howe was a peacock among the contented American chickens. Henry Longfellow ran into her on September 11 and noted in his journal that there was "a great sadness about her mouth."[14] The marital troubles of the Howes were no secret in Boston.

Julia recovered quickly from her first testy reactions and set herself to mending her relationship with Julia Romana and Flossy. I am "living very quietly at G.P.," she wrote to Annie, "enjoying my children, my Swedenborg, and my nocturnal walks round the house, just as if I had never been away,—no, not as if I had not had the relief of a year of rest and absence. So far, my nerves are steadier and my temper more tranquil than of old."[15] As long as the weather stayed warm, Chev and Julia kept a sort of truce. In her absence, he had hired an efficient new housekeeper, Mrs. Stanwood, who handled everything. Julia didn't like her; she never liked the women Chev hired for the house, whom she suspected of watching her and reporting her ineptitude to Chev. On the other hand, having someone else taking charge of the housework gave her time for study and writing. She was reading Comte's *Philosophie Positive*, which Wallace had given to her. Following Comte's recommendations of the study of science, she took up astronomy.

If Chev's querulous voice was stilled, it was because he had other things on his mind. Like Julia, he too was facing separation from his dearest friends, the men who truly understood him. Horace Mann was heading to Ohio to become president of Antioch College. Worst of all, while Julia was in Rome in April 1851, Sumner was chosen by the Massachusetts General Court as the replacement for Robert Winthrop in the Senate. It had been a ferociously contentious election, which dragged on for three months and twenty-six ballots. Cornelius Felton and George Hillard had supported the Compromise of 1850 and were put off by Sumner's vehemence on behalf of banning slavery in Kansas; the jolly Five of Clubs dinners were over, as the members split over abolition. When Julia came home, Sumner was getting ready to move to Washington and take his senatorial seat, and Chev was dreading their separation. A week before Sumner left, he was tormented by the thought that he would not be able "to get near you for comfort & sympathy when I am sad."[16] The reality was even worse than he had anticipated. Without Sumner to confide in, he was lonely and distraught. On December 6, he wrote, "I miss you, more even than I supposed I should. It makes me sad and almost sick at heart to think you are where I cannot reach you, be my need of sympathy ever so great."[17] And until the end of December, Julia was still nursing eighteen-month-old Laura, who shared her bed. Sexual abstinence was Julia's preferred method of birth control, but after their long separation Chev felt deprived of all kindness and affection.

It is sad how desperately each of the Howes needed comfort, compassion, tenderness, and trust, and how little they were able to get from each other. Rather than admitting his feelings of loneliness, Chev retaliated for his exclusion from her bed by retreating to the library and working silently by himself in the evenings. On her side, Julia was annoyed by his withdrawal after her long day with the children and saw his silence as a punishment. She withdrew, too, into her studies and writing. In an undated poem from this period, she gave a bleak picture of their chilly life together:

Between us the eternal silence reigneth
The calm and separation of the tomb.

He did take on one project in December 1851 in which they could be partners: the editorship of *The Commonwealth*, a struggling small newspaper, highly polemical, which offended many with its fulminations against slavery and its promotion of the Free Soil Party. Cornelius Felton was so outraged by its "vulgarity, violence and insolence" that he canceled his subscription.[18] Julia contributed an occasional column on the arts—lectures, plays, concerts—and her essays on George Sand and *Uncle Tom's Cabin* gave her a chance to speak to a sympathetic audience throughout the next few years. The paper hung on until September 1854. Chev was also an active member of the Vigilance Committee in Boston, fighting against the notorious Fugitive Slave Act of 1850, which commanded New Englanders to return runaway slaves to their "owners" in the South. He was transferring his attention and moral passions to the question of slavery, which would take over his life for the next fifteen years.

In March, Chev refused to accompany Julia to the theatre, considering it a waste of time; she was grateful to join the Longfellows when they attended. While she had been touchy about turning to "Longodingdongo" for judgments of her poetry and resented what she saw as his patronage, she began to be more at ease with him, trust him more, and consult him for advice about publishing her work. Another poet, Arthur Hugh Clough, came to Boston from England in the fall of 1852, sponsored by Emerson. Chev invited him to Green Peace, and Julia found him a cheerful addition to the household. Behind his boyish mask of joviality, though, Clough was a sharp observer of the Bostonian transcendentalists, ministers, and advanced women. His report of Julia for his male friends back home was that she dressed "so low that I'm always in terror lest she should come bodily up out of it, like a pencil out of a case."[19] He didn't like her showy singing either; she was no "Diva" to him. To her daughters, however, Julia reigned over an idyllic home. Laura's first recollection of her mother was "standing by the piano in the great dining room at Green Peace, in a black velvet dress, with her beautiful neck and arms bare, singing to us."[20]

When summer came, Julia wrote to Louisa that she was getting better at coping with Chev's coldness and irritability: "I acquired a little firmness and independence during my year of freedom, and no longer quiver at a cold look, or weep at a sharp word."[21] Then Annie was having another baby, and Julia spent two months with her while the children remained at Green Peace with Chev. No sooner did she leave for Bordentown than Julia Romana fell sick, and alarmed Chev with her expressions of guilt and remorse for imaginary sins. Religious self-castigation was Julia Romana's way of explaining why her mother was always going away, and an expression of anger and resentment. This episode was an early sign of the depression that she increasingly displayed throughout her childhood and adolescence. It is possible that Julia saw Wallace in Bordentown. He had gone to Louisville when his sister Mary died in May 1852, and then returned to Philadelphia, close to the Mailliard estate.

Little Napoleon Mailliard was born in July, and in August, Julia, Annie, the Longfellows, and all the children went to Newport. They stayed in a boardinghouse near the beach called the Cliff House and enjoyed a holiday of parties, charades, and beach life. A photograph of the group shows Fanny Longfellow and Augusta Freeman, Julia's upstairs neighbor in Rome, smiling in white summer dresses; Longfellow, buttoned up in a heavy black velvet-trimmed coat and a top hat at least a foot tall. Another visitor was Count Adam Gurowski, a radical journalist who had come to the United States from Warsaw in 1849. Gurowski, who had lost an eye in a duel, was a brilliant but eccentric aristocrat, noted for his rudeness and bad table manners, and a famous freeloader. He drove Sumner crazy by coming uninvited to his house, reading his newspapers, and staying until late at night. At communal dinners, he broke the crust of the chicken pie with his fist and ate it with his fingers but scolded the children for their bad table manners. Gurowski was such a pest that in Newport, one man hid in the loft and pulled the ladder up after him when the Count was in the neighborhood. It was Gurowski, though, who renamed Cliff House the Hotel de Rambouillet, after the seventeenth-century French salon of the bluestockings, and called Julia their Madame de Sévigné. Among Julia's pleasures were charades and theatricals; she acted Juliet taking the sleeping potion, to great applause. Juliet, because of the name and the theme, remained her favorite Shakespearean role.

Chev came to join them towards the end of the month, but he was cranky and difficult, and shuttled back and forth between the Perkins Institution and Newport. Julia complained lightly of his behavior, but her indifference to his feelings is striking; she attributed his irritability to jealousy. As she recapped the vacation to Annie in October, "Chev's sourness of disposition becomes so dreadfully aggravated by any success of mine. He was miserably sick every time he came to New Port, and fearfully cross—would not go out any where, and was strangely indignant at my enjoyment of society which was indeed very moderate."[22] Chev had some reason to be sour; Julia had been away for months, and he was bored by the idle society of Newport. Each of them, however, held the worst interpretation of the other's behavior. They had not learned how to talk to each other.

On one of his solitary wanderings away from the beach, however, Chev decided on impulse to buy Lawton's Valley, a small and dilapidated Newport farmhouse. He used Julia's money to pay for it but put his own name on the deed. The house featured a lovely setting, with a brook Chev dammed up and redirected, and a picturesque old mill by a small waterfall. Over the next few summers, Julia made a studio for herself in a tiny attic room that held just a little pine table and a chair but had the great advantage of a heavy door. It was hot and buzzing with wasps, but in this room of her own, Julia could write as she pleased. After doing housekeeping and taking a morning walk, she went to her study to read and write. The children knew they must not interrupt her P.T.—her "precious time." Edward Twisleton, a British friend who had been on their ship to London in 1850, came to visit in the early fall, and she enjoyed having him as a dinner guest; they shared literary interests.

In Chev's kingdom of the blind, everyone seemed to complain of failing eyesight. That fall all of them were having eye problems. In September 1852, Wallace declared that his eyesight had completely broken down, and that he was unable to rest. He sought the advice of several doctors in Philadelphia; one grudgingly allowed that there might be "congestion of certain optic vessels at the base of the brain," but another said there was nothing "the matter with his eyes at all."[23] Visual disorders could also be hysterical symptoms, physical ways of expressing psychological pain. Both Chev and Julia also suffered from eye problems. Julia always thought a northern light was responsible for her ocular afflictions, and indeed they both did a lot of reading and writing in poor light. Eye problems nevertheless seem like an apt metaphor of their problems of vision and insight.

Chev had long been a health fanatic, and in the fall he abruptly banned wine at parties. The Longfellows came for dinner in November and found to their dismay that they had only cold water to drink. "The Dr. does not mean to do his penance alone," Longfellow wryly observed.[24] Chev gave Julia permission to have her friends over for tea and whist, a concession she found belittling and condescending. "What an ass he must take me for!" she wrote indignantly to Annie. "Do you think that Giant Despair ever gave tea-parties?" She was feeling like Giant Despair, lamenting that "my books are all that keep me alive."[25]

Adding to her depression was Wallace's departure for Europe on November 8. He sailed on the *Arctic* from New York to Liverpool, headed to Paris, and took lodgings at the Bains de Tivoli, a hydrotherapeutic spa, under the care of a Dr. Bertin. On December 13, he went to visit Comte. He did not write to Julia, while she continued to write to him. A letter of January 7, 1853, from Boston shows how indiscreetly she had confided in him about her unhappy marriage: "I have been made happy by hearing that you are miserable in Paris . . . so anxious am I to have my best friend on the same side of the water with me again . . . It was so unkind of you to go and I miss you so much." She especially missed his help with her book of poems. "I have felt often tempted to publish my poems, separately, this winter. *Putnam's New Monthly* would do very well to bring them out, but I shall keep them all to myself, waiting for your advice." She chided him for his failure to write. "You must not forget me. I am too lonely, too helpless, too orphaned to be deserted by you, my brother." Wallace obviously knew about her unhappiness; she wrote that "I have been leading a very lonely and unsympathetic life ever since I came from New Port." Her language is much like Chev's to Sumner, and she emphasized her sadness in her self-characterization: "I am very thin and ugly this winter—this alone consoles me for being unseen of you. Farewell, my dear, dear friend—God bless you. Let me know when I may see you again. Glauko."[26] Wallace had called her Glaukopis, using the Homeric epithet for Athena in *The Odyssey*, meaning bright-eyed, and she had thought of using "Sybil Glauko" as a pen name. Chev had never given her a pet name. Calling herself Glauko was doubly significant; Wallace had praised her eyes, and unseen by him, she felt that she had lost her beauty and health.

She was unable to mail the letter, though, because she did not have Wallace's address in Paris. When Annie came for her usual winter visit, Julia asked if the Mailliards could provide it. Annie turned away in tears. It was thus Julia learned that Wallace had committed suicide in Paris on December 16, 1852. He had cut his throat. Three days before, he had written to his brother John, imploring him to come to Paris. "I am exceedingly nervous . . . I have sometimes been in the deepest depression and alarm . . . Come if conveniently you can."[27] On the same day, his last social act had been to call on Comte and leave him the first deposit of an annuity.

Julia was devastated. "This sorrow departs not from me day or night," she confided to Annie, "I always loved him but I did not know how much until I lost him."[28] To Louisa she wrote more guardedly. "Surely, surely he was insane. I believe it, and can almost fancy that I saw the elements of it in some of his ways . . . My sensibilities are much exhausted. I shed few tears for him—it was rather like having had a limb amputated while under the influence of Chloroform, and then waking and feeling the loss in the *want.*"[29] Even Chev expressed sympathy for her. Before she knew that Wallace was dead, she had planned to look pretty again for his return, ordering a new wardrobe from Madame DuWavran near the Opera in Paris. When the packages arrived on January 22, including a gown in violet silk, another in white and gold, a third in green with three flounces trimmed in satin ribbons—she wanted only to wear black.[30]

Her feelings were intense, agitated, tumultuous, and confused. Only a few days before writing that calm letter to Louisa, she had composed a frantic letter to Comte, in French, ostensibly to ask for information about Wallace's death, and reassurance about the immortality of his soul, but mostly for the relief of pouring out her feelings. It is an astonishing document. Never before or again would Julia reveal herself so openly:

You do not know me, and even my name can scarcely explain to you who I am. Allow me to tell you rather what I think I am. I need only use a name that will be dear and sacred for you as for me, to introduce myself to you as a friend, rather than as a stranger. This name is that of a person who informed me of your precious works—it is he who encouraged me to undertake the study of positivism, the science of sciences. It is to him I owe what I owe to you, sir. He was my adopted father, my support, my encouragement. He was, for he is now only a holy and precious memory. You will already have guessed, I hope, that I am speaking of Horace Binney Wallace, your ardent disciple, the one who, perhaps in all America, understood you best.

She told Comte about their friendship, which she cast as one between a mentor and devoted disciple:

I met him in Rome in the winter of '50 and '51. He found in me abilities too little disciplined, an imagination loving to exhaust itself, a genius without the corresponding study. I have an ardent temperament—I suffer and am happy to excess. Nature gave me the gift of poetry, which I have used rather to embellish my happiness and console my sorrow, than for a noble and reasonable purpose. I tossed off poems here and there, as a child tosses flowers—if someone picked them up, that was good, I was grateful—if they were left to perish, that did not bother me much. That is the way Horace saw my poems and took an interest in my studies. I was busy with the Hebrew Bible, which I enjoyed reading under the guidance of an erudite rabbi—I studied Swedenborg (I have studied a lot)—but at the same time, I went to balls, I danced, I sang, I gave dramatic recitations they still talk about in Rome. Horace followed me faithfully through this life, so agitated, so full of sensations. He finally made me understand that my life was not worthy of my talent—he begged

> *me to cultivate the latter, to undertake studies that were more solid and more satisfying. I promised to do so.*

Towards the end of the letter, she described the "dull calm" of her life in South Boston in despairing terms.

> *I live in a sad little country place, not far from a rather provincial town, whose society has few charms for me. No more music! No more of that electrifying thrill in the rapport of one soul with others. I make myself poorer than I am (I have enough to live in comfort) in order to be sober in all things—I make myself obscure in order not to shock other women, who, however, resent me and do not like me. My health is weakening—I exhaust myself struggling against the melancholy that consumes me. I am alas one of those exceptional women who can not relate* ["do not love" has been crossed out] *to their children—mine are very young, and charming, but I do not enjoy them as I would like to.*

Of course she did not send the letter; it was not written to be sent. Yet she kept it among her papers.[31]

Bostonians did not know about Wallace, and she had no close women friends to confide in about her loss. That winter she gave up trying to make friends. "I cannot swim about in this frozen ocean of Boston life," she complained to Louisa, "I feel as if I had struggled enough with it, as if I could now fold my arms, and go down."[32] From that point on, she became determined to publish a book of poems—partly as a memorial to Wallace, partly as solace for her grief. To both sisters, she lamented that without her books, without her poetry, without her project, life would be empty and unbearable. Over the next few months, the Book, as she called it, took on an increasingly powerful symbolism in her mind. As a first step, she submitted a poem called "Eloise and Abelard" to George

Putnam for his monthly journal. She was furious when he rapidly sent it back, with a short letter saying that "people watch very narrowly the tone of his magazine" and "there were some lines in the poem which made it inexpedient to use it." However tactless the letter, Putnam deserves credit for picking up on the throbbing emotion in the poetry. Julia was indignant in denial; how dare he imply that there was "some impropriety of thought or expression" in her writing? She considered penning a sharp reply called "How to Write for Putnam's."[33]

Chev, too, was working on a book. In May, it was rejected by James T. Fields, who wrote candidly that it was "too wordy and not welded together strong enough to hold the . . . public attention."[34] He must have been furious, but he probably didn't share the news of his rejection with his wife.

Julia sent her manuscript to James Fields as well, and in the middle of October, Ticknor, Reed, and Fields agreed to publish it anonymously. They must have seen that, unlike the Doctor's essays, it would attract a lot of public attention. She spent the next several weeks revising her poems, and by the end of November had sought advice from Longfellow about further revisions and the title. All autumn, she wrestled with whether or not to tell Chev about the book. She was inclined to keep it a secret. As she wrote to Annie, "I have a great mind to keep the whole matter entirely from him, and not let him know anything until the morning the volume comes out. Then he can do nothing to prevent its sale in its proper form. Dear Annie, could one do this? he has known all summer that I intended publishing, and has made no objection, and not much comment."[35] Certainly Chev disapproved of women publishing, and had the power to prevent her from making her work public, and she also knew that he had little sympathy with poetry and little understanding of literary ambitions. In one sense, though, Chev's lack of interest in poetry made it safer for her to go ahead with publication, and to convince herself that he would not understand the implications of her poems. In any case, it was important for Julia's pride not to seek Chev's permission to write or publish.

At last in December the proofs arrived, and checking them was unexpectedly taxing. She complained to Annie about it:

> *. . . the endless, endless plague of looking over these proof-sheets—the doubts about phrases, rhymes, and expressions, the perplexity of names, especially, in which I have not been fortunate. To-morrow I get my last proofs. Then a fortnight must be allowed for drying and binding. Then I shall be out, fairly out, do you hear? So far my secret has been pretty well kept. My book is to bear a simple title without my name, according to Longfellow's advice. Longfellow has been reading a part of the volume in sheets—he says it will make a sensation. Chev knows nothing, as yet. I feel much excited, quite unsettled, sometimes a little frantic. If I succeed, I feel that I shall be humbled by my happiness, devoutly thankful to God. Now, I will not write any more about it.*[36]

Chapter Six

PASSION-FLOWERS

Julia's first book did make a sensation. Titled *Passion-Flowers* (a name thought up by Emmanuel Scherb and approved by Longfellow), it was published by Ticknor, Reed and Fields on December 23, 1853. Julia quickly sent copies to her family and to prominent Boston poets. And true to her word, she finally showed the book to Chev.

It must have been a painful conversation and the start of a tense Christmas weekend. There were wounds aplenty for Chev in this revelation. Not only did he learn that his wife had secretly published a very personal book of poems, but also that his beloved old friend Longfellow had conspired with her to keep it from him. Moreover, the publisher who had rejected his book had accepted hers. Above all, while Chev had privately indulged his anger towards Julia, he could not have imagined that she would humiliate him publicly, or indicate that she did not love him. *Passion-Flowers* made that possibility achingly clear.

Julia admitted to Annie that he had taken the news "very hard." His anger was a "bitter drop" in her overflowing happiness. Chev, however, did not say anything more about it in the days afterwards; he and Julia collaborated as usual to make a jolly holiday for the children, and she thought that the crisis had passed. He was consoled by the book's success, she told Annie, and "behaves very well indeed."[1] With the ordeal of confronting Chev behind her, she allowed herself to feel excited about the book's early reception and hopeful that it would establish her reputation as a serious American poet. She was pleased when Theodore Parker quoted from *Passion-Flowers* in his Christmas sermon. Chev did not go to church, even on Christmas, so he was not there to hear Parker or to watch the reaction of other parishioners. Julia hoped that the worst was over.

Passion-Flowers is a book of forty-four poems, arranged to tell the story of a poet-pilgrim's spiritual and aesthetic quest during a time in Rome. Julia had been thinking of herself as a pilgrim for many years. While the title of the book might allude to the flower symbolic of the passion of Jesus, it is also tauntingly ambiguous. The passion-flower is never specifically mentioned in the poems, although many other flowers are named, especially roses. The word *passion* appears in the book in romantic and sexual contexts.

Julia would claim that the book was about the revolutionary political events of 1848, plus slavery and religion. These are not, however, the themes that stand out and shock most readers. The first-person voice of the poems is that of a woman poet or artist confessing her ambition and her unhappiness. In "Salutatory," she addresses "brother and sister poets dear!" seeking admission to their "shining ranks," and, like "a mournful Anne Boleyn" awaiting her death sentence, inviting severe criticism from "the headsman of our tribe." In "Mother Mind," she writes about an imperious male muse who fertilizes her imagination:

My Master calls at noon or night;
I know his whisper and his nod. . . .
I bear a thought within my breast
That greatens from my growth of soul. . . .
Its greatens till its hour has come;
Not without pain it sees the light.

Metaphors of childbirth came readily to Julia's mind; the Master also sounds uncomfortably like Chev.

One of the longest poems, "Rome," clearly alludes to her own experience in Rome away from her husband:

The winter, like a college boy's vacation,
Seemed endless to anticipate, and lay
Stretched in a boundless glittering before me,
Unfathomable in its free delight.
Or if horizon-bounded like the sea,
I saw new seas beyond—the sweeping line
Limits the known, but not the possible.

Julia also defiantly included the poem George Putman had turned down as risqué, retitled "Thoughts, at the Grave of Eloisa and Abelard." "Often at midnight, on the cold stone lying," Eloisa laments, "My passionate sobs have rent the passive air." Other poems about suffering women were just as fervent and disturbing.

For Julia's contemporaries and her family, the poem that attracted the most gossip and attention was "Mind versus Mill-Stream," a parable about a miller who wants "a mild, efficient brook" to help him grind his corn. Unfortunately for him, the Miller has "a brilliant taste" and "a love of flash and spray," so he is attracted to a tempestuous stream with fierce depths beneath its deceptively quiet surface. He convinces himself that this wild, bright stream is actually the "beautiful and bland" companion that will serve him in a "snug and shady nook," although other men have tried and failed to "bridle" her by "artifice and force." When its "depths were stirred," Julia warns, in the slangiest and most forceful line she ever published, "Wow! but it wrought its will." (This may be the earliest use of "wow" in non-Scottish literature; it appears in Burns and in Scott, but the first English usage cited in the *OED* is 1892.)

Then after a brief "summer's glow" of a honeymoon, the Miller settles down to tame and bridle his bride. He builds a waterwheel and orders her to turn it. She defies him:

"Your mill-wheel?" cried the naughty Nymph,
"That would indeed be fine!
You have your business, I suppose,
Learn too that I have mine."

When the miller tries to punish and control the "perverse" stream by building a strong dam to contain her, all hell breaks loose.

"What? Will you force me?" said the sprite;
"You shall not find it gain",
So, with a flash, a dash, a crash,
She made her way amain.

Then, freeing all her pent-up soul,
She rushed, in frantic race
And fragments of the Miller's work
Threw in the Miller's face.

The Miller does not confront the stream but rebuilds the dam and diverts the water's course. "Aha! I've conquered now!" he crows. But the stream, goaded to fury, rises up, floods the mill, and flings "to utterness of waste / The Miller and his mound." In case any obtuse reader missed her point about domination and resistance in marriage, Julia appended an explicit and mischievous moral:

If you would marry happily
On the shady side of life
Choose out some quietly-disposed
And placid tempered wife,

To share the length of sober days,
And dimly slumberous nights,
But well beware those fitful souls
Fate wings for wilder flights!

For men will woo the tempest,
And wed it, to their cost,
Then swear they took it for summer dew,
And ah! their peace is lost!

The poem is a barely veiled summary of the courtship, honeymoon, and marriage, with Chev's insistence on damming up Julia's creativity and shutting her up in isolated houses. Calling the Miller "Reason" and the stream "Rhyme," she emphasizes the difference between their kinds of work. To Chev, Louisa, and Annie, moreover, there were obvious allusions to Lawton's Valley, where Chev had actually dammed up a brook and diverted the stream. Julia even made the brook a redhead, "coiffed with long wreaths of crimson weed." The threat to Chev's peace in the conclusion could not be more clear. *Passion-Flowers* was the stream's revenge on the Miller. Julia's conviction that Chev would not understand what she was saying shows how little she understood him. Or perhaps she knew he *would* understand and wanted to hurt him. In this she succeeded.

The finest poem in the book, in my judgment, is "The Heart's Astronomy," which deals with the confinement of maternity. Julia uses the metaphor of a comet, rather than a stream, to express the poetic nature and fiery drive that forces her out of a steady orbit. Since Wallace's death she had been reading about astronomy, following up on Comte's recommendations. Comets had been in the news in the 1840s. In 1847, Maria Mitchell, one of the first female astronomers in the United States, had discovered a comet, which won her acclaim and induction to the American Academy of Arts and Sciences. Named "Miss Mitchell's Comet," it lit up the New England press. Comets in general fascinated both scientists and the general public. As John Herschel, the British Astronomer Royal, explained in 1848: "The extraordinary aspect of comets, their rapid and seemingly irregular motions, the unexpected way in which they often burst upon us, . . . have in all ages rendered them objects of astonishment, not unmixed with superstitious dread to the uninitiated, and an enigma to those most conversant with the wonders of creation in the operations of natural causes."[2] Within the Howe family, "the comet" was a metaphor for the restless, explosive, and unpredictable Chev; the daughters would later attribute Julia's disorientation in the early years of her marriage to being "caught up as it were in the wake of a comet, and whirled into new and strange orbits." They acknowledged too that "life with a Comet-Apostle was not always easy."[3]

If Chev was a "Comet-Apostle," Julia was a comet-apostate, or comet-opposite; she was the one tied down to regular patterns and routines. In the poem, she begins with an image of captivity. The poet describes herself walking around the outside of her house, desperate to escape, if only for a little while, the confinement of domesticity. Her three children watch her from inside the front window. Using a metaphysical conceit, like Donne's compass in "A Valediction: Forbidding Mourning," Howe compares her trudging to the fixed orbit of a star. From the children's point of view, the mother revolves around them, and although she sometimes disappears from view behind the house, they are confident she will come around again.

Yet Howe suggests that she is not a steady maternal star, but a poetic comet, a creature with no fixed orbit, driven by inner compulsions, and capable of suddenly shooting off into space:

They watched me as Astronomers
Whose business lies in heaven afar,
Await, beside the slanting glass,
The reappearance of a star.

Not so, not so, my pretty ones,
Seek stars in yonder cloudless sky;
But mark no steadfast path for me,
A comet dire and strange am I.

But Comets too have holy laws,
Their fiery sinews to restrain,
And from their outmost wanderings
Are drawn to heaven's dear heart again.

And ye, beloved ones, when ye know,
What wild, erratic natures are,
Pray that the laws of heavenly force,
Would hold and guide the Mother star.

In her conclusion, she raises the possibility that her wild, erratic poet's nature might not be held back forever.

Julia wrote proudly to Annie that the book had been a hit in its first week of publication. "Its success became certain at once. Hundreds of copies have already been sold, and everyone likes it. Fields foretells a second edition—it is sure to pay for itself. It has done more for me, in point of consideration here, than a fortune of a hundred thousand dollars."[4] Despite its anonymity, everyone in Boston knew immediately that she had written it—the publishers themselves might have spread the word—and she hoped news of her authorship would help sales in other cities. "The authorship is, of course, no secret now, and you had best talk openly of it, all of you, as it may help the sale of the book in N.Y."[5]

Longfellow, who had been such a friend to her and the book, did not respond right away. He may have been startled, when he saw it all in print, by its themes—sorrow, anger, and defiance. On Christmas Eve he confided to his journal that the book was "full of genius, full of beauty; but what a sad tone! Another cry of discontent added to the slogan of the *femmes incomprises*!"[6] A few days later, he was still thinking about the troubling revelations of these "brilliant lamentations"; despite a "great deal of feeling, poetic and otherwise . . . here is revolt enough, between these blue covers."[7] (The first edition has brown covers, the second, blue.)

On a more enthusiastic note, the Quaker poet John Greenleaf Whittier, a warm supporter of women writers in general, wrote from the country with unmixed praise for the book, which he took as a passionate statement on the political issues of the day. "A thousand thanks for thy volume! I rec'd it some days ago, but was too ill to read it. I glanced at 'Rome,' 'Newport and Rome,' and they excited me like a war-trumpet. To-day, with the wild storm drifting without, my sister and I have been busy with thy book, and basking in the warm atmosphere of its flowers of passion. It is a great book—it has placed thee at the head of us all. I like its noble aims, its scorn and hate of priestcraft and Slavery. It speaks out bravely, beautifully all I have felt, but could not express, when contemplating the condition of Europe. God bless thee for it!"[8] Whittier went on to write a positive notice of the book for the *National Era*.

The senior transcendentalists held back. Emerson wrote a thank-you note for the gift copy but managed to avoid saying anything about the poems, with the excuse that he was busy packing for a long absence. He had only had time to peek at the pages, he said, but looked forward to reading the "private lyrics, whose air and words [are] all your own."[9] Emerson could be a master of social as well as philosophical indirection.

Julia did not send a copy to Nathaniel Hawthorne, who was living in Liverpool as the American consul. The social relations of the Howes and the Hawthornes were not of the warmest; Hawthorne had a well-known dislike of women writers, although he might have been even more irritated by Chev. He was also uncomfortable with social events. The Howe daughters write that when their parents once went to call on the Hawthornes in Concord, they were welcomed to the parlor by Sophia Hawthorne and saw Nathaniel coming down the stairs. "Mrs. Hawthorne called out 'Husband! Husband! Dr. Howe and Mrs. Howe are here!' Hawthorne bolted across the hall and through the door without even looking into the parlor."[10] The Howe family excused him as "shy," and he was; but he had made his feelings clear.

Nonetheless, William D. Ticknor was also Hawthorne's friend and publisher, and passed the book on to him. "The devil must be in the woman to publish them," Hawthorne replied; the poems "seemed to let out a whole history of domestic unhappiness." He was impressed by the vigor of the writing but appalled by the book's candor. "What a strange propensity it is in these scribbling women, to make a show of their hearts," he wrote. "However, I, for one, am much obliged to the lady, and esteem her beyond all comparison the first of American poetesses. What does her husband think of it?"[11] A few years later, in 1857, his opinion had hardened against her. "She has no genius or talent, making public what she ought to keep to herself—viz. her passions, emotions, and womanly weaknesses. *Passion Flowers* were delightful, but she ought to have been soundly whipt for publishing them."[12] His terminology makes the book sound like a slightly pornographic volume designed for male titillation.

James Fields sent a copy to Elizabeth Barrett Browning, who wrote to her friend Mary Russell Mitford that while some of the poems were good, "many of the thoughts striking, and all of a certain elevation," overall she was unimpressed. "There's a large proportion of conventional stuff in the volume. She must be a clever woman. Of the ordinary impotencies and prettinesses of female poets she does not partake, but she can't take rank with poets in the good meaning of the word, I think, so as to stand without meaning. Also there is some bad taste affectation in the dressing of her personality."[13]

Still more malicious speculation was heading across the Atlantic in the opposite direction. Francis J. Child, the Boylston Professor of Rhetoric and Oratory at Harvard, had become a close friend of Clough's when he came to Boston, and dashed off a letter to London making fun of Julia's talent as a poet, her self-regard, and her scandalous behavior. "The vanity of the woman is most amusing throughout her poems," he sneered. "She sets up to be a good dancer, to be a famous musician, a dab at theology, cooking, languages, and all the accomplishments. She hints at a time when she was a leading belle, and gives you to understand that her beauty as well as her cleverness led her to that distinction . . . She does *not* pretend to be a model wife and there are several obscure pieces addressed to different men unknown which might reasonably give offense to her husband, who by the way never saw the book until it was printed." He was dismissive of the poems themselves. They "showed a sympathy with poetical feeling without being poetical"; a "total want of ear," and thoughts "crude in themselves and vaguely expressed."[14]

In Boston, too, there was acid comment even among Julia's circle of friends. Mary Jane Quincy wrote to Mary Peabody Mann, "Some of the flowers are doubtless too passionate. What a pity they were not cut off!"[15] Louisa May Alcott did not say anything about the poems, and probably couldn't afford to buy them; but when she was invited to meet Julia at a party in January, she declined. I "can't bear her so I wouldn't go."[16] Julia was mercifully unaware of this hostility; she fielded some barbed questions about the identity of the allegorized figures in the poems but generally thought the Boston reception was "tolerably civil."[17]

Reviewers, however, were exceedingly civil. They were startled and impressed by the apparent autobiographical nature and intellectual range of the book. George Ripley, an ardent transcendentalist who had set up Brook Farm with his wife, Sophia, had become the literary critic of the *New York Tribune* after the community collapsed. Like other reviewers, he stressed the personal nature and unconventionality of the poems, especially coming from a woman, and praised *Passion-Flowers* as "a product wrung with tears and prayer from the deepest soul of the writer . . . We should not have suspected these poems to be the production of a woman. They form an entirely unique class in the whole range of female literature." Moreover, he found the language of the poetry "marked by strength and vigor, which betokens an intellect of masculine self-concentration and force."[18]

Edwin Whipple's short review in *Putnam's Monthly Magazine* could not have been more admiring. "The book is full of a remarkable power and an unusual experience, and is evidently the work of a woman," he wrote. "It betrays more subtlety of emotional analysis than we had anticipated from the title. For, if we are not mistaken, the title was the result of consideration. But it does not describe the book. The poems indicate a shrewd intellectual sympathy with passion, but they are not passionate. They are the result of a searching glance upon the author's shifting moods of experience, and a glance determined that these moods shall be variations of passionate emotion . . . They are so full of life, so audacious, so evidently the natural product of the author's experience and self-knowledge . . ." And they are full "of generous human sympathy . . . an unblenching heroism and social independence."[19] The review would have been even more gratifying if Edwin Whipple had not been a good friend of Julia's.

Ednah Dow Cheney was the only woman who reviewed *Passion-Flowers*, and she saw it as a breakthrough for American women's poetry, a huge advance on the sentimental lyrics of the ladies' annuals and the patriotic anthologies. "It really is a grave thing, and in this country, a rare thing, to publish such a book as this. Lively description and subtle sentiment have been the highest characteristics of the almost infinite . . . brood of female songsters which the Rev. Griswold has harbored under his wings; timidly yet earnestly, we have demanded something deeper than these, something truer to the idea of American womanhood. Shall we say that now, for the first time, we have been answered? We surely believe that this work stands for such a want in our Literature, and it is one that very many will not willingly let die."[20] Sales were good; *Passion-Flowers* did indeed sell out its first edition in a few weeks.

Chev had held his peace for a few weeks, but in secret he was writing to Nathaniel Parker Willis and Sumner to get their opinions of the book. Willis, the editor of the conservative *Home Journal* and the brother of the feminist writer Fanny Fern, replied on January 10, saying he hadn't read the book itself, but he had looked at the reviews and opined that Julia had "volcanic resources, and may do what she pleases in the way of fame"—i.e., the book was a dangerous eruption by a woman eager for attention and celebrity.[21] Sumner did not answer his request right away, and Chev wrote despondently to prod him, asserting in a transparent display of bravado that he needed to hear the truth and could take it. "You have not said a word about Julia's book: I wish you would say to me what you think of it—though I know well it is a vain wish,—you would not wound me by saying all you think, I know."[22] Sumner wrote back a few days later that the book stood comparison with the poetry of Elizabeth Barrett Browning, and was a work of genius. These words did not reassure Chev, however; and somewhere else he heard snide insinuations about the book and faced questions about his part in it.

And then, towards the end of January, Chev erupted in a violent confrontation with Julia, which left them both shaken and exhausted. She was dazed by his anger and alarmed by his paranoia and instability. She had never seen him so out of control. Her intended visit to Annie had to be postponed; she was too frightened to leave him alone. In February, she confided to Annie:

> *I have been able to calm and soothe him, somewhat. . . . The Book, you see, was a blow to him, and some foolish and impertinent people have hinted to him that the Miller was meant for himself—this has made him almost crazy. He has fancied, moreover, that every one despised and neglected him, and indeed it is true that I have left him too much to himself. I will not expand upon the topic of our miseries—he has been in a very dangerous state, I think, very near insanity . . . we have had the devil's own time of it, and as I tell you,*

I hardly know myself, after all that I have endured. You must not blame poor Chev, however, he could not help it.[23]

Behind his authoritative façade, Chev was thin-skinned and insecure; he feared ridicule and gossip. Competition from his wife was the last straw in the burden of resentment towards Julia he had been carrying during the ten years of their marriage. His belief that he was being persecuted and laughed at, that he was an outsider, came to the surface and made him frantic. Nevertheless, Boston appearances had to be kept up, if possible. In the face of his rage and pain, Julia felt remorse and tried instinctively to protect him. Her response to the crisis was to project the blame onto other people and to deny that she had indeed caricatured him as the Miller. But it was too late.

In exchange for agreeing to tolerate Julia's perfidy, Chev demanded severe concessions. First of all, she had to make changes in the book. When the second edition of *Passion-Flowers* came out in February, "Mind versus Mill-Stream" had already been changed to "The Mill Stream," and the last verses of the "Moral" had been cut.[24] After the third edition appeared in March, Chev's opposition escalated even more. Now he was offended by the sexual innuendo he detected in the book. During a trip to Washington that spring, he wrote to her about his concerns: "There are things in the book which made my cheeks tingle a little with a blush. They border on the erotic." These interpretations were unlikely to have been the result of Chev's newfound sensitivity to poetry, but probably reflected his conversations with other friends about the sensual language of *Passion-Flowers* and its images "such as a pure minded & sensitive lady should not write." Topping these insults off, he suggested that their pure little daughters would be harmed by reading the book.[25] Julia could not go back and rewrite the poems, but a possible fourth edition did not appear.

A far more devastating consequence of the confrontation in January was Chev's insistence that they resume their sexual relationship, suspended for the previous eighteen months. If she refused, he threatened to divorce her and keep custody of Julia Romana and Harry. Divorce was legal in the United States and had become much more frequent by the 1850s, so this was a possibility. As Julia explained sorrowfully to Louisa, she had no choice but to accept his terms:

> *After three years of constantly increasing unkindness and estrangement, no alternative presented itself before me, but that of an attempt at a reconciliation or a final separation. The latter had been all along in Chev's mind, and was so favorite a project with him that he would bring it up in our quietest hours, when there was nothing whatsoever to suggest it. His dream was to marry again—some young girl who would love him supremely. Before God, Louisa, I thought it my real duty to give up everything that was dear and sacred to me, rather than be forced to leave two of my children, and those two the dearest, Julia and Harry. In this view, I made the greatest sacrifice I can ever be called upon to make. God must accept it, and the bitter suffering of these subsequent months, as some expiation for the errors of my life . . .*

Chev's fantasy of the "young girl who would love him supremely," and presumably, give up her identity to please him, as to a father, sums up his paternalist marital expectations. He could not cope with an adult woman, his equal in intelligence and spirit. But what could Julia do? Comparing herself to the actress Fanny Kemble, who had lost custody of her children in a notorious divorce case in 1849, she declared that she could "suffer and die with my children, but I cannot leave them." The letter ended dramatically; "Burn this—I shall never speak of these things again."[26] Sex, which had never been enjoyable for her, became a kind of punishment, a sentence, a silent transaction of duty. By the middle of February, she was pregnant again. Chev wasted no time in extracting his fee.

She was then allowed to visit Annie. While she was in Bordentown, Chev informed her in a letter that he was moving the family out of Green Peace, putting it up for sale, and taking them all back to Perkins. Julia pleaded with him not to sell Green Peace, and he eventually gave in, but he had determined on the move. To Uncle John Ward he explained that he would both save $2,000 a year by living rent-free and please the Perkins trustees by moving back into the Doctor's Wing. He also agreed on a plan to house the pupils of the Idiot School at Green Peace temporarily. "I am to go to the Institution for good. The idiots are to have our house," Julia wrote scornfully.[27] But she had lost the battle, and lost any semblance of control over where they lived. From then on, Chev moved them frequently from house to house.

From her perspective, the move was insensitive, if not spiteful. Soon she was back at chilly Perkins, coping with "loneliness, desolation, much fault finding, a cold house, no carriage, weary walks in and out of town, these things go far to counterbalance any pleasure that my Book has given me." She felt such "horrible depression" that she broke down, and had "one fit of raving hysterics, I was perfectly mad, and rushed from room to room like a wild creature."[28]

Chev witnessed the attack, and was sufficiently alarmed to ease up on his grouchiness and fault finding.

By June the pregnancy was visible, and her social life was even more curtailed. On Perkins Institution notepaper, she confided to Annie that she was bursting out of her clothes. "I have grown dreadfully out of shape since you saw me, darling . . . I still adhere to corsets, but with difficulty, and am going to have some with elastic and without a bone in front. I keep out of sight as much as possible and make myself as genteel as possible when I do go out." She could just "squeeze into my green dress—the Paris one."[29] The growing shabbiness of the lovely green Paris dress became one of the metaphors of Julia's life for the next few years.

Despite Julia's sexual concessions, Chev remained emotionally distant and physically absent, and she began to suspect him of having found the docile young girl he dreamed of. Writing to Annie in June 1854, she said that Chev was "as cold and indifferent to me as a man could be. I sometimes suspect him of having relations with other women, and regret more bitterly than ever the sacrifice which entails upon me these moments of fatigue and suffering. God will help me through, I hope. But it all looks very dark before me."[30] In a few months' time, she had lost her home, her sexual autonomy, her literary control, and any pretense at a companionate marriage.

When summer came, they moved back to Lawton's Valley, where Julia spent the two hundred dollars she had made on *Passion-Flowers* to buy furniture. We have no letters from Chev giving his point of view about the pregnancy. His anger and alienation expressed itself, however, in his tacit encouragement to Theodore Parker, who wanted to adopt the prospective baby. Parker and his wife, Lydia Cabot, were childless, and that was a source of misery for the preacher. He complained in his journal and his letters that "a Parker or a Cabot that has no children is something unheard of in the history of our families."[31] According to Parker's letters, Howe did not refuse.[32] Years later, the Howe daughters recalled different versions of the incident. Laura said the plan had never been taken seriously and wondered lightheartedly how her rambunctious sister would have turned out if she had been brought up by the Parkers.[33] Maud, the subject of the transaction, told a more dramatic story; according to her memoir, Parker rode to the Institution as soon as he heard of the baby's birth. There, like a fairy-tale gnome, he said to Chev: "A fourth daughter, a fifth child! You and Julia have your hands full already. Give the baby to my wife and me; we will bring her up as our own, call her Theodora, and make her our heir!" According to Maud, Chev dismissed the idea at once and told it to Julia, who exclaimed, "Parker can certainly have no idea what it means to have a child!"[34]

Julia never liked being pregnant, but this pregnancy was the worst of all. November 4, approaching her confinement, she wrote to Louisa:

> *You ask whether I am glad or sorry. I can scarcely trust myself to speak of it, so bitter and horrible a distress has it been to me. You recommend ether—my dear Wevie, my mental suffering during these nine months nearly past has been so great that I cannot be afraid of bodily torture, however great. Neither does the future show a single gleam of light. I shall not drag this weary weight about me, it is true, but I cannot feel that my heart will be any lighter. I dread to see the face of my child, for I know I cannot love it. I must not write further in this strain—it brings tears, and I never give way to these, lest I should lose the little eyesight I have left.*[35]

On November 8, she instructed Annie to give her manuscripts to George Ripley if she died in childbirth.[36]

The next day, Julia, alone in the main room reading a French poem, endured her labor pains until Donald insisted that she go to bed. The "great, stout baby" was born immediately.[37] Chev wanted to call her "Thyrza," but Julia must have prevailed; they named their daughter Maud.

How good a poet was Julia Ward Howe, and how important is *Passion-Flowers*? Most specialists in nineteenth-century women's poetry would dismiss this question as irrelevant. They argue that the primary task of literary historians is recovery of the lives and texts of the scores of women who wrote, and that raising aesthetic questions means applying elite male standards to a group of writers whose intentions were different and for whom sentimentality was a technique like any other poetic mode.

Nonetheless, poetry is an artifact of language. We can judge its range and versatility, the originality of its images, its use of words and meter. By these standards, only a few of the hundreds of men and women composing and publishing their poetry in nineteenth-century America are among the great. The male poets Howe knew personally, Longfellow and Whittier, belonged to the genteel school called the "Fireside" or "Schoolroom" poets; no one reads them now. Dickinson and Whitman are the great exceptions, but they were iconoclasts who challenged tradition and found strategies to allow them to stay on their own paths. Dickinson never married and never published her poems; she did not have to ask permission to write, and she did not need critical approval to keep writing. Among nineteenth-century American women poets, only Emily Dickinson continues to be read and studied.

The pioneering group of Julia Ward Howe's biographers were dismissive of her poetry. Deborah Clifford thought that "except for a few intense poems which touch on then-forbidden subjects, there is little true poetry in *Passion-Flowers.*" In her view, the book's popularity came mainly from its notoriety.[38] Mary Grant too found all Howe's writing except *The Hermaphrodite* "derivative in form and content."[39] Valarie Ziegler thinks it does not matter whether the book was good or bad; Howe had published a book, one that got attention and good reviews, she had won a literary reputation, and that was a major achievement.[40] That was certainly how Julia herself treated *Passion-Flowers* in later years. She had earned acceptance by the literary community: "The great performers in the literary orchestra of writers answered to its appeal, which won me a seat in their ranks."[41]

More recently, however, Howe scholars who have worked extensively with the archives and know the broad historical and theoretical literature on nineteenth-century American women's poetry have given *Passion-Flowers* higher praise. Gary Williams calls it a benchmark of "antebellum literary achievement . . . that represents a claiming and settling of territory that permanently alters the map of the world."[42] Cheryl Walker sees in Howe's poetry "a dark and thrilling mystery . . . which refuses to unveil itself."[43]

To understand the plusses and minuses of the book, I think we need first to understand the horizon of expectation for women poets in the 1850s. On the positive side, American women were encouraged to write and publish their poems, and there was a steady market for their work. Annuals and newspapers were packed with women's verse, usually anonymous, but clearly feminine in terms of subject, imagery, and tone. On the negative side, female poets' standard themes were disavowals of poetic ambition or desire for fame; women poets bragged mainly about their modesty and self-abnegation. They insisted that they sang as artlessly as birds, or that divine inspiration spoke through them, not that they practiced a craft that required study, effort, revision, and originality. Technically they were not experimental, depending on quatrains, usually based on hymn meter; and when they sat down to write poetry, they abandoned conversational naturalness for an archaic, artificial language that signaled "This is a poem! Stop smiling and sit up straight!"

Julia's technical and verbal style in *Passion-Flowers* is generally conventional. With a few variations, she casts her thoughts in blank verse, heroic couplets, and hymnlike quatrains; uses feminine rhymes as line endings; and, as in the Griswold anthology, depends on a stilted vocabulary of poetic effusions, such as *raiment, boon, olden, gladsome, spake, forsook,* or *methinks*. She could use the vernacular freely and forcefully in her correspondence with her sisters (*tittie* and *pipi* come up with relation to babies); and she was a skillful satirist who continued to produce clever comic poems throughout her life. But Chev had been angry when she showed him the verses on the old woman of Portsmouth, and while she carefully kept copies of serious poems, she was careless with her humorous verse. Comic verse was not "poetry"; the comic Muse got no respect, and the wordplay Julia enjoyed when she was writing for friends or family had to be set aside when she auditioned for the literary orchestra.

Yet there are places in *Passion-Flowers* where she does defy verbal and thematic convention, as in the "wow!" of "Mind Versus Millstream."

When the poet confronts a scornful audience in "From Newport to Rome," she declares her independence after long submission, in language that is vigorous and direct:

I've sat among you long enough,
Or followed where your music led,
I've never marred your pleasure yet,
"But you shall listen now!" I said.

No affected medievalisms—*amongst* or *ye* or *thy*—show up in this claim to an irrepressible poetic voice.

Whitman's case is very instructive in terms of highlighting the profound disadvantages of women poets. Julia Ward and Walt Whitman were born in the same year. They both grew up in New York. But in the 1830s, while Julia was confined to her home, unable to move without a chaperone, hemmed in by restrictions of her reading and theatregoing, he was already working in Brooklyn and freely exploring the city. As he remembered, "I spent much of my time in the theatres . . . going everywhere, seeing everything, high, low, middling—absorbing theatres at every pore."[44] He avidly absorbed the slang and dialect of the streets, while Julia was restricted to a decorous and ladylike vocabulary.

By the early 1850s, both were ambitious young poets hoping to make their mark on American literature, yet the options open to a male poet and a female poet could not have been more different. Whitman was determined to take full advantage of all the resources of self-promotion and self-advancement available to a writer. In 1854, he was unmarried, unemployed, and living with his family in Brooklyn. He typeset ten pages of the first edition of *Leaves of Grass* himself, at the printing shop of some Brooklyn friends, and had two hundred copies bound in green cloth at his own expense. Whitman's initial efforts to find a bookstore to sell the book failed, but he convinced the firm of Fowler and Wells, which sold phrenological and health-fad books, to take it on. It appeared on July 4, 1855.

Although the book was anonymous, Whitman used a steel engraving of himself, bearded, casual, one hand in his pocket, the other on his hip, in an open-necked shirt and a black slouch hat, as the frontispiece. It was taken from a daguerreotype he had commissioned from the Brooklyn photographer Gabriel Harrison and was meant to reinforce the image of individualism and immediacy in the poems. His gaze, as biographer David S. Reynolds observes, radiated egalitarianism; the expression of his face is "full of emotional shadings, insolence, arrogance, calmness, compassion, even a touch of sadness."[45] Even the beard was a bardic symbol.[46]

The first edition of *Leaves of Grass* did not make the splash Whitman had hoped for. The copies piled up; as Whitman recalled, "none of them were sold—practically none—perhaps one or two, perhaps not even that many."[47] There were only a few reviews; they were hostile and stressed the reader's outrage at the book's "indecency." Whitman, however, was not discouraged or dispirited. He wrote several rave reviews of the book himself and published them anonymously. In the *United States Review*, for example, he began: "An American bard at last! . . . Self-reliant, with haughty eyes, assuming to himself all the attributes of his country, steps Walt Whitman into literature."

Still nothing happened. Fortunately, he had sent a copy of the book to Emerson, who soon responded with a glowing letter of thanks, congratulating Whitman on "the beginning of a great career," and praising his "free and brave thought" and "courage of treatment." Emerson's cultural power was immense, and his eloquent assessment was a priceless publicity asset. How could Whitman make use of a personal letter? After holding on to it for a few months, Whitman passed it on to the editor of the *New York Daily Tribune*, who printed it, without Emerson's permission, in October. It also played a prominent role in the "publicity apparatus" of the second edition in 1856, although Emerson himself began to rethink his appraisal; in May 1856, he wrote to Carlyle, *Leaves of Grass* was "a nondescript monster, which yet had terrible eyes and buffalo strength, and was indisputably American."[48] Overall, Whitman got his work published through confident initiative and tireless self-promotion, and if some reviewers found it scandalous, their views had no impact on his life. Certainly no woman threatened him with divorce for publishing his work, however intimate or revealing. When Whitman wrote "I celebrate myself," this was no poetic exaggeration.

Julia Ward Howe also wanted to be an American bard. No woman poet, however, could ever have attempted the same confident methods of self-branding and self-advertisement available to Whitman. Women did not include photographs of themselves in their books. To judge by the pictures of Julia at this period—demure, genteel, bonneted, beshawled, buttoned-up, eyes downcast—her image is more of concealment than engagement. She would not have dared to write a preface that was in fact a manifesto for a particular vision of American poetry, or to assume the attributes of her country. Had she dared, she would have been denounced for it. Male experience could be seen as symbolic of the nation, but certainly not female experience. Julia could not have written a "song of myself" and could not have claimed the verbal range open to Whitman. She could not have imagined writing an anonymous review of her own book. Worst of all, she did not have the freedom, as Whitman did, to revise and expand her work, and to argue for it. Howe was a poet with the irresistible force of her talent, the subversive intellect of an Emily Dickinson, the political and philosophical interests of an Elizabeth Barrett Browning, and the passionate emotions of a Sylvia Plath. *Passion-Flowers* was her best collection of poems, an impressive and promising debut. But Chev was an immovable object in her path, a powerful censor, her worst critic; and mid-nineteenth-century America did not allow her to grow.

By Christmas 1854, Julia had recovered enough from her depression to preside graciously over the annual party at Perkins. A Christmas tree had been set up in the large drawing room, and she sat at the piano and struck up a march, while the blind pupils and all their teachers and attendants entered. "At the end of the procession came Laura Bridgman, dressed as the Fairy Queen of the Festival, in fluttering gauze and tinsel, seated in the Howe children's donkey carriage, which was filled with gifts, waving a gilded scepter over the merry throng. Her face was radiant, her slender figure trembling with joy. A smile hovered on her lips but was not allowed to break out. With royal dignity she presided over the distribution of gifts by her maids of honor."[49]

For Julia this celebration was a charade, the final performance of a painful year. Like the Duke in Robert Browning's "My Last Duchess," Chev had given orders, and all passion ceased. Behind her accustomed mask as the smiling matron, she was in despair. In a Christmas letter to Annie, she anticipated the bleak decades ahead: "Why should I add a chapter to the complaining of Job? . . . But oh! the weary, tasteless life, without a single point of interest in it! This life, which is a waste, without hope, love, or courage to help me to the future."[50]

Chapter Seven

THE SECRET SIX

In the fall of 1856, Louisa May Alcott met Julia Ward Howe at Theodore Parker's house, and found her to be "a straw colored supercilious lady with pale eyes & a green gown in which she looked like a faded lettuce."[1] Alcott, proudly poor, with one good dress, which she carefully tended, saw Howe as a haughty society lady. She could not have known how much Julia had treasured that green Parisian gown with its filmy, now bedraggled, flounces. When she had ordered it, she had been young, fresh, hopeful, and crisp; now she felt washed-out and limp. Maud's birth had not resolved her quarrels with Chev. He continued his efforts to get control of her income and property, and harped on the issue of a divorce. The sisters were concerned for her, and so was her brother-in-law Tom Crawford. He wrote to Louisa, who had visited Julia in the summer and was spending some months with Annie, that "I am really alarmed by what you tell me of poor Jules's treatment by Chev. The man must be mad, and Jule will be if she allows him to get possession of property. I do hope Uncle John will take the matter in hands and cleanup the difficulty by actually separating them, allowing Chev a small portion of her income to bring up the child he is determined to keep. I think Jule is justified in leaving him whenever she pleases. Certainly such a dog's life is insupportable, as there can be no object in continuing it any longer."[2]

In public, Julia and Chev put on their best faces, and at home they concealed all their frustration, suspicion, even desperation, from the children, who remembered only glorious years of parties, music, books, and games. As parents, they poured all their affection, playfulness, and imagination into creating an idyllic home. Every spring the Howes gave a famous children's party in the garden at Green Peace, with a play, a donkey carriage, bowling outdoors, and delicious sweets, and a comic play written by Julia. At home, too, she played the piano energetically every afternoon while the children danced, or taught them songs and ballads. She wrote a play for their doll theatre and played all the parts, alternately grunting and squeaking the voices while Chev operated the puppets. Chev read to the children, took them horseback riding, and dressed up as a bear in his fur coat and chased them, growling, around the dining room. While they were constantly moving around and changing schools, tutors, and modes of education, their sense of a stable and enchanting family life kept them secure, and as adults, even when they read the letters and journals, they found it hard to believe that their parents had been unhappy together.

Much more vivid were their memories of antislavery activism. In the 1850s the Howes gradually became converted to Abolitionism. Both had been resistant to abolitionist ideas; Julia had indeed looked down snobbishly on the abolitionists, believing them to be "men and women of rather coarse fibre, abounding in cheap and easy denunciation, and seeking to lay rash hands on the complex machinery of government and of society." She had a particular aversion to William Lloyd Garrison, whom she had never seen, "but of whose malignity of disposition I entertained not the smallest doubt."[3] Chev, who generally agreed with the opinions of the abolitionists, nonetheless disapproved of their methods. It was Parker who persuaded the Howes to meet Garrison at his home, which was the headquarters of radical discussion. Julia ended up sharing a hymnbook with Garrison as they sang around the piano, and was humbled to find him "gentle and unassuming in manner," sincere and benevolent in his ideals. She also came to respect Maria Weston Chapman, the editor of *The Liberty Bell*, and Wendell Phillips, one of the great orators of the day and an early supporter of women's suffrage.[4]

The most fiery and committed abolitionist of their circle was Sumner. His strong opinions, the harsh and vehement way he delivered them, and his elaborate oratory made him one of the most unpopular men in the Senate, hated by his fellow senators for what they saw as his pretensions and "sanctimonious idealism."[5] In the 1850s, according to Carl Sandburg, Sumner became "the most perfect impersonation of what the South wanted to secede from"—self-righteousness, humorlessness, arrogance.[6] Speculating on the sources of his bachelorhood, gossips wondered wickedly whether he avoided marriage to avoid reducing a woman to slavery.

On May 19, 1856, Sumner gave a blistering three-hour speech in the Senate on "The Crime Against Kansas," excoriating the campaign to make Kansas a slave state. He had memorized the 112-page oration to enhance his delivery, and a large crowd gathered in the Senate to hear it, spread over two days. On both days he singled out Senator Andrew P. Butler of South Carolina as a Southern Don Quixote, who "has chosen a mistress to whom he has made his vows, and who, though ugly to others, is always lovely to him; though polluted in the sight of the world, is chaste in his sight . . . the harlot, Slavery." There was much more invective, including mockery of Butler's speech impediment. Sumner meant the speech to insult and offend, and it did. Butler was not in the chamber to hear himself attacked, but Southern congressmen were enraged, and Sumner's friends feared for his safety.

Three days later, Butler's cousin, Congressman Preston S. Brooks, entered the Senate chambers determined to avenge the honor of his family and South Carolina. He accosted Sumner, who was sitting at his desk reading some papers, and beat him unconscious with his gutta-percha cane, which splintered and broke with the force of the blows. Afterwards, Brooks boasted of giving Sumner the flogging he deserved, and Southern newspapers inflamed mob sentiment by editorializing that antislavery senators were "a pack of curs" who needed to be "lashed into submission." For every insult to the South, blustered the *Richmond Enquirer*, "they will suffer so many stripes," that "they will soon learn to behave themselves like *decent dogs*—they never can be gentlemen."[7]

In the North, however, Sumner's bloody coat became an emblem of martyrdom, and Brooks was denounced as a savage thug. Boston welcomed Sumner home in November with a grand parade on Beacon Hill, but he was far from recovered. For three years, he would be absent from the Senate, unable to concentrate or return to work, suffering from headaches that made him fear a brain injury, limping, shaky, and unable to get up from a chair without assistance. He wandered from health resort to spa to specialist, and eventually went to Europe, for two lengthy trips in 1857 and 1858, combining frenetic sightseeing and compulsive socializing with frequent medical consultations.

At last, in Paris in June 1858, he saw a distinguished physician who gave him hope that he would recover. Dr. Charles-Édouard Brown-Séquard was one of the strangest characters in this strange story. Born in Mauritius, of French and American ancestry, he was trained in France, but for sixteen years in the middle of his career, traveled back and forth across the Atlantic, teaching and practicing in Richmond, New York, Boston, Glasgow, Edinburgh, Dublin, London, and Paris. He taught at Harvard Medical School and the Collège de France, and is credited with some important discoveries in the field of neurology; but he was also an eccentric and controversial physician, whose enthusiasms led him to endorse some bizarre remedies. The most spectacular of these was the "elixir of life," a treatment for male aging and erectile dysfunction. In

1889, he would publish an article in *The Lancet* on the dramatic rejuvenating effects of injected extracts of the testicles of guinea pigs and dogs. After three injections, he wrote ecstatically, "I had regained at least all the strength I possessed a good many years ago . . . With regard to the facility of intellectual labor, which had diminished within the last few years, a return to my previous ordinary condition became quite manifest."[8] The article created a sensation, and the use of animal testes, tissues, and glands became an enormous fad. A 2002 study of Brown-Séquard's research concludes that his reported effects were the result of a placebo response.[9]

After a three-hour examination of Sumner, Brown-Séquard diagnosed injuries of the spinal cord produced by blows on the head and prescribed a course of applications of a powerful cauterizing agent called moxa. Used in ancient Chinese medicine, moxa is a cylinder of dried mugwort ignited and burned directly on the skin. It is excruciatingly painful, but Sumner wished to begin at once and refused chloroform, lest it make the moxa less effective. Over the next two weeks, Sumner endured six applications of fire on his bare back. "I have never seen a man bearing with such fortitude . . . the extremely violent pain of this kind of burning," the doctor noted. It was months before the burns healed. "The torment is considerable," Sumner wrote to Chev, ". . . I walk with pain; lie down with pain; rise with pain."[10] Chev thought that Brown-Séquard was a quack, and his prescriptions ridiculous, but fully supported Sumner. Nonsensical as a medical remedy, moxa was a peculiar placebo that assuaged Sumner's post-traumatic stress disorder. His wounds were psychological as well as physical. Brooding about the unmanly shame of being so badly beaten, and knowing that the newspapers accused him of malingering, he needed to restore his sense of masculinity, prove his courage, and assuage any remnants of guilt about his actions. Word spread about his heroic endurance of treatment, and the rumors of shamming stopped. After Sumner's treatment, David Herbert Donald suggests, "identifying himself with the martyrs of the past erased any unconscious doubts about the correctness of his course," and he came to regard himself as "a symbol of a righteous cause," rather than a vulnerable and defeated man.[11] Brown-Séquard, however, never used moxa again, regarding the pain it caused as too severe.[12]

The combination of "bleeding Sumner" and "Bleeding Kansas" had immediate consequences in 1856. After hearing about the attack on Sumner, John Brown, a fanatical abolitionist who wanted to start an armed slave insurrection, led his ragtag band of guerrillas to take violent revenge on the proslavery settlers in Pottawatomie, Kansas. They massacred five men in the settlement, beheaded one, and mutilated their bodies. Brown denied knowledge of the infamous raid. He escaped and went underground, trying to raise funds to carry out his plans.

In January 1857, he came to Boston to stay with Theodore Parker. Chev met the fugitive at Parker's home and was captivated by the simple strength and Puritan conviction Brown displayed. By March, along with Parker, he became an enthusiastic member of a group dedicated to funding Brown's antislavery campaigns. The other members of the "Secret Six," as they were known, were Franklin B. Sanborn, an abolitionist activist, transcendentalist, and disciple of Emerson; Thomas Wentworth Higginson, a minister, reformer, and literary critic; George Luther Stearns, a wealthy businessman; and Gerrit Smith, a philanthropist. Their antislavery beliefs did not preclude racism. Like Emerson, Thoreau, and Bronson Alcott, each of them regarded black slaves as an inferior race. Abolitionism and white supremacy were not contradictions. They were drawn into the conspiracy, however, for humanitarian and ideological reasons. In addition, Chev brought the romantic fervor of his youth to the Secret Six, and based his military support of Brown's mad schemes on his memories of guerrilla warfare in Greece. Once more he was reminded of the exhilarating insurgency in the mountains of Arcadia. "The prospect of a slave stampede on a large scale was quite in Dr. Howe's line," Higginson wrote.[13] But thirty years after the Greek revolution, Chev was no longer the passionate youth who had eaten raw snails in Athens and reveled in waving a scimitar or a pistol. He was caught up in a Boys' Own Adventure with terrible consequences.

Julia did not stop writing. Indeed, 1857 was the peak of her literary career in terms of the amount of work she produced, published, and had performed. In February 1857, she braved Chev's anger by publishing her second book of poems, *Words for the Hour*, with Ticknor and Fields. Signed by "the Author of *Passion-Flowers*," the book included fifty-four poems on topical subjects, including two on Sumner's martyrdom, "An Hour in the Senate" and "The Senator's Return." The hour had room for personal history, too. Other poems defiantly revisited her friendship with Horace Binney Wallace. In 1854, Wallace's brother John had brought out a limited edition of his writings, *Art, Scenery and Philosophy in Europe.* Julia composed a sorrowful poem on receiving the book, in which she expressed her longing to visit the shrine of his grave:

But, held by ties that let me not depart,
On grief's wild sweeping opinions any whither,
I can but send my pilgrim wishes thither,
Folding thy dear, dumb volume to my heart.

She also wrote "Via Felice"—the happy way—named for the street he lived on in Rome, and, imagining them back in Rome forever, while she waited at her window for him to come with her morning violets.

But in the ancient city
And from the quaint old door,
I'm watching, at my window
His coming, evermore.

For Death's eternal city
Has yet some happy street;
'Tis in the Via Felice
My friend and I shall meet.

As in *Passion-Flowers*, Julia wrote best when she was angry. Two poems on Florence Nightingale criticize those people (probably she had Chev in mind) who put the exceptional woman on a pedestal but continued to oppress ordinary women:

If you debase the sex to elevate
One of like soul and temper with the rest,
You do but wrong a thousand fervent hearts,
To pay full tribute to one generous breast.

She also took an injudicious shot at the Brownings, whom she believed had snubbed her in Rome, and she used their names.[14] "I am told you do not praise me, Barrett Browning, high-inspired," she declared in "A Word with the Brownings."

Nor you, Robert, full of manhood, with your Angel interlyred;
In my sometime invocation the poet-brotherhood,
'Twas a word from you I wanted, in a word, a sentence,—good.

That was risky enough, but "One Word More with E.B.B." hinted that Barrett Browning attempted "unmeasured heights" in her poetry with the help of opium, while Howe herself more morally shrank "before the nameless draught / that helps to such unearthly things, / and if the drug could lift so high, / I would not trust its treacherous wings." She might be the lesser poet, but she filled her pages "with pictures of the things I see." These imprudent lines made lifelong enemies of the Brownings, scandalized by her sense of entitlement. Howe attacks us, Browning wrote to his friend Isa Blagden, "because we didn't *praise* her!"[15] Ironically, some of the poems in *Words for the Hour* were imitations of his dramatic monologues.

The new book received respectful but muted reviews. "After the reign of the myriad Lady Magazine poetesses," the editor George Curtis wrote in *Putnam's*, ". . . ladies who have written the most graceful good grammar about emotions they never had, it is truly refreshing to encounter a torrent of lava streaming out of the heat of real experience." He judged it "a better book than its predecessor," but accurately predicted it would "probably not meet with the same success."[16] Other reviewers found it deeply sad. "The wail of private sorrow which forms the keynote of these remarkable poems can never harmonize with universal sympathies . . . If the author stands before us like Niobe, she exhibits nothing effeminate, maudlin, or sentimental. Her compact and resolute intellect seems armed as with triple steel."[17]

Julia was also writing plays and channeling her volcanic emotions through the representation of powerful heroines. On March 16, 1857, her tragedy in blank verse *Leonora, or The World's Own* was performed in New York at Wallack's Lyceum Theatre. Set in sixteenth-century Italy, *Leonora* is the story of a young woman whose seduction and cruel betrayal by the cynical Lord Lothair violates the sexual codes of her society, stigmatizes her as damaged and dangerous, and precipitates her ejection from the village. So far, the familiar plot, in which the woman pays. Yet Leonora does not meekly accept her shame, but plots to punish her seducer and takes on the identity of a veiled and vengeful madwoman. In the fourth and fifth acts, aided by a sympathetic prince who loves her, she becomes "the Lady of the evil eye," whose power "shows its malignant presence everywhere." Mercilessly she plots to destroy Lothair, his wife, and his son, only to realize in the end that she has become the demon of her own disguise. She stabs herself, and in her last few moments envisions herself as a young girl once more, dressed in white, dancing with the "maiden band," and "taller than the rest." The ebbing of her "life blood lets the madness out," and she is restored to "the peaceful visions of my youth."

Howe's brother Sam was an enthusiastic supporter of the production, as always; but the New York critics did not like the theme or the treatment, and the play closed after a brief run. As the *New York Times* reported, "the critics quite unanimously concede that Mrs. Howe's new play 'The World's Own,' is a poetic success and a dramatic failure . . . And they all have a great deal to say of the immorality, if not indecency, of the play." The *Times* critic agreed that "in working up the material there are great faults of taste, misconceptions of the laws of dramatic art, and an unnecessary prolixity." Moreover, he felt, "there are offensive expressions which should be cut out, as there are whole scenes and characters by whose entire removal the play would gain in unity, force and interest."[18]

Later critics, however, have seen much to admire in *Leonora.* Arthur Hobson Quinn, who included it in his anthology of American plays in 1925, saw it as a projection of Howe's rebellion in the medium of romantic drama, and saw its fate as another example of her creative silencing. "With any real encouragement," he argued, she "could have contributed plays to our stage that would have enriched our literature as well as our theater."[19] Zoe Detsi, in 1996, described it as "a self-conscious attempt at the creation of feminist theatre," which attacked the sexual double standard and portrayed a "powerful, assertive, Mediterranean female character."[20]

For all its melodramatic extravagance, *Leonora* has some strong lines and some exciting scenes; writing dialogue forced Howe to be direct and clear. It belongs to the tradition of the mad female double who expresses the heroine's rage, as in *Jane Eyre.* Later that summer, Howe, like Louisa May Alcott and many other American women, was reading Elizabeth

Gaskell's newly published biography of Charlotte Brontë. Alcott was moved and inspired. "Read Charlotte Brontë's life. A very interesting, but sad one. So full of talent; and after working long, just as success, love, happiness, she dies. Wonder if I shall ever be famous enough for people to care to read my story and struggles. I can't be a C. B., But I may do a little something yet."[21] Howe resisted identification with Brontë. "Charlotte Brontë is deeply interesting," she wrote to Annie, "but I think she and I should not have liked each other, while still I see points of resemblance, many indeed, between us."[22] There were certainly resemblances between them, especially the attraction to Gothic images, but Brontë did not have five children or a difficult husband. Why Howe thought they might have disliked each other is harder to guess. She was not sufficiently intrigued by their similarities to read *Jane Eyre*.

Fanny Longfellow took obvious pleasure in gossiping to her Cambridge circle about the scandal of *Leonora*. "Julia Howe's play has been abused by all the papers here and in New York except in one or two cases," she wrote a friend, "but she is serenely indifferent and thinks it was a success. The sudden virtue of the *Herald* about it is amusing, but it is strange so clever a woman should have chosen so hackneyed a story and so wretched a heroine, and should not see there is tragedy enough in life to inspire a drama without condescending to vice . . . The poor Doctor must feel it painfully as a thing he cannot give his daughters to read."[23]

In her wasp-ridden attic room at Lawton's Valley, Julia, undaunted by the failure of *The World's Own*, was writing another play, for the young actor Edwin Booth, whose Boston performance as Hamlet had made a strong impression on both the Howes. When Booth's manager asked her to write a play for him, she was honored and chose the subject of Hippolytus, based on Euripides's *Hippolytus* and Racine's *Phaedra*. The part of Hippolytus seemed to her like a perfect fit for Booth: "his austere beauty, his reserve and shyness, all seemed to her the personification of the Hunter Prince."[24] Between the composition and the production, however, many years went by, as Booth became an increasingly famous American actor. At last in 1864, E. L. Davenport, the manager of the Howard Athenæum, agreed to produce the play with the celebrated actress Charlotte Cushman as Phaedra. To Julia's dismay, Davenport suddenly decided *Hippolytus* was too shocking, and it was withdrawn; according to local gossip, Mrs. Davenport was unhappy with her part. Julia was crushed. "This was, I think, the greatest letdown that I ever experienced. It affected me seriously for some days, after which I determined to attempt nothing more for the stage."[25] Fifty years later, she still felt the disappointment: "This with much other of my best literary work has remained a dead letter on my own shelves."[26] *Hippolytus* was not performed until March 24, 1911, after Howe's death, starring the future movie actor Walter Hampden as Hippolytus.

Chev barely noticed the book or the plays; he was preoccupied that spring with his own dramas. He confided in Julia that he had met "a wonderful man, an apostle, a Puritan of the old type, who had devoted himself to an elaborate plan for the emancipation of the Southern blacks, with the zeal and courage that ever characterized the saviors of mankind."[27] On March 7, he identified the man "who wished to be a savior for the negro race" as John Brown, and told her Brown was coming to their home that afternoon. As she told the story in her *Reminiscences*, "At the expected time, I heard the bell ring, and, on answering it, beheld a middle-aged, middle-sized man, with hair and beard of amber color, streaked with gray. He looked a Puritan of the Puritans, forceful, concentrated, and self-contained."[28] Brown remembered Julia Ward Howe too: "A defiant little woman, all flash and fire."[29] While he was in Boston, he also went to see Charles Sumner, who was still recovering, and asked to see the blood-soaked coat he had been wearing in the Senate. He gazed upon the garment silently for some minutes, as if it were a holy relic. For Brown, it was.

Julia may have responded to Brown's charisma, at least in retrospect; but she and Chev were hardly ideological partners. Through the spring and summer, the Howes were traveling and quarreling. Julia and Flossy accompanied Chev on the Middle Western leg of a trip to Kansas. "Heaven knows what I have not been through since I saw you," she grumbled to Annie, "—dust, dirt, dyspepsia, hotels, railroads, prairies, Western steamboats, Western people, more prairies, tobacco juice, captains of boats, pilots of ditto, long days of jolting in the cars . . . There ought to be no chickens this year, so many eggs have we eaten."[30] Chev bought land in Grasshopper, Kansas, on this stage of the trip, another in his long line of bad investments.

That summer, the tension between Julia and Chev was obvious to their friends and family. In July, Parker wrote to Julia, appealing to her generosity and suggesting that she take the initiative in working out a compromise between them. "It grieves me sadly to see you both unhappy—each made so by the other . . . It seems to me not difficult for one so richly gifted as you to turn out such a silver lining in the house as to fill it all with brightness, & charm it into love. Chev has his faults—some of them you bear with great sweetness—but there is such a soul of *Generosity* in him that it seems to me you might make such music as would charm all the little household duties about him & so gladden & bless all the family—making the seven into one."[31]

She did make an effort—she always made an effort—and the summer months seemed to have calmed the waters. But by October, Chev was once more urging divorce. "Down comes Chev with his fall madness of separation and a week or so of misery undoes all the summer's gain. The ground this time is that there is no unkindness between us, and that for the present is the best time to make a decision. I will not amplify on all this, but will only say that I have not made one drop of good blood since this most strange and unexpected turn of matters."[32]

Still, she had learned how to recover and bounce back. On one particularly bad day, she quarreled with Chev and he "pummeled me until I was black and blue in the soul."[33] The rhetoric of Sumner's thrashing had entered their marriage. But somehow they got over it, wound the clock, and went to bed. Quarreling had become a routine; there was no point in losing more sleep over it.

Chev was feeling even more depressed than Julia. He missed his friends—Sumner still in Europe; Mann in Ohio; Parker, whose tuberculosis he had diagnosed in December, slowly dying. His close friendship with Longfellow had not survived the affair of *Passion-Flowers*. In the winter of 1859, when Parker decided to go to Cuba and Santa Cruz for his health, he pleaded with the Howes to join him and Lydia for the first part of the trip. Before they sailed, Chev wrote a letter of introduction to a wealthy Bostonian for John Brown: "He is of the stuff of which martyrs are made. He is of the Puritan order militant."[34]

Julia described their expedition in *A Trip to Cuba*, travel letters that had been commissioned by the *Atlantic Monthly*. It contained some of her wittiest and most candid observations. She made fun of herself being seasick on the trip down:

> *A woman, said to be of a literary turn of mind, in the miserablest condition imaginable. Her clothes, flung at her by the Stewardess, seem to have hit in some places and missed in others. Her listless hands occasionally make an attempt to keep her draperies together, and to pull her hat on her head; but though the intention is evident, she accomplishes little by her motion. . . . This woman, upon the first change of weather, rose like a cork, dressed like a Christian, and toddled about the deck in the easiest manner . . . is supposed by some to have been an impostor, and, when ill-treated, announced intentions of writing a book.*[35]

Chev appears in the text as The Philanthropist, or occasionally, The Phrenologist. She also gave scathing and uncensored descriptions of the Nassauese, Cubans, Creoles, and slaves. In Nassau, she reflected "it is a dolorous thing to live on a lonely little island, tied up like a wart on the face of civilization." She was dismayed by the docile subordination of the society women, who accepted "an Oriental submission. In the public street they must on no account set foot, . . . without the severe escort of husband or brother" or "the black coachman who escorts the wealthiest women to shop and pay visits." After a few days in Havana, Julia concluded that Cuban men had so much "animal vigor" and could be so sexually aggressive in the street, that "women must be glad to forgo their liberties for the protection of the strong arm." She thought the Cubans overall had poor taste and little artistic talent.

Her most offensive comments were about race and slavery. She recorded her views that "the Negro of the North is an ideal Negro; it is the Negro refined by white culture, elevated by white blood, instructed even by white inequity;—the Negro among the Negroes is a coarse, grinning, flat-footed, thick skulled creature, ugly as Caliban, lazy as the laziest of brutes, chiefly ambitious to be of no use to any in the world." Her racist prejudices underlay her feeling that emancipation should come gradually as slaves grew intellectually and morally through exposure to white society and culture. The slave, she concluded, "must go to school to the white race, and his discipline must be long and laborious."[36] It's astonishing to think that she had been serving tea to John Brown a month before, and that in another year she would be writing about the Christian duty to abolish slavery. When the book on Cuba came out in 1860, she was attacked for her views by William Lloyd Garrison in the *Liberator*. Chev was mildly disturbed; "some things in it made me sad," he wrote to Parker, "e.g. the question whether viewing the actual condition of the Negro, enforced labor is not best!—As if anything would justify the perpetuation of such wrong by the stronger race."[37]

When they got to Havana, Theodore and Lydia Parker departed for

Santa Cruz, en route to Italy, where they hoped he might recover. The Howes were melancholy to be parting, probably forever, from "the great fighter. How were we to miss his deep music, here and at home! With his assistance we had made a very respectable band; now we were to be only a wandering drum and fife—the fife particularly shrill and the drum particularly solemn." They said a sad good-bye. "And now came silence, and tears, and last embraces; we slipped down the gangway into our little craft, and looking up, saw bending above us, between the slouched hat and the silver beard, the eyes that we can never forget, that seemed to drop back in the darkness with the solemnity of the last farewell. We went home, and the drum hung himself gloomily on his peg, and the little fife *shut up* for the remainder of the evening."[38]

On the way home, the Howes traveled through the South and stopped at the South Carolina plantation of a wealthy couple, Wade Hampton II and his wife, whose company they had enjoyed in Cuba. They were planning to stay for two days, but the visit grew into two weeks. It was Julia's first experience of Southern slave owners, and she was impressed by their civilized and hospitable manners. She could not connect this charming couple to the brutality of slavery, and Chev, for all his abolitionist fervor, was similarly attracted to their gracious lifestyle. The trip to Cuba had brought the Howes closer; in April she conceived her sixth child.

John Brown returned to Boston in May, and Chev invited several prominent Bostonians to meet him as "a practical, not a talking abolitionist," who would be glad to tell them "in his rough way something about his mode of abolitionizing."[39] Brown also tried to persuade Frederick Douglass to join him in a raid of the US Armory at Harpers Ferry, Virginia, and get weapons for the army of slaves he was sure would escape and join them in their insurrection, but Douglass thought the plan was doomed and refused to help. In August, Brown's son John Jr. went to Lawton's Valley to see Chev, who gave him fifty dollars. Brown then rented Kennedy Farm in Maryland, near Harpers Ferry. That was the last the Howes heard of him for several months. All summer Chev was preoccupied with worries about Julia Romana, who was studying too hard. He wrote to Sumner in July that he "had been in great alarm & distress about my dear & beautiful daughter Julia breaking down under her course of study." She had been so upset he had feared that "there was danger of aberration of mind, but happily all the . . . symptoms have passed away & she is doing well."[40] His dear friend Horace Mann died on August 2, and Chev busied himself raising money for a monument.

On the evening of October 16, Julia read in the *Boston Transcript* about a disturbance at the Virginia Armory at Harpers Ferry and drew it to Chev's attention. "Brown has got to work," he nonchalantly remarked. Everyone soon knew the bloody nature of that work. Brown had launched an attack with only twenty men, including two of his sons. The siege lasted less than thirty-seven hours. Easily defeated by the federal troops led by Captain Robert E. Lee and Lieutenant J. E. B. Stuart, Brown was wounded but captured alive. He was tried and convicted at the end of October for murder and treason, and sentenced to hang on December 2.

During the six weeks he spent in prison, Brown impressed not only New England abolitionists but many citizens, with his dignity, serenity, and courage. His speech before the sentencing judge on October 30 spoke eloquently about his motives: "If it is deemed necessary that I should forfeit my life for the furtherance of the ends of justice, and mingle my blood further with the blood of millions in this slave country whose rights are disregarded by wicked, cruel, and unjust enactments, I say, let it be done." Deciding he could best serve his cause as a speaker, writer, and Christian martyr, Brown became a hero to writers including Melville and Whitman. The leading transcendentalists passionately took up his defense. Thoreau was among the first to compare him to Jesus; Emerson rebranded Brown as a holy warrior rather than a mad fanatic, and called his death sentence a crucifixion of "the new saint awaiting his martyrdom, and who, if he shall suffer, will make the gallows glorious like the cross."[41] Bronson Alcott described him as "the manliest man I have ever seen."[42] No wonder that Chev had been so drawn to him.

To his death, Brown refused to name his supporters, but the Secret Six panicked when their letters were discovered in the rented farmhouse and printed in the *New York Times.* The media rapidly spread the story. On October 27, the day of Brown's trial, the anti-abolitionist *New York Herald* printed a lurid editorial about the Secret Six, titled "The Exposure of the Nigger-Worshipping Insurrectionists," calling for the arrest of Frederick Douglass and Gerrit Smith as accessories to the crime. Douglass was gone; he had fled the country and stayed away in England. Gerrit Smith had a mental breakdown, convinced that he was responsible for the bloodshed, and tried to join Brown in the prison at Charlestown. Lured by friends who told him they were taking him to Brown in Virginia, Smith was committed for six weeks to the New York State Lunatic Asylum in Utica. Frank Sanborn hastily destroyed his manuscripts and letters. Chev was panicking and terrified that he would be arrested. Only Parker and Higginson stuck by their support of Brown.

Julia always insisted the Howes were unaware of the plans for the Harpers Ferry raid, despite admiring John Brown. "I confess that the whole scheme appeared to me wild and chimerical. Of its details I knew nothing, and have never learned more. None of us could exactly approve an act so revolutionary in its character, yet the great-hearted attempt enlisted our sympathies very strongly."[43] She was most concerned to persuade Annie that Chev was innocent. On November 6, she wrote that "Chev is not at all annoyed by the newspapers, but has been greatly overdone by anxiety and labor for Brown. Much has come upon his shoulders, getting money, paying counsel, and so on. Of course all the stories about the Northern Abolitionists are the merest stuff. No one knew of Brown's intentions but Brown himself and his handful of men. The attempt I must judge insane but the spirit *heroic.* I should be glad to be as sure of heaven as that old man may be, following right in the spirit and footsteps of the old martyrs, girding on his sword for the weak and oppressed. His death will be holy and glorious—the gallows cannot dishonor him—he will hallow it. . . ."[44] In these words we can see the hint of the "Battle Hymn" to come—the vision of Brown as one of God's martyred warriors.

This was the only time that Julia deliberately misled her sister. Chev and George Stearns fled by train to Montreal, and on November 16, Chev published an open letter in the *New York Tribune* denying any knowledge of Brown's plans and expressing shock that this prudent and peace-loving man could have committed such a bloody act: "It is still to me a mystery and a marvel."[45] His flight and his continued denials infuriated his compatriots and injured his reputation as a courageous hero. "Is there no such thing as honor among confederates?" Thomas Wentworth Higginson demanded of Sanborn.[46]

Meanwhile, Julia was becoming anxious about the forthcoming birth. Her sixth pregnancy had been her most uncomfortable; she was trying to cope on her own, and fearful that she might die in delivering the child. In late November, she wrote to Chev that she was having a lot of pain, and "should give up altogether but for my red hair."[47] Chev reassured her by mail from Montreal with his customary hearty insouciance. "Dear child, do not be hypochondriacal—like me; you have no cause for it. Look! You inherited a sound and vigorous constitution: you did not marry until it was fully matured. Childbearing when the number does not exceed eight . . . & is not too frequent, & if the system is healthy, tends to prolong, not to shorten the duration of life."[48]

When Brown was executed on December 2, still calm and at peace with his acts and motives, New England radicals, intellectuals, and abolitionists were brought together in grief. Bronson Alcott, Emerson, and Thoreau attended a memorial meeting in Concord to honor Brown. In Montreal, on the execution day, Chev had taken his usual morning ride. Returning to Boston about December 6, he wrote anxiously to Sumner about his legal position and was reassured that he would not be charged.

Julia was not ungrateful for his presence. By December 22 she was too uncomfortable to sleep, and appreciative, albeit with many qualifiers, for Chev's "on the whole kind treatment . . . He has really been very good & and has seemed quite fond of me," she reassured Annie.[49] Their second son, Samuel, was born at 3:00 a.m. on Christmas Day. The baby weighed twelve pounds; no wonder Julia had trouble sleeping. Within a week, Chev had returned to Canada, allegedly to study "methods for the education of the blind," always his cover story and euphemism for whatever adventures he might pursue.

He had agreed to testify before the Senate committee investigating Harpers Ferry, and finally did so on February 3, 1860. His self-protective testimony, in which he answered most questions by saying he could not remember, got him off but left a dent in his knightly image. In May, the Howes learned that Theodore Parker had died in Florence. He was buried in the English Cemetery, where Elizabeth Barrett Browning would also have her tomb. His Florence physician, William Wesselhoeft, was the son of the German homeopath of the same name who had run the Brattleboro Water Cure spa Chev had frequented. Wesselhoeft thoughtfully sent the Doctor a jar containing Parker's pickled brain. Chev hid the brain in a cupboard; it was not so easy to conceal the guilt of his repudiation of Brown.

In Julia's mind, Sammy's birth would always be connected with the death of John Brown. "The time of your birth was a sad one," she wrote to the infant. "It was the time of the imprisonment and death of John Brown, a very noble man, who should be in one of the many mansions of which Christ tells us." The delivery could not have been as easy as her others. But Sammy was an enchanting baby. She nursed him for thirteen months, slept with him lying on top of her, dressed him in silk and velvet, and took him with her everywhere. But she did not go out very much. When she came home, she was happy to be with the infant. "It was always sweet to come to the bed, and find you in it, sound asleep, and lying right across. . . . I learned to sleep on a very little bit of the bed, you wanted so much of it. This winter, I bought you a pair of snow-boots, of which you were very proud. . . ." Sammy took up all her attention and love. "I used to think: this Baby will grow up to be a man, and will protect me when I am old," she wrote in her journal.[50] She could not depend on Chev to protect her, but Sammy would be there to take his place.

Chapter Eight

THE CIVIL WAR

The 1860s were the ten most momentous years of Julia's life. In 1860, she was forty-one years old. She had given birth to her sixth child, but she may have expected to have more; the average age of menopause in the 1850s was forty-six, and Chev thought eight children were a reasonable and healthful number for a family. She had accepted matronly middle age and had even begun to take up the once-despised domestic crafts of needlework, cross-stitch embroidery, knitting, and hooking rugs. A photograph labeled "circa 1862" shows her with shiny dark hair in a bonnet trimmed with flowers, a full silk dress, and a black velvet cloak, her hand resting on a Bible lying on an elaborately embroidered cloth-draped table. Another photograph from the 1860s shows her with a heavy braid wrapped like a crown around the top of her graying hair. Worried that her hair was thinning, she was attempting to disguise it with a hairpiece.

The winter of 1861 began cheerfully. For once, the Howes had a good German cook, and Julia was enjoying her baby boy. She bought him warm winter clothing, loved coming home from a party and joining him in their bed. But the parties ended abruptly in April with the attack on Fort Sumter and the declaration of war. Fathers and sons in Boston enlisted; mothers and daughters in Boston were making lint bandages; but Julia felt depressed by her inability to contribute to the fight. "I could not leave my nursery to follow the march of our armies, neither had I the practical deftness which the preparing and packing of sanitary stores demanded," she recalled. "Something seemed to say to me, 'You would be glad to serve but you cannot help anyone. You have nothing to give, and there is nothing for you to do.' "[1] That mocking and belittling inner voice was probably an echo of Chev. He had been serving as a member of the US Sanitary Commission during the summer and had submitted his first report in July. "Soap! Soap! Soap!—I cry but none heard," he complained to Governor Andrew. But he was discouraging about women's efforts to help the commission.

Julia was grateful for Chev's invitation to accompany him to Washington for commission meetings in the fall of 1861. Setting out as a woman with nothing to give and nothing to do, she would return as the author of the greatest American war anthem in history. Departing from Boston, the Howes traveled by ferry and train, accompanied by James Freeman Clarke; governor John Andrew and his wife, Eliza; and critic Edwin P. Whipple and his wife, Charlotte. Julia was apprehensive, but also excited "to meet the grim Demon of the War face to face," rather than imagine it from newspaper reports and men's conversations. As they reached the outskirts of the city of Washington, the Bostonians saw clusters of armed men seated by campfires; Chev explained that these were pickets, Union soldiers protecting the capital against a feared invasion from Confederate troops stationed across the Potomac. The Howes stayed at the bustling Willard's Hotel on Pennsylvania Avenue in the middle of Washington, a place described by Hawthorne in 1862 as "more justly . . . the centre of Washington and the Union than either the Capitol, the White House, or the State Department."[2] Rooms at the Willard cost four dollars a night, about sixty in contemporary terms. That was high for a hotel; the Willard was in demand and had doubled its prices. Now the broad avenue was crowded with mounted officers and horse-drawn ambulances bringing the wounded into the city hospitals. The Washington offices of the *New York Herald* were next door, and across the street was "the ghastly advertisement of an agency for embalming and forwarding the bodies of those who had fallen in the fight or who had perished by fever."[3]

Embalming had become one of the images of death in the war. Dr. Thomas Holmes, a coroner's physician from New York, had developed an embalming technique and was given a commission from the Army Medical Corps to treat Union officers. His services were in so much demand that he extended the service to enlisted men, and after the war he estimated he had embalmed about four thousand soldiers in all. Other physicians advertised too, even handing out cards to soldiers marching out to battle; but death on the field was too abrupt and bodies too numerous to allow for many funeral obsequies.

While Chev was busy at meetings, Julia went with Clarke and William Henry Channing, another Unitarian minister, to visit hospitals and army camps. At the headquarters of the First Massachusetts Heavy Artillery, Colonel William Greene asked her to speak to his men. She had never spoken in public; Chev was strongly opposed to such activities for women, although Parker had encouraged her. At first she was overcome by shyness, and tried to run away and hide in one of the hospital tents, but at last, "as well as I could," she told the soldiers "how glad I was to meet the brave defenders of our cause, and how constantly they were in my thoughts." That first public address was legitimized in a way that overruled Chev and was well received by the audience. She began to think it might be possible to share her ideas on other platforms.

Chev's account of Julia's activities in Washington, or rather his assumptions about the way she would be occupying herself, presented her as a social butterfly enjoying the opportunity to charm a new audience. "Your Mama is having a very delightful time," he wrote to twelve-year-old Laura; "the weather is delicious: there are expeditions every day, to camps, objects of curiosity. In the evening there are many people gathered in the Salon of the hotel . . . people who can appreciate talent and wit and conversational power are sure to be drawn to her." He, meanwhile, was doing the serious work: "I go about inspecting camps and hospitals and doing what I can to help the cause of freedom."[4]

Chev wasn't there when she spoke to the soldiers, or when John Andrew arranged for the Boston contingent to meet President Lincoln in a drawing room at the White House. She remembered "a tall, bony figure, devoid of grace; his countenance almost redeemed from plainness by two kindly blue eyes."[5] All except Andrew, "whose faith never wavered," felt disappointed by the man who was then regarded by many intellectuals as simple and clumsy, his leadership most charitably credited as meaning well. Julia was not impressed by his conversation and shocked by his uneducated backwoods accent, pronouncing "heard" as "heerd." Leaving the White House, James Freeman Clarke ruefully noted, "We have seen it in his face; hopeless honesty; that is all."[6]

They joined the thousands of civilians who rode out in carriages to watch General George B. McClellan's elaborate troop reviews, designed to display the splendor and discipline of the Army of the Potomac. On November 18, Julia and her companions drove out to watch a parade at Munson's Hill in Northern Virginia. While they were watching, there was an attack by Confederate soldiers on a small group of outliers, and some of the soldiers went to defend them; the parade broke up, and the remaining men were ordered back to their barracks. In the slow drive back to Washington, the Bostonians were surrounded by troops and passed the time by singing army songs including "John Brown's body lies a-mouldering in the ground; his soul is marching on," which had become especially popular with the Massachusetts regiments. "The soldiers seemed to like this," she recalled, "and answered back, 'Good for you!' Mr. Clarke said, 'Mrs. Howe, why do you not write some good words for this stirring tune?' I replied that I had often wished to do this, but as yet had not found in my mind any leading toward it."

That night she found powerful words in her dreams:

I went to bed that night as usual, and slept, according to my wont, quite soundly. I awoke in the gray of the early morning twilight, and as I lay waiting for the dawn, the long lines of the desired poem began to twine themselves in my mind. Having thought out all the stanzas, I said to myself, "I must get up and write these verses down, lest I fall asleep again and forget them." So, with a sudden effort, I sprang out of bed, and found in the dimness an old stump of a pen which I remembered to have used the day before. I scrawled the verses almost without looking at the paper. I had learned to do this when, on previous occasions, attacks of versification had visited me during the night, and I feared to have recourse to a light lest I should wake the baby, who slept near me. I was always obliged to decipher my scrawl before another night should intervene, as it was only legible while the matter was fresh in my mind. At this time, having completed the writing, I returned to bed and fell asleep, saying to myself, "I like this better than most things I have written."[7]

This often-repeated account suggests she had written in the dark so as not to wake the baby. But Sammy had been left behind in Boston. Chev was not in the bedroom either; they had taken separate rooms at the Willard. He did not read the lines in Washington, although she had scribbled them on the notepaper of the US Sanitary Commission. Two days later, on the way home, she read the verses to James Clarke, who liked them very much. The composition of the "Battle Hymn" was a repetition of the composition of *Passion-Flowers*, a secret only to her husband; but this time, Chev could not grumble. Her minister had given her permission to write. Even more than her book, the "Battle Hymn" would change the balance of power in their marriage.

Back in Boston, she made a small number of revisions and sent the poem to James Fields at the *Atlantic Monthly*, with a playful note: "Do you want this, and do you like it, and have you any room for it in the January number? I am sad and spleeny, and begin to have fears that I may not be after all, the greatest woman alive."[8] It was an unusually self-deprecating cover letter, but her self-mocking admission to Fields showed how low her confidence had fallen. Fields paid her five dollars, came up with the title "Battle Hymn of the Republic," and published the poem anonymously on the cover of the magazine in February 1862.

The same month, Chev published a letter "To Mrs.—and other loyal women" in which he asked women not to send supplies to the troops. "Our men in the field do not lack food or clothing or money," he wrote to discourage charitable ladies, "but they do like noble watchwords and inspiriting ideas such as are worth fighting and dying for."[9] He had no idea that those words and ideas were on the way, or that his wife would supply them.

The "Battle Hymn" attracted little notice at first. Julia explained that "we were all too much absorbed in watching the progress of the war to give much heed to a copy of verses more or less."[10] But slowly it caught on, and her six-stanza contribution to the Union struggle ultimately outweighed all her husband's lengthy reports. By December 1863, she was reciting the "Battle Hymn" at the dedication of a statue of John Brown in Boston. By February 1864, the "Battle Hymn" was being performed to cheering audiences in Washington in front of President Lincoln.

Why was the "Battle Hymn" so much more successful than any of Julia's other writings? Of course, it is about a great national conflict, a life-and-death struggle, rather than a marital quarrel. Julia had linked or projected her own emotions onto a moment of historical mythmaking. But it is also a better poem. Her lifelong knowledge of biblical imagery, her decades of training as a poet, and her own longing to be part of the war effort, fueled and fused her creative imagination. She drew upon images from her reading, from sermons, from her dreams, from her unconscious, from her anger at her husband, and from her view of the Civil War as a holy war.

Above all, the syncopation of the music got her away from the predictable quatrains and peculiar stanzas of her usual verse. Written to be sung, the words were meant for the ear and not the eye. Instead of the ungainly feminine rhymes of her passion poems, ending on a weak syllable, her lines ended on a forceful final rhyme. Her language is elevated, but she does not impose awkward contractions to make the meaning fit the meter. There were many who wrote new words to "John Brown's Body," but the "Battle Hymn" had the most serious and uplifting language; there were many who composed new music for Julia's lyric, but unsuccessfully. As her daughters wrote, "it is inseparably welded to the air for which it was written, an air simple, martial, and dignified: no attempt to divorce the two could ever succeed."[11] The "Battle Hymn" was specific to an occasion, but it could also be adapted for chorale and eulogy, memorial and inspiration. As David Reynolds comments in his cultural biography of John Brown, "without Julia Ward Howe, John Brown may not have become fused with American myth. . . . She caught the essence of John Brown, a devout Calvinist who considered himself predestined to stamp out slavery. She had coupled his God-inspired antislavery passion to the North's mission and had thus helped define America."[12]

Almost every family in Boston was in mourning during the war. But back at home, the Howes felt safe: Henry was only fifteen; Sammy a four-year-old child. Then, in May 1863, Sammy came down with croup, which rapidly turned into diphtheria. Now prevented by vaccination, diphtheria was a terrible scourge in the nineteenth century, characterized by a barking cough, high fever, and swelling of the throat. The family physicians tried their futile remedies of steam, beef tea, and water by injection. On the fifth day, Chev returned from Washington, but Sammy died in his parents' arms at 3:00 a.m. Chev was too crushed by grief to attend the funeral on May 19; instead, James Freeman Clarke rode in the carriage with Julia to Mt. Auburn Cemetery. "Your little funeral, dear," she wrote that evening in the journal she had just begun to keep, "was bitter and agonizing. . . . The small white casket was placed on the front seat in the carriage. We came near the gate of Mount Auburn, when I began to realize that the parting was very near. I now opened the casket, took your dear little cold hand in mine, and began to take silent farewell of you." [13]

A few days later, the Howes went to New York, seeking comfort from the family at 8 Bond Street. Chev stayed in a hotel, since Uncle John's house was full; he was sick and bedridden most of the month, and Julia visited him there. The celebrated abolitionist minister Henry Ward Beecher had promised to make a condolence call at Bond Street, but he didn't show up; on Sunday all except Chev went to hear him preach on "Variety of Opinion in Minor Matters of Religion," a topic "not at this moment of special interest to me," Julia noted bitterly. On her birthday, May 27, she wrote "the one thing I desire now is reunion with my darling baby boy." For weeks she dreamed that she was trying to nurse him in the dark. Most heartbreakingly, Julia and Chev seem to have been unable to share their grief or console each other. "We take a different course about dear Sammy," he told her. "You seem to cherish his memory,—I strive to let him go." [14] There would be no more babies; her childbearing years were over. When he recovered from the first wave of his grief, Chev buried himself in ever-expanding reform work. On June 2, she went to see a medium named Foster who gave her vaguely consoling messages about Sammy in heaven, but said "nothing definite."

Julia turned to her studies and, writing for refuge and distraction, and perhaps unconsciously, expressed her conflicted feelings through six essays on philosophy and religion: "How Not to Teach Ethics," "Doubt and Belief," "Moral Triangulation, or The Third Party," "Duality of Character," and "The Fact Accomplished." "The Third Party" was the keynote of the series, and a metaphor for her state of mind. In it, she compared the bonds of matrimony to the compact uniting the States. Under what conditions, she asked, were divorce and secession justified? And "if North and South agree to set aside their bonds of union, and to become two republics, why should they not do it?" Ultimately, she concluded, the sacredness of the bond precluded cancellation. Somehow, the parties had to find a way to stay together.

She called her lecture series "Practical Ethics" and determined to offer it to a Boston audience. She doesn't say whether Chev read the lectures, but he insisted that if she gave them, she could not accept payment. In November 1863 she invited some of her friends to a Monday-night lecture series in her home. Attendance was excellent, the audience was attentive, and questions were respectful. Emerson, although unable to be present, was especially interested in "The Third Party." Julia took advantage of the meetings to work on her presentation and rhetoric. She tried to avoid anticlimax and to aim for clarity. Giving a lecture was midway between acting and teaching, which she approached through inducing a kind of trance-state: "on the morning of the day on which I was to give my lecture, I would read it over, and a curious sense of the audience seemed to possess me, a feeling of what it would and what it would not follow."

Her hopes that she had established herself as the preeminent civic poet of Boston, however, were soon dashed. At the November ceremony to dedicate the great pipe organ at the Boston Music Hall, the largest in the United States, the celebrated actress Charlotte Cushman recited an ode that had been commissioned from Annie Fields, the young wife of James T. Fields. It would be Annie Fields's first published poem. Julia had expected to be invited to write the ode; instead, she had to smile politely at the reception given by the Fieldses after the ceremony, when the authorship of the anonymous ode was revealed. Most unwisely, in an indication of her emotional vacillation during this difficult year, she used her position at the *Commonwealth* to write a nasty unsigned review of the poem:

> The ode which was now presented to the public, judged from a literary point of view, deserves neither praise or criticism. It had no characteristic of a poem other than phrase and rhyme, and pre-

> sented the mere wardrobe of poetry, without a body or soul . . . with no stamp of originality, and with no line that will remain . . . The false ambition of this attempt merely blocked the way from something better. Surely, among the literary men and women of Boston, among those who really *could*, might have been found someone who *would* have spoken the word for the hour which, whether in prose or in verse, was what the public wanted to hear.[15]

The review offended Annie Fields and her husband; even Longfellow reproached Julia for having been unkind. In her notebook, Mrs. Fields wrote: "Julia Ward Howe has said and sung her last as far as Boston goes. Her jealousy of the Odist got the better of her better judgment and she has written out her gall for the *Commonwealth*. Alas! Where was her good genius?" At a dinner party given by Mary Ward Dorr, she added later, the company picked "Julia as clean as any duck for the spit." Julia eventually wrote a note of apology, and Annie Fields graciously accepted it, but she never really forgave those snide remarks. She joked with friends that Julia resembled Mrs. Jellyby in Dickens's *Bleak House*, bursting in upon a newly organized society of working women "like a whirlwind," interrupting their discussion, and "bringing her little narrow personality into a meeting occupied with business and heated with high enthusiasms."[16] If Julia was to recover her literary reputation and her ethical high ground, she had a fight ahead of her.

Despite this setback, she wrote new philosophical lectures, and in January 1864 told Chev that she intended to take them on the road to New York, Philadelphia, and Washington, and ask for honorariums. Chev was predictably outraged, and her promise to give her profits to the Sanitary Commission did not mollify him. On January 16, they had a bitter quarrel; she wrote in her journal that "some illusions left me today, giving place to unwholesome facts." Did this cryptic message mean, as some Howe scholars surmise, that Chev had told her he was having an affair? Certainly she had been suspecting him of infidelity for years. He could also have been passing on sexual gossip, which would have disillusioned her almost as much. But not even unwholesome facts could stop her. A few days later, she read her lecture on "Duality of Character" in the vestry of James Freeman Clarke's Indiana Place Church. There she introduced her white lace cap, which both covered her hair attractively and became her trademark. "Quite a full audience" showed up, including the steadfast Mary Ward Dorr.[17]

In the spring she went to Washington, where her friend the *saloniste* Fanny Eames had offered her parlor as a venue. Sumner not only refused to support the lectures but also wrote to women in the city to dissuade them from attending and refused to attend himself. On the subject of women's rights, Sumner was yesterday's man; in the 1860s, a decade of rapid social change, he could not keep up. Yet her confidence as a speaker was rising. Departing from Washington, she confided to her journal her determination to face the challenge. "I have no one to stand for me there, Sumner against me, Channing unknown to me, everyone else indifferent." Nonetheless, she went "in obedience to a deep and strong impulse which I do not understand or explain, but whose bidding I cannot neglect."[18] Sumner did not show up, but William Henry Channing, Stephen Foster, and Salmon P. Chase were in her audience.

On November 6, 1864, against Chev's usual fierce opposition, she went to the Century Club in New York to participate in the celebration of the seventieth birthday of William Cullen Bryant, the only woman invited to read. She knew that she was there as a token woman and "the author of the most stirring lyric of the war," but she was proud to be included just the same. On the train, she sat next to Oliver Wendell Holmes, who apologized that he could not make conversation because he was saving his voice to read his poem for Bryant. Julia had the satisfaction of assuring him that she too had a poem to read. In the event, she was the star of the evening. The *Chicago Tribune* commented: "She has just the pathetic and well measured voice for oracular manifestations . . . and looks remarkably inspired. She was received with much applause."[19]

On the train home, Holmes made lively conversation, and gave her the teasing nickname of "Madame Comment," for all her questions and answers.

The first months of 1865 found her hard at work, and trying to juggle the care and chaperonage of her growing daughters with her reading and writing. She turned to philosophy, especially Kant, to calm her down and give her moral ammunition in her arguments with Chev, although domestic duties and the children's demands cut maddeningly into study time. "Much tormented by interruptions," she wrote in February; "could not get five quiet minutes at a time. Everybody torments me with every smallest errand. And I am trying to study philosophy!"[20]

Among the new essays was "Polarity," a key to her views on relationships between men and women. In this lengthy unpublished essay, in the Julia Ward Howe Collection at the Library of Congress, she argued that the relations of men and women were not fixed and innate, but the product of social forces and customs. The polar opposition of masculine and feminine, of man and woman, did not rest upon the superiority of men. If society could come to understand that progress required the equal development and growth of both sexes, polarity and opposition could evolve towards complementarity and a "sublime unit" coming from the liberty of the individual. Although she was laboring to prove this intellectually in the 1860s, Julia made it the basis of a philosophy of gender that enabled and inspired her feminist actions for the rest of her life.

Julia Romana's birthday in March led her to meditate on her oldest daughter's reserve and the strains in their relationship: "Twenty-one years old, and almost a stranger to me."[21] Both Julia Romana and Flossy took Chev's side in protesting against her public speaking and traveling away from home. When she insisted on giving a lecture that month despite his fury, he stomped off to Newport with Julia Romana.

The Howes called a temporary ceasefire on April 9, when Lee surrendered at Appomattox, and there were flags, decorations, festivities, and parades in Boston. Less than a week later came the terrible news of Lincoln's assassination. For Julia, the news brought personal pain as well as patriotic grief. Edwin Booth was a friend and neighbor; she had attended the funeral of his young wife. The whole family admired him as an actor and had often seen him on the stage, as well as his brother John Wilkes Booth. The week of the assassination, Edwin Booth was performing in Boston; the Howes had tickets to the Saturday matinee. All theatres closed, and it was rumored that Edwin would never act again. In her journal, Julia recorded her anguish and added, "this atrocious act, which was consummated in a very theatrical manner, is enough to ruin not the Booth family alone, but the theatrical profession."[22] The day of Lincoln's funeral, April 19, she wrote a poem called "Parricide." Then on April 27, she heard that John Wilkes Booth had been found and shot, refusing to give himself up—"the best thing that could have happened to himself and his family."[23] That day she wrote a second poem, "Pardon," which some readers took as a premature forgiveness of Booth. It was her gesture of closure for the vengeful passions of the Civil War.

But the Howe truce was short-lived, and Julia's domestic war was also coming to a head. April 23 was her wedding anniversary, often a day of sad solitary reflection. This year she announced her intention to spend the night of the anniversary giving a sermon to the inmates at the Charlestown Women's Prison. First, Flossy tried to stop her, and then Chev erupted. He "attacked me with the utmost vehemence and temper, calling my undertaking a mere courting of publicity, would not argue, nor hear me at all." Julia gave in for the last time; but in her diary she recorded a forceful repudiation of her marriage. "I have been married twenty-two years today. In the course of this time I have never known my husband to approve any act of mine which I myself valued. Books—poems—essays—everything has been contemptible or contraband in his eyes, because it was not *his* way of doing things."[24] Chev read this entry the next day—he may have been reading her diary all along—and demanded that she destroy the whole journal, which she absolutely refused to do. She did not get to preach at the prison, but, as Valarie Ziegler points out, "no one knew better than she what life governed by an unyielding warden could be . . . [she] had spent her entire life in confinement."[25]

The marital civil war did not end with surrender, assassination, a jail break, or a funeral. From April 1865, however, it was in a new phase. Julia felt some loyalty towards Chev, but she was no longer dependent on his permission or support to do what she wished. If he occasionally behaved well, she was amazed that "he shows any kind of liking to me."[26] She would never break their marital vows, but she would follow her own conscience. The national conflict had enabled her to resolve the personal one. Despite all its tragic losses, she observed, the Civil War not only had emancipated the slaves but also had liberated women, who "found a new scope for their activities, and developed abilities hitherto unsuspected by themselves."[27]

In the autumn, the Howes once more were searching for a new house and bought one at Boylston Place, where they bickered constantly over Chev's insistence on keeping the rooms healthily cold and Julia's complaints that she was freezing to death. At her cold desk, Julia was editing a collection of her poems called *Later Lyrics*, and she did not enjoy the task. "The labor of looking over the manuscript nearly made me ill . . . Had a new bad feeling of intense pressure in the right temple." Still, "nearly disabled by headaches," she pushed on.[28] A group of war poems, including "The First Martyr," on the execution of John Brown, were less dramatic than "The Battle Hymn," with which the section concluded. She was still sniping at the Brownings; in "Kenyon's Legacy," named for John Kenyon, who had funded them in Italy, she made fun of the poets dwelling in Casa Guidi, who "yawn at common people," and set a lofty table where

The chairs are queer and rotten,
The board is bare, the talk divine,
The teapot long forgotten.

In addition, Julia declared her difference from the advanced women of Boston, who supported "the woman's standard, new unfurled," by ventilating their anger against men. "I am not with you, sisters, in your talk," she wrote in a poem called "The Tea-Party"; "My life has striven for broader scope than yours." Advising them to keep to their own turf, she reminded them that "in carpet counsel ye may win the day; / But keep your limits—do not rule the world." Their "pettish will," she warned, would lead to strife and discord, "No lengthened wars of reason, but a rage, / Shown and repented twenty times a day." She might have been talking about herself. In any case, she was not quite ready to join a movement for women's rights.

She saw copies of her book at Tilton and Company in December, and although she liked its appearance, her expectations for its reception were very low. Her usual supporters were prudently noncommittal. Oliver Wendell Holmes claimed to be too busy to read it. Longfellow wrote a bland note of thanks for his copy, "declining to praise or criticize, most strangely, I think," she observed.[29] In the aftermath of the publication, Julia felt defeated by the silence: "Literary affairs confused, I have no market, Chev takes away my voice, and I do not see how or where to print."[30]

Yet if the door of print was closing, speaking invitations were still expanding. A reading in September had been well attended and well received, and ended with a call to recite the "Battle Hymn." In October, she had read some poems at the newly founded New England Hospital for Women and Children, and the next day was applauded by a crowd at the boys' reform school in Westboro, as the woman who wrote "that Battle Hymn of the Republic."[31] These were humble venues, but proof that her voice had not been entirely taken away.

In 1866, she built on that foundation. February saw her in Washington giving a series of philosophical readings to small audiences. Uncle John Ward died in April, leaving a much smaller bequest to the Ward sisters than they had expected. "Dull, sad, and perplexed," she reflected on her chances of earning some money and some reputation: "My uncle not having made me a rich woman, I feel more than ever impelled to make some great effort to realize the value of my mental capacities and acquisitions. I am as well entitled to an efficient literary position as any other woman in this country—perhaps better than any other. Still I hang by the way, picking up ten dollars here and there with great difficulty. I had as lief die unless I can be satisfied that I have delivered the whole value of my literary cargo."[32]

Chev was also at an impasse and seeking a new direction. He had not been active at Perkins for years and had been trying to resign for almost a decade. Hearing that the Greeks in the Cretan Islands were rebelling against Turkish rule, Chev thought he could escape his disappointments by returning to the site of his heroic youth, as head of the American mission to Greece. Julia thought his chances were poor but kept her reservations to her journal: "Chev full of the Greek commission, which I think he cannot get. I wish he might, because he wishes it. Surely a man so modest and meritorious in his public career might claim so small an acknowledgment in life as this."[33] She went to Washington to plead his case with General Grant, President Johnson, Vice President Foster, and other officials. To her annoyance, Sumner, who had promised to support Chev's application, did not come to see her at the hotel. He probably knew it was a hopeless cause; Chev was controversial enough in his own right, but the support of Sumner, one of Johnson's chief antagonists in the Senate, could not have helped him. Johnson received her civilly, but his most notable remark was that she must be much younger than the Doctor.

Indeed, the nearly twenty-year age difference between Julia and Chev was now working to her advantage. On May 31, a few days after her forty-seventh birthday, Julia received a letter from Vice President Foster telling her that a younger man than Chev had been nominated for the Greek mission. "This gave me an unhappy hour. Chev was a good deal overcome by it for a time, but rallied and bears up bravely. The girls are rather glad. I am content, but I do not see what can take the place of this cherished object to Chev."[34] Sumner gave Chev the bad news and Julia wrote a sympathetic but pitying poem "To S.G.H. on his failure to receive the Grecian mission which he had been led to think might be offered to him, 1866."

Let, then, the modern Embassy float by,
Nor one regret in thy high bosom lurk:
God's mission called thy use to that soft sky;
Wait God's dismissal where thou build'st His work.[35]

Wisely, she did not try to publish the poem; Chev would have been livid to see himself described by his wife as failing, especially when she seemed to be succeeding. He pretended not to mind his rejection, but he was wounded nonetheless. "Had either the Pres. or the Minister been persons of delicacy or generosity," he griped to Sumner, they would have told him early on "that there would be no use in pressing the matter. That they lack delicacy & generosity is their misfortune." He would seek solace once more in his work "in other fields, while my little of life remains."[36] He was reminded of his age that fall, when Sumner, then fifty-five, wed Alice Mason Hooper, a twenty-eight-year-old widow with a seven-year-old daughter. Sumner was beginning a new life; Chev was living out the old diminished one.

Julia called upon the newlyweds on her next visit to Washington. She also went to Mount Holyoke to read *Passion-Flowers* to the inmates of the lunatic asylum. They seemed to like it. And she took on a job as the editor of a weekly magazine, *Northern Lights.* She was hopeful that Henry James might contribute a story. Still, the end of the year found her uncertain about her readings. "The bitter opposition of my family renders this service a very difficult and painful one for me. I do not, therefore, seek occasions of performing it, not being quite clear as to the extent to which they ought to limit my efficiency; but when the word and the time come together I always try to give the one to the other and always shall."[37]

Chev, meanwhile, was not ready to go gently into his retirement. He was as handsome as ever; why should he not make a last stand? In January 1867, he went to speak at the Boston Music Hall to raise funds for Crete, and he made a sensation, a star returning to the stage. According to his daughters, "he was sixty-six years old, but looked much younger. When, at the first meeting called by him, he rose and said, 'Forty-five years ago I was much interested in the Greek Revolution,' the audience was amazed. His hair was but lightly touched with silver; his eyes were as bright, his figure as erect and martial, as when, in 1826, he had fought and marched under the Greek banner and slept under the Greek stars."[38] Julia gave a cooler account: "In the evening attended meeting in behalf of Crete, at which Chev presided and spoke. Excellent as to matter, but always with a defective elocution, not sending his voice out."[39]

Basking in the applause of his comeback, Chev decided he must go to Crete himself on an errand of mercy, and wanted Julia, Julia Romana, and Laura to join him as well. Julia had belatedly received a bequest from Uncle John giving her an annual income between $1,400 and $2,500. Out of habit, and sympathy, she handed most of it over to Chev; it would finance the trip. The timing seemed right for the family; Harry was an undergraduate at Harvard; Flossy was engaged to a young lawyer, David Hall. Julia convinced herself that the trip would be a turning point for her oldest daughter. Almost twenty-four, Julia Romana was shy, odd, unhappy, and single. On March 13, they all sailed on the *Asia* bearing $37,000 for Cretan relief.

Their first stop was in London, where Julia picked up her former social life. She went to parties, teas, and dinners; noticed the latest fashions—Lady Baker wore a necklace of lion's teeth—and found herself seated next to Robert Browning at a dinner. He was gracious about her satiric poems, and she was grateful for his magnanimity. (He would be less magnanimous in years to come.) Then she and Laura headed to Rome for Easter with Louisa, now remarried to the American expatriate artist Luther Terry, and living in the enormous Palazzo Odescalchi, as big as a Boston square. Chev and Julia Romana went on alone to Greece, allegedly to save the expense of two more passages; but Julia understood his real concerns: "he objects . . . probably more to an indefinable fear of my predominance where he would wish to be the sole figure, which of course he would and ought to be."[40] Against Laura's advice, she read one of her essays to the American colony in Rome, which included Charlotte Cushman. Then Chev unexpectedly invited them to join him in Athens in June. Once there, she was again popular and in demand, and gave two readings to the English-speaking colony. In Crete, she and her daughters attracted a huge crowd when they distributed the clothes made by Boston sewing circles for the refugees. Chev did not enjoy this competition for the spotlight.

Julia also made use of the seven-month trip to write another travel book, *From the Oak to the Olive: A Plain Record of a Pleasant Journey*, in which Chev is called "the veteran" and barely mentioned. Her journal gave some glimpses into her emotions on returning to Rome in middle age; there were ghosts in every square, including that of Horace Binney Wallace, but on this third visit she no longer felt haunted by them.

In at least one respect, the trip paid off handsomely. In Athens, Chev and Julia Romana met a bearded young Greek philosophy student, Michael Anagnostopolous, an ardent disciple who wished only to serve the great philhellene. He acted as Chev's translator and secretary. When the Howes left, he accompanied them back to Boston, where he rapidly mastered English, changed his name to the more pronounceable Anagnos, and became the Doctor's assistant at the Institution. He also continued to tutor Julia in Greek, a project they had begun in Athens.

Their homecoming in October was troubled, nevertheless. When they docked in Boston, they learned at once that Sumner's marriage had scandalously broken up after Alice was seen in public with another man, the German aristocrat Friedrich von Holstein. She had gone off to Europe, and it was widely rumored that Sumner was impotent. Chev wrote letters of consolation to Sumner, blaming Alice. Then, five days later, John Andrew died, and the Howes were both bereft. Julia wrote a memorial poem about John Andrew and wanted to read it at his commemorative service, but Chev forbade her to go. Moreover, without consulting her, he had rented their homes on both Boylston Place and Lawton's Valley; they had to move back to the gloomy Institution, where she spent another lonely winter.

Finally, she read a lacerating unsigned review of *Later Lyrics* in the *North American Review*, which had come out the April before. "Mrs. Howe's prevailing fault is that she is too vague, too general, too lax; and it requires a more constant patience of fact, linear divisions, and of shades of meaning, than properly belongs to her genius, to call back into being phases of life and character so alien to our actual circumstances."[41] She was sure that James Russell Lowell and Charles Eliot Norton, the editors of the *NAR* from 1864 to 1868, had commissioned the review, and she was outraged. "It seemed to me mean in motive and obliterating criticism. No one of real culture handles in that way a book which, whatever be its faults, is literature and not any ballad. Lowell and Norton are both of them responsible for this critique although I should have supposed it too stupid for the one and too bad hearted for the other."[42] She was still seething in November when she wrote a vengeful poem on the *NAR*, for her eyes only. "Please God," she vowed, "the N. A. review, with all Ticknor and Field–dom to back it, shall not take away my office from me."[43]

But there were also some pleasures. She loved the company and instruction of Michael Anagnos, "looked forward to her Greek lesson as girls do to a ball," and referred to him in her journal as "a dear son to me."[44] To her surprise, she was invited to read a paper before the august Radical Club, which met monthly to discuss and debate, and included such luminaries as Emerson and Higginson. Elizabeth Peabody was among the handful of female members. Joining such an elite society made Julia feel that she had arrived as a Boston intellectual, and she believed that the Civil War had made it possible for people, even women, to break down barriers, share ideas, and argue with civility. They could also have fun. At a meeting of the Brain Club, a sociable women's group Howe had started, she gave a comic narration of her Cretan trip:

Oh! Who were the people you saw, Mrs. Howe?
When you went where the Cretans were making a row?
Kalopathaki—Rodocanachi—
Paparpopoulos—Anagnostopoulos—
Nicolaides—Paraskevaides—
These were the people that saw Mrs. Howe
When she went where the Cretans were making a row.

Oh! Give us a specimen, dear Mrs. Howe,
Of the Greek that you learned and are mistress of now.
Potichomania—Mesopotamia.
Tatterdemalion—Episcopalian—
Megalotherium—monster inferium—
Scoulevon—auctrion—infant phenomenon.
Lyrie ticamete—what's your calamity?
Pallas Atheneae Aun,
Favors no Fenian.
Such is the language that learned Mrs. Howe,
In the speech of the gods she is mistress of now.

Julia had long enjoyed the social opportunities of Boston clubland. After 1867, however, she replaced Chev's all-male Five of Clubs, and all the men's clubs that had excluded her for decades, with pioneering women's clubs. Indeed, she started so many groups that she jokingly called herself the Mother of Clubs—"I have one every year."[45] In 1871, she became president of the New England Woman's Club and remained in office until 1910.

Chev was not so resilient. In the fall of 1868, he learned that Julia intended to be a delegate at a New York Conference of Unitarians, and, much worse, to attend a women's suffrage meeting at Boston Horticultural Hall. The letter of protest he wrote to her shows how obstinately and obtusely he interpreted her religious and political interests as vanity and narcissism. His letter obsessively repeated the word *passion*, to remind her of the crime of *Passion-Flowers.* "Your note of yesterday gives me new pain & sorrow, for it almost crushes the hope I had begin to form that you would yield to my most earnest entreaties & to the consideration of family wishes & interests, and forego further indulgence in your passion for public appearance & display." In a crescendo of self-pity, he wildly hinted that one of their children might have another father: "When I reflect that only a few days ago I pleaded with you earnestly but tenderly, that I tried [to] set forth the consequence upon me & the family of another form of passion, my life long suffering, my blight of heart, my fear of family disgrace, the worst of my domestic happiness & hopes, the occasional inquiry of doubt about the paternity of offspring; when I imagined other sad effects upon our family, you seemed to be moved & changed of purpose. I had a right therefore to hope that you would yield to my request and to the wishes of the family and make no more engagements for public appearances."

In a final blow, he invoked the tragedy of Sammy's death to keep her in line: "By our old affection, by the memory of our dear dead boy, by the years of heart ache & misery which you acknowledge to have brought on me by your own indulgence in another form of passion, I entreat you to forego indulgence in this one."[46] He had gone too far. The letter was so extreme in its paranoia, self-pity, and manipulative tactics that Julia found it easy to resist, although very painful to read. Chev took out his frustration on his employees at Perkins: he found out that Miss McLane and Mr. Hallard were cohabiting, and he fired them. There, at least, his word was law.

Chev had the upper hand, but he understood the subtext of her activity and her determination. She was escaping from his control, and control was his major weapon of power. He had played his strongest hand, and it had failed. At the beginning of the war, Julia had felt useless. She wanted to serve, but her domestic circumstances prevented her from serving. She wanted to give inspiration but felt that her writing was unwanted and misunderstood. She wanted to act in a public role but was opposed and excluded. "There is nothing for you to do," she heard from the world. Now at last, she was breaking out of the fixed orbit of the Mother Star. The word and the time and the need had come together, and she was about to take flight.

Chapter Nine

A NEW WORLD

As she approached her fiftieth birthday in 1869, Howe had a vision of a new world of womanhood and endeavored to become part of it. "During the first two thirds of my life," she recalled in her memoir, "I looked to the masculine ideal of character as the only true one. I sought its inspiration, and referred my merits and demerits to its judicial verdict. In an unexpected hour a new light came to me, showing a world of thought and of character quite beyond the limits in which I had hitherto been content to abide. The new domain now made clear to me was that of true womanhood,—woman no longer in her ancillary relation to her opposite, man, but in her direct relation to the divine plan and purpose, as a free agent, fully sharing with man every human right and every human responsibility. This discovery was like the addition of a new continent to the map of the world, or of a new testament to the old ordinances."[1] Hitherto her models and mentors had been great men—her father, her husband, Theodore Parker, James Freeman Clarke, Spinoza, Kant. As she looked to women for evidence of intelligence, morality, courage, and purpose, she was strengthened and transformed.

With this revelation, Howe began to apply philosophic insights to the situation of women, and to her own life. Reasoning from women's divinely given maternal responsibilities, she concluded that they must be the moral and spiritual equals of men. The next step was to demand for women "the full dignity of citizenship" that had been granted to the slave.[2] Northern women had fought for abolition and emancipation of the slaves; now their turn had come. They "had labored incessantly to supply the needs of those at the front," and had "worked to build, maintain, and fill the churches throughout the land with a patient industry akin to that of coral insects. Surely we should be invited to pass in with our brothers to the larger liberty now shown to be our just due."[3] Like the microscopic insects that had gradually built up the great coral reefs of the Pacific, women were the anonymous, almost invisible agents of change. They must channel that patient industry into creating a place of their own in the halls of government. And she herself must break away from the confines of Chev's approval and become a free agent, a free woman.

Nonetheless, when she was invited to take part in an organizing meeting for women's rights in Boston in 1868, Howe was uneasy, expecting the suffragists to be eccentric, ugly, strident, and belligerent—to embody, in short, the stereotypes of strong-minded harridans she had read in the newspapers and heard from Chev's friends. On a wet November morning, she slipped into Horticultural Hall as inconspicuously as possible, respectably dressed in her "rainy-day suit," and hoping to be unnoticed by the officers of the group. On the platform were men she honored and respected—William Garrison, Wendell Phillips, Thomas Higginson, and James Freeman Clarke. Also sitting on the platform, however, was the suffragist and reformer Lucy Stone, who had graduated from Oberlin College and taken the bold step of keeping her maiden name rather than combining it with her husband's. Perhaps these signs of challenge to traditional womanly behavior antagonized Howe; perhaps she was envious. In any case, she had made Stone "the object of one of my imaginary dislikes." Yet when Stone rose to speak, Howe was astonished; her nemesis was "sweet-faced and silver-voiced, the very embodiment of Goethe's 'eternal feminine.'" Furthermore, Stone's views on women "harmonized with my own aspirations."[4] Suddenly Howe felt her prejudices dissolve: "The object of my distaste had been a mere Phantom, conjured up by silly and senseless misrepresentations. . . . These champions, who had fought so long and so valiantly for the slave, now turned a searchlight of their intelligence upon the condition of woman, and demanded for the mothers of the community the civil rights that had recently been accorded the negro. When they requested me to speak, which they did presently, I could only say 'I am with you.'"[5] On the second day of the conference, she was elected president of the New England Woman Suffrage Association.

Howe clearly presents this conference as a conversion experience, and she wrote about it explicitly in those terms. She had to exorcise the image of the suffragist as an unsexed monster and see her instead as the noble figurehead of the movement; as she sat on the platform, she recalled, "for the first time I met the monster woman suffrage face-to-face. My conversion was instant . . . I embarked then on the good ship, woman suffrage."[6] More likely, her conversion had been building for a long time, and at the conference she came out in public as a suffragist, a view she had privately held but had been unwilling to declare.[7] She had told herself that women must hold back until black men had citizenship and the vote, and the ratification of the Fourteenth Amendment in 1868 and the Fifteenth Amendment in 1869 relieved her scruples. Personally, Howe had also reached a dead end in her efforts to make a career as a lecturer on philosophical ethics. She had sadly recognized in the late '60s that her lectures on metaphysics went over the heads of her baffled audience. Reading a paper on "Ideal Causation" one night, she realized that no one was "greatly interested."[8] Finally, she herself had become wearied by a purely mental life. After another unsuccessful presentation at the Parker Fraternity Rooms, a memorial site for Theodore Parker, she told Maud that she "determined to live from experience, from thinking about people and about life, and to think no longer about thoughts."[9] The suffrage movement offered a solution to this split between mind and spirit and united all her gifts in a grand public role.

Susan B. Anthony and Elizabeth Cady Stanton had left the Republican Party to organize a women's party campaigning for suffrage, but their insistence on women's entitlement to the vote brought them into a conflict with black rights, a conflict that would evolve into racism. "If intelligence, justice, and morality are to have precedence in the government," Anthony argued in a debate, "let the question of woman be brought up first and that of the Negro last."[10] In reaction, a group of moderate New England reformers, most of them abolitionists, decided to call for a convention on "the woman question," the genteel euphemism for feminism. The conveners of the conference avoided naming women's suffrage as their goal, but they proposed "the equality of the sexes before God . . . And the rights of the individual as set forth in the ever memorable words of the Declaration of Independence" as their subject.

When the American Woman Suffrage Association was formed in 1869, Howe became its foreign corresponding secretary, making use of her language skills and broad European contacts to communicate with feminists abroad; she was also one of the editors of its publication, the *Woman's Journal.* In the first issue, she described the cause as renewal and revitalization for middle-aged women. "We who stand beside the cradle of this enterprise are not young in years. . . . Some of us have been looking thoughtfully forward to the final summons, not because of ill health or infirmity, but because, after the establishment of our families, no great object intervened between ourselves and that last consummation. But these young undertakings detain us in life. While they need so much care and counsel, we cannot consent to death."[11]

The women's movement was especially precious to Howe because it brought her women friends. She had understood sisterhood through Louisa and Annie, and Mary Ward Dorr had remained a loyal friend in Boston. But she had never had the experience of working with intelligent women who shared her energy and values. "Words could not express the comforting instruction which has come to me in the later years of my life," she wrote, from "the better acquaintance with my own sex."[12] On the road, the suffragists taught each other, supported each other, learned from each other, and mothered each other. Howe really loved their expeditions, however uncomfortable the rooms where they slept, however cold the halls where they spoke, however indigestible the food they ate, and however hostile the audiences they had to convince.

Her closest ties were with Lucy Stone and Mary Livermore, the editor-in-chief of the *Woman's Journal.* They were almost the same age, and Stone was the same height, while Livermore was tall, stout, and comforting, the maternal "dear big Livermore!" who often rescued her in an unfamiliar town.[13] To Livermore, a suffragist who became "the Queen of the Platform" as a professional public speaker with the Lyceum Bureau, Howe was "the *darlingest darling* of all my women friends."[14] On a chilly trip to Vermont with Stone and Livermore in the winter of 1870, Howe cheerfully noticed that the evergreens "were hung with icicles, which glittered like diamonds in the bright winter sun."[15] The comparison to jewels is always a sign of her happiness. When the three women got to their meeting room in Burlington, however, they found "a vulgar and silly ballad" that described them as three old crows. Howe volunteered to talk first, promising that she would not be disturbed even if the audience threw chairs at her. They did not; Mary Livermore stared them down, and Howe's reasonable speech calmed them down. On the other hand, Vermonters were not persuaded to pass a suffrage measure. Some women who went to the meetings in Rutland, Montpelier, and Burlington found Howe out of touch with their lives and were offended when she addressed them as if they were spoiled socialites. "It touches our sense of the ludicrous," one wrote sharply in the *Vermont Watchman*, "to see people coming to the hard-working women of Vermont to tell us we are dying of ennui."[16]

Howe learned from that awkward experience that she had to pay more attention to class diversity and to the interests of her audience.

With the help of Stone and Livermore, she was soon teaching herself to be a better public speaker. Her first task was to move up from the polite parlor discussions of Boston ladies, and the arcane intellectual debates of the Radical Club, to rowdy political gatherings where she had to master parliamentary procedure and win over a bored or unruly crowd. With a broader experience of public speaking and argument, she learned to lower and control her operatic voice, and figured out how to gauge the amount of information and persuasion an audience could tolerate. Most of all, she became aware of her own snobbery and the need to speak to a group of women on their own terms, drawing on her sense of humor as well as philosophy. For years she had been trying on her own to improve as a lecturer; at last, these experiences of trial, error, and mastery gave her a genuine sense of accomplishment and growth. She was also watching the style of the suffragists.

Maria Mitchell, professor of astronomy at Vassar, came to the Women's Congress in 1868, and Howe noted approvingly that she wore a well-made, rich black silk dress, to which her silver curls presented a striking contrast. Then as now, the black dress was the best look for professional women, although on one visit to a girls' school, twelve young ladies "acted in graceful dumb show the stanzas of my Battle Hymn," four dressed all in red, four in white, and four in blue.[17] Watching Lucy Stone and Henry Blackwell, she became aware that *some* husbands were devoted partners in the battle for women's rights. As with Theodore and Lydia Parker, however, she did not notice the submerged competition and tension between the exemplary couple.[18]

Soon her days were filled with meetings and protests. In snow, rain, frost, dust, and heat, she went on lecture tours from Buffalo to Minneapolis, anywhere with a spare room and a church hall. She organized a woman preachers' convention and became president of that, too. Decades ahead of Elizabeth Cady Stanton's *Woman's Bible* (1895), she was thinking about women's absence from theological doctrine. "I felt how much the masculine administration of religious doctrine had overridden us women, and I felt how partial and one-sided a view of these matters had been inculcated by men, and handed down by man-revering mothers. . . . We need to have the womanly side of religion represented."[19]

Finding a community of women gave her confidence to resist the disapproval of her family. "One of the comforts which I found in the new association was the relief it afforded me from a sense of isolation and eccentricity. For years past I had felt strongly impelled to lend my voice to the convictions of my heart . . . always with the feeling that my course in doing so was held to call for apology and explanation . . . I now found a sphere of action in which this mode of expression no longer appeared singular or eccentric, but simple, natural, and, under the circumstances, inevitable."[20] Freed from the inner pressure to apologize when she followed her convictions, she bloomed, and her friends noticed the change. Higginson observed "a new brightness to her face, a new cordiality in her manner."[21]

Finally, having a group of female allies and women friends helped Howe separate from her daughters as they married and left home. On December 30, 1870, Julia Romana married Michael Anagnos and went to live at the Institution for the rest of her life. In June 1871, after a long engagement, Laura married Henry Richards, an architect trained at Harvard. In November 1871, Flossy married David Prescott Hall, a young lawyer who had been her childhood sweetheart. Three down. Of the daughters, only Maud was left at home, and she was more interested in parties and dances than education and reform. Chev thoroughly disapproved of her frivolity and blamed Julia for indulging her. "Silly Mama, has not the heart to restrain her; but lets her get intoxicated, daily and nightly, by the admiration & compliments of silly men, by the fumes of fashion. Heaven grant she may not become permanently & fatally injured, in moral character."[22]

Julia Romana's marriage was a miraculous combination of compatibility, mutual need, and plain good luck; it was also an Oedipal threat to both parents. Anagnos was being groomed to take over the Institution;

by 1871, he was already the "resident superintendent" and had sealed his rights to the succession by marrying into the family. His career would mirror and rival Chev's. For Julia Romana, becoming Mrs. Anagnos was as close as she could get to marrying her father. Always shy and uncomfortable with parties and dances, she could devote herself to serving her husband and his pupils. She also snatched away her mother's beloved Greek tutor and took her place as the First Lady of Perkins. Living in the rooms where she had been a child suited her, too; she did not have to start from scratch with a new household and could settle easily into the familiar roles and routines. Julia says almost nothing in her journal about the Anagnos household. She was in fact relieved to have her difficult and depressed oldest daughter settled and out of the house, and to cede the Doctor's Wing to another bride; she also kept Michael as a trusted adviser. For Chev, however, the marriage of his most devoted daughter was a painful loss that he felt for the remainder of his life. Of the three married daughters, Julia missed Laura most: "Today my dearest Laura married and left me . . . This marriage cuts into my heart, taking away my pet child. Let her know, if she reads this when I am dead and gone, that she had the inside fold of my heart."[23]

Howe's first major feminist act was to launch a women's movement for peace. In 1870, during the Franco-Prussian War, Howe started to think about the nature of war itself. She had sanctified the battle between the States as a holy war. Now she was struck by the unholiness of war and the ways it could be avoided. "Why do not the mothers of mankind interfere in these matters," she asked, "and prevent the waste of that human life which they alone bear and know the cost?"[24] She called on women to initiate a Mother's Day for peace on June 2 every year:

> Arise, then, women of this day! Arise, all women who have hearts, whether our baptism be of water or of tears! Say firmly: We will not have great questions decided by irrelevant agencies. Our husbands shall not come to us, reeking with carnage, for caresses and

applause. Our sons shall not be taken from us to unlearn all that we have been able to teach them of charity, mercy and patience. We, women of one country, will be too tender of those of another country, to allow our sons to be trained to injure theirs. From the bosom of the devastated earth a voice goes up with our own. It says: Disarm, disarm! The sword of murder is not the balance of justice. Blood does not wipe out dishonor, nor violence vindicate possession.[25]

As Julia stepped forward into the public spotlight, Chev was longing for a final knightly adventure. As usual when he was stymied or bored, he looked backwards to his glory days in Greece, and this time he yearned to become the US ambassador to Greece. Unfortunately for him, all the signs were against it; President Grant was no more amenable to naming him a diplomat than President Johnson had been. Then in the mid-1870s, his desire for a little kingdom of his own led him to become embroiled in the tawdry campaign for the annexation of Santo Domingo, now the Dominican Republic. Grant wanted to get control of the harbor of Samana Bay for a naval base. Backed by a group of politicians, businessmen, and land speculators, he offered a treaty of annexation to the Dominicans, with an original payment of $1.5 million, and appointed a three-man commission including Ben Wade, a radical ex-senator from Ohio; Andrew D. White, the president of Cornell; and Dr. Howe. They left for an exploratory trip to the island in 1871; Chev loved the tropical climate, was charmed by President Buenaventura Báez, and persuaded himself that the Dominicans were virtually unanimous in desiring union with the United States.

Sumner, however, thought the Dominican project was a disgraceful mixture of greed, exploitation, and imperialism. He brought all his political passion and relentless oratory to opposing the treaty of annexation in the Senate; and the project was tabled. For once, the old friends could not agree. "I cannot see anything in this business as you see it—nothing!"

Sumner wrote to Chev.[26] Sumner's intransigence was the most intense challenge faced by the two friends. For decades they had fought on the same side. Chev could not accept or endure Sumner's refusal to support him. He let off steam in a strongly worded letter to Andrew White, invoking the most extreme images of madness and betrayal: "I have been slowly & painfully led to the sad conclusion that Charles Sumner has become morally insane. The great moral influence over the public which he has gained by a noble and brilliant career, he is now wielding to gratify personal hate & envy. God help him; for he knows not what he does. Much as I love him, I have a duty now to guard the public by all my feeble powers, against the evil which this once great and good man is now doing, in his blind phrenzy . . . He has deceived and misled the public. He has vilified & abused innocent men . . . He has imperiled the acquisition of territory by the U.S. which would be a vast advantage to the country; to commerce; & to the progress of freedom & humanity . . ."[27]

Despite the setbacks, Chev was determined to go back to the island and take his family with him; he still had hopes for the Dominican project, if only as a business venture. He invested his money—or rather, Julia's money—in the Samana Bay Company, along with a group of speculators and shipping merchants. In February 1872, he and Julia set sail on the *Tybee* for a rough and stormy voyage, accompanied by Maud and one of her friends; Chev's three nieces; and his devoted secretary Mary Paddock. While Chev was courted by President Báez, Julia was entertaining the girls and enjoying the opportunity to give a lavish ball for them during Easter carnival, something they could not have afforded at home. She also gave weekly sermons in the small black church.

Early on, Chev had uneasily noticed that speculators were making their own use of the capital of the Samana Bay Company: "money was squandered prodigally on fabulous salaries, traveling expenses, and bonuses to officials who accomplished nothing."[28] Unfortunately, he stifled his doubts, and the swindle soon collapsed. The Samana Bay Company went bankrupt, and Chev was lucky to get out without losing his entire investment and paying the company's debts as well. Writing about his adventure, though, he used the rhetoric and imagery of the knight-errant that had carried him so far: "Parts of it are like a romance. Parts read like the hopes and fears of the adventures of the pioneers of the East India Companies. Parts recall the South Seas Bubble, and parts the Spanish pursuit of Eldorado in Mexico and Peru; parts the French Buccaneers, while parts were enacted by lovers of chivalrous adventure, imitators of the noble Quixote, whose high aim ever was to redress wrongs, put down evil doers, and lift up the fallen and oppressed."[29]

In April, Julia left Chev and the others behind and returned to Boston to pack for a short trip to London. She had proposed that an international Peace Congress for Women be held in London, preceded by planning meetings in New York. Now it was taking place. But the London congress was disappointing. She was snubbed by the British delegates, "as hard as billiard balls, charged with electricity . . . But I may be a little nettled by the entire neglect with which I was treated, altho I was prepared for this."[30] She also had an unpleasant encounter with Robert Browning at an afternoon reception. He was "ruder and more brutal to me than I supposed any man would have been to any woman," she wrote in her journal. "Moral, avoid a devilish big tomcat." Browning had been gracious and suave to her at an earlier visit to London; now, a decade after Elizabeth Barrett Browning's death, he seemed ungentlemanly and rude. Julia didn't record his words, but she did record her shock. "No American, not drunk, would treat a woman so."[31] She had underestimated the impact of her satiric poems about Elizabeth Barrett Browning's opium addiction in *Words for the Hour*. Obsessing about the encounter back in Boston, she was still trying to minimize his insult: "I have loved E. B. B. though I have written one crooked word about her, which, among many loving ones, seems to be the only one remembered."[32] Barrett Browning herself had shrugged off the crooked words, as she wrote to a friend: "if you could know how little I have thought of it, & how when I do consider the subject, the strongest feeling I am conscious of is pity for *her* & that she should have felt vexed *through me.*"[33] Her husband was not as forgiving.

However disagreeable the Browning incident, meeting him made Howe ruminate for the next few months on the literary life she had abandoned for public life and pacifism. "When I hear literary performances praised, & remember my own love for it, & for praise, I think of all this I have sacrificed in these later years for a service which has made me enemies as well as friends. I felt called upon to do this, and I still think that if I made a mistake it was one of those honest mistakes which it is best to make."[34] Listening to Ednah Dow Cheney's lecture on English literature at the New England Woman's Club in October, she was pained to hear herself mentioned as a *former* poet: "though she pleasantly alluded to me as one who has laid aside the laurel for the olive branch, she said nothing whatever about my writings, which deserve to be spoken of in characterizing the current literature of the day."[35] Her fame as the author of the "Battle Hymn" grew every day; but giving birth to a great cultural anthem was a burden as well as an honor. The New York literary editor and critic Edmund Clarence Stedman could see how the fame of the "Battle Hymn" could also be "a Frankenstein's monster . . . when it has become the sacred scroll of millions." Howe knew that the glory of the "Hymn" marked the end of her career as a poet. "It was a joy to her to be associated with the 'Battle Hymn,'" her daughters wrote, "yet she sometimes grieved a little because this so greatly overshadowed all her other literary productions."[36]

Back home, Chev was feeling neglected and forgotten, too; one October morning he had chest pains he believed to be a heart attack and insisted they take the 7:20 a.m. train into Boston to see the doctor. Julia went with him; it was nothing serious. Once on the train home, "people congratulated him on his good looks," and he quickly recovered.[37] Being admired made him feel young, and looking young won him admiration and restored his self-confidence. At Laura's wedding, he had worn the bright blue suit from his own wedding to Julia; he was proud that it still fit him perfectly.

In December 1872, Howe went to a meeting at the New England Woman's Club and was annoyed when the guest speaker, Dr. Edward H. Clarke from Harvard Medical School, gave a paper "on the education of women, considered from the physical point of view. It was an argument against the coeducation of the sexes, based entirely upon the monthly indisposition if so it may be called of women."[38] According to one historian, "the clubwomen thought they had invited an ally to speak on the subject of 'women's fitness for entering practical life.' Likewise, Dr. Clarke anticipated a friendly and supportive audience before whom he could unveil his new theory that higher education unfit women for motherhood and made them ill. Both sides thought wrong."[39] Clarke believed that the neglect of menstruation in youth, especially if accompanied by the intense brainwork of higher education, doomed women to a lifetime of disease and infertility. In 1873, he published *Sex in Education, or a Fair Chance for the Girls*, which became one of the most notorious antifeminist works of the 1870s, going through seventeen editions in thirteen years and provoking furious rebuttals from women in the United States and in Europe.[40]

Howe joined a large group of feminists, doctors, and suffragists to refute Clarke's claims. Fussing about "the monthly indisposition," she wrote, was an old-fashioned holdover from the "elder generation . . . Many young women who are allowed to eat, dress, live, and behave as they like, are periodically kept from all violent exercise and fatigue, so far as the vigilance of elders can accomplish this." The elders might even be right, but, she sarcastically noted, "the wilfullness and ingenuity of the young . . . are often more than a match for this vigilance; and a single ride on horseback, a single wetting of the feet, and indulgence in the irresistible German, may entail lifelong misery, which the maternal or friendly guardian has done all in her power to prevent."[41] In any case, Clarke's contention "that women in America particularly neglect their health, that women violate the laws of their constitution as men cannot violate theirs, and that the love of intellectual pursuits causes them to do so, . . . is the fable out of which Dr. Clarke draws the moral that women must not go to college with men."[42]

Euphemistic and impersonal though it is, this essay is nonetheless the most explicit discussion of menstruation in all of Howe's writings, including her journals and letters. She had no problems discussing childbirth, breast-feeding, or toilet training; but like other nineteenth-century American women, she could not bring herself to write about menstruation or menopause. These do not seem to have been problems for Howe, or for her two sisters, or four daughters; at least she doesn't mention them. Only in one reference to the "course of nature" happily relieving her fear of another pregnancy does she allude to a process that took much time and ingenuity for women to manage and conceal. Although Clarke's book stands in women's history as benighted and infamous, it also made it permissible for women to discuss menstruation in public, and for women doctors like Dr. Mary Jacobi to do the research to remove its stigma.

Chev was feeling tired, and in March 1873 Julia accompanied him back to Santo Domingo to see the end of the Samana Bay Company. President Báez had been overthrown, and Chev made a little speech as the flag of the company was lowered for the last time. She admired his pluck, and this time called him "the old Crusader" whose "beautiful chivalry stood in the greater contrast to the barbarism and ingratitude which dictated this act."[43] The Howes stayed on for a tropical vacation; Julia went shopping for jewelry while Chev recovered his appetite, optimism, and strength enough to go riding every morning. For a time, he was considering buying a retirement home on Samana Bay, among the palms and fruit trees; but that plan was quickly abandoned. They both realized it would be their last visit.

It was in Santo Domingo that they got the news of Sumner's death of a heart attack in Washington on March 11. "He never seemed to me exactly a great man," Julia wrote, "but a great place is left empty by his death." Chev was shocked; he had known that Sumner was in poor health, but their political disagreements kept them distant. He was unable to get back to Cambridge for the funeral, where Emerson and Longfellow were among the pallbearers. Despite his grief, he could not resist criticizing Sumner's role in blocking the Dominican annexation. Their mutual friend Francis Bird reproached him; "Alas! Alas! Alas! That before the sod is green over dear Sumner's grave *you* should speak of *him* as 'blinded by passion & prejudice'— . . . I have never told you . . . How dearly he loved you, & how tenderly he moaned over the change in your feelings towards him."[44] Chev apologized: "Would I were worthy of the affection which he accorded to me during so many years . . . Dear Charlie! The hope of renewed useful intercourse, makes immortality all the more desirable."[45] Now he felt truly alone.

The Howes returned to New York in April in time for their son Henry's marriage to Fannie Gay. Despite headaches, rheumatism, and prostate problems, Chev kept up his work routines and attended Sumner's memorial service in the Boston Music Hall at the beginning of June. In a letter to an Athens friend, George Finlay, he lamented the deaths of Horace Mann, Theodore Parker, and Sumner. "All my well beloved and intimate friends, and all have gone before me."[46]

In Santo Domingo, Julia had started to feel compassion for Chev, but in Rhode Island that summer—he had sold Lawton's Valley in 1871 and bought a new home, Oak Glen, twenty-five miles from Newport—he was not easy to live with. He swore loudly all the time, even at dinner; grumbled, fretted, and found fault with all the arrangements. He griped about Julia's political activities in a letter to his friend George Finlay: "Mrs. Howe grows more and more absorbed in the public work of obtaining women's suffrage; and, like most of her co-workers, shows more zeal than discretion; and, in my opinion, does more harm by subordinating domestic duties to supposed public ones."[47] Writing to Laura, he took a jokier tone: "Mama is in high feather, and is organizing all kinds of Clubs and Associations, under the guise of advancing the cause of human progress, civilization, women's rights, etc., etc., but with the appearance of good times at picnics, aesthetic teas, lobster salads, clam bakes, etc., which are to be taken inwardly, while the breath of eloquent exhortation is vented outwardly. *Vive le suffrage quand meme!*"[48]

Chev was working on his forty-third annual report to Perkins, an overview of his career and work there. In his final discussion of Laura Bridgman, he compared her unfavorably to Oliver Caswell and concluded that there was something abnormal about her indifference to men. She "never seems to pine for that closer relation in sympathy with one of the other sex, which ripens so naturally into real and sympathetic love between normal youth, placed in normal circumstances."[49] Even Laura had failed to live up to his expectations of feminine devotion to men.

By Christmas 1874, Julia was feeling the strain of his irritability; "If I do not soon have an interval of entire freedom from care & responsibility of any kind, the thin cords of sanity will snap."[50] During the first half of 1875, the cords of her sanity were stretched to their limits. Chev kept the furnace at Green Peace turned up high, "making the house a perfect hell of heating suffocation, abuse, and ill-humor." She and Maud snuck down late at night, "opened the cold air flue, & the house became comfortable at once."[51] Throughout the winter, she turned to her journal for relief. "Chev dreadfully provoking. Wrote my peace festival circular, but all the time am weary to death with his coarse & irrational violence. I grieve to use those epithets, even on paper which [is] intended only for my own sight, but they are just. The lesson is, that the indulgence of self-will & temper through life will in the end make even a good & great man, & such I hold him to be, an insupportable companion."[52]

By May, however, she had realized that he was in decline, and began to feel more patient with his outbursts: "A morning game of whist with Chev. Alas! I do not make sufficient allowance for the pain & weariness of the decline of life."[53] He was eating very little, taking digitalis three times a day, and napping in his chair. As he grew weaker, so did his inhibitions. She did not stop giving her talks despite his illness, and he protested by refusing her help. When she came back from an evening talk one night, he "would not let me help him to undress, & told me to go to hell. I was rather angry, in consequence, but saw that he was very feeble."[54] In her absence, Julia Romana gave him his morning massage; when Julia "wanted to rub him instead of letting Julia [Romana] do so. I went into his room & told her to leave it . . . He shook me violently, from head to foot, threatened to jump out of the open window. I have been very sad all day in consequence. . . . Poor Chev at bed time asked me to forgive his ill humor, which I was very glad to do."[55]

By the end of November his temper tantrums had subsided, and he began to talk honestly to his wife. In response, Julia called him "dear Chev" again in her journal, although her accounts of these discussions suggest that he had confessed to her about his affairs. "I have had some sad revelations from dear Chev of things about some of my own sex which greatly astonish me," she wrote. "From these I learn that women are not only sensual, but lustful, & that men are attracted, rather than shocked by this trait. The privacy of offices, or at least their remoteness from domestic visitation, is eagerly made available by these women for the vilest purposes." Were these offices at the Institution? Was the man Dr. Howe? It is generally assumed that Chev confessed to affairs in the 1850s, but it's hard to believe that Chev was seriously involved with another woman. He was too prudish, too sexually reserved, to have undertaken a risky escapade. Yet that initial disclosure was followed by a more explicit "sad talk" that apparently named a name and left Julia haunted by "the great injustice done me and the other's self by a course of conduct most treacherous & worthy of reprobation. If thought has a grave, may this ghost be laid & appear no more."[56]

The next day they reached a solemn reconciliation, with mutual forgiveness. Julia recorded "a most touching & comforting talk with dear Chev, in which I felt once more all the moral beauty which has been my faith & delight in him. I have solemnly sworn to him never to allude to any thing in the past which, coming up lately, has give us both pain . . . *Gloria in Excelsis Deo!* I have reached the bottom of these years of estrangement, in wh[ich] there has been fault & wrong on both sides, & we shall begin to rebuild our life in common." Poignantly, she had her double bed moved into his room, "in order that we may have the comfort of being near each other in the dark & silent hours."[57] Two double beds in one room was as close as they wished to be.

The ghost of the sensual woman did not stay buried, but Julia wrestled with it. At night alone on a speaking trip to Leominster, she fantasized a confrontation with the woman she called "B.," discussing "her 'shameful conduct' and the wrong done me. I wished to see her ghost more than I ever dreaded to see one. I remembered with joy that she died by inches a painful death, in poverty alleviated by the care of friends."[58] Who was B.? Louise Hall Tharp speculates that she might have been a woman named Becky mentioned in a few letters in the late 1850s. Becky had relatives who taught at the Institute and she visited there often; Julia had mentioned her in a letter to Annie: "Did I tell you of Becky's visit? She came one PM and staid [*sic*] to tea and I had to send her to the cars in from Milton. Then Chev took her on to Newport and cunningly slipped off next morning, finding it not so strange that people could have enough of her. She wore her bosom too low, even for him."[59]

Becky sounds like a temptress, but there could have been another B. or more than one woman. In any case, Julia determined to blame herself rather than B. or Chev. "It seemed a great comfort to have the burden of offence laid on my shoulders. Strange as it may seem, it was comparatively delightful to me to accuse myself, & to make my own sins point out the hypocrisy & unkindness of which I have had so long an experience, without in the least understanding the facts, as they were."[60]

Chev had dinner with his family and friends on Christmas Day 1875 and also managed to get to Sunday dinner January 2. Two days later he had a convulsive attack and fell into a coma from which he never recovered. The family gathered around his bed; on the morning of January 9, Julia brought Laura Bridgman to his side to bid him good-bye. Her account of Laura's final farewell was Dickensian in its emotion; "She could not see—she never had seen him, but she knew that she was in his presence for the last time. She was allowed to touch his features very softly, and a little agonized sound, scarcely audible, alone broke the silence of the solemn scene. All who were present deeply felt the significance of this farewell."[61] They may have misinterpreted that sound; Laura told Sarah Wight that she had been frightened and repelled by the touch of the Doctor's warm, moist skin.[62] On January 9, 1876, Chev died shortly after noon; the cause of death is uncertain, although a stroke, a brain tumor, or cancer have been suggested as the cause.

The next morning Julia went to his room and laid her bridal veil across his bed. She had already written her farewell poem of repentance:

A mother and grandmother,
A widow, long a wife,
I recognize the childhood
That follows me through life.

Oh! Take me yet, dear Master
Where thy disciples stand;
And set me down before them
With thy instructing hand.

Show them the faulty record,
The willful brow and face,
And tell them this offender
Is conquered by thy grace.

An entry in her journal the day after he died contains a rare misspelling: "Now, the death of my darling husband makes a new chapture [*sic*] for me."[63] Chapter? Capture? Picture? Closure? Departure? It was all of these. She had been married to Chev for almost thirty-three years; she would live another thirty-four. Chev's funeral was on January 13; the next day she wrote: "Began my new life today."

And then on January 15, Chev's will was read. Julia had not known its contents. Sitting with the family, she learned that he had left her nothing. "My wife, Julia Ward Howe, having ample means of her own," he wrote maliciously, would not need any legacy from him. As he knew, he had lost most of her family fortune; she had an income of about $2,000 a year. Chev's estate was to be divided equally among the daughters; it was left to Julia to help Harry start his career. She accepted the news of her disinheritance stoically, mentioning in her journal only that everyone thought the will to be unfortunate, especially Flossy's lawyer husband, David Hall. The will had probably been written and signed long before; he would not have had time to change it after their deathbed talk. But disinheritance sounds like a gesture of disapproval he would have enjoyed. From beyond the grave, his dead hand continued to punish Julia and attempt to exert control.

Julia also had to go through Chev's personal papers with Michael Anagnos, who refused to let her read a number of his letters and insisted on burning them. But the letters kept on turning up all spring. She found two more from a mysterious Mrs. Motley in a locked drawer, which she burned; and another two from Sumner, which she threw in the privy. As late as July, she destroyed another letter from Sumner, "with many clauses in it which I shall never forget, the matter treated of being entirely personal."[64]

Chev was honored at a grand memorial service on February 8 at the Boston Music Hall, with speeches by Boston notables and readings by poets and sages. Julia observed all the proprieties. She memorialized Chev with formal and ceremonial language, in a short pamphlet, printed in raised type for his students; her daughters stress the intended audience to excuse its brevity and obscurity. In her journal, a few entries around what would have been their anniversary describe her remorse over their estrangement: "Would to God that I had done a thousand times more for him than I ever did. I learn more deeply than ever before how happy one is in being able to make sacrifices for other people, especially for those to whom we are bound by sacred ties. I thought I made many sacrifices for dear Chev, that I now feel that I ought to have done far more."[65] But her ethical mourning for Chev, and her regret for making too few sacrifices on his behalf, could not compare with her deep sorrow and grief over Sammy's death. Only rarely did she dream of Chev, and when she did he was scolding her.

She had to move on, and she had to make some money. Green Peace was in her name, but the taxes were so high she could not afford it, even though she rented it out and moved to Oak Glen with Maud. The Christmas after Chev's death, she was lecturing in Chicago. Then in the New Year, having made enough money to pay her bills, Julia unexpectedly decided to take Maud on a Grand Tour of Europe. Maud had been left behind on other trips and had been lonely and envious of her sisters; she was flirtatious and unsettled, and needed a good dose of European culture. In her journal, Julia was explicit that "my European tour was undertaken for dear Maud's sake. It took me away from the dear ones at home, and from opportunities of work which I should have prized highly." If she had stayed at home in Boston, she would have been president of the Women's Congress.[66]

Yet there were obvious advantages for Julia in getting away from Boston and starting her new life. This time she would plan the itinerary and set the pace. In the event, the trip lasted over two years, from May 1877 to July 1879; they saw everything, met everyone, and went everywhere. In London, Maud was considered a great beauty and went joyfully to dinners, dances, garden parties, cricket matches, football matches, boat races, horse races, and "shows of pictures, flowers, vegetables, dogs."[67]

Julia meanwhile gave talks, went to meetings—including some on antivivisection—and was escorted about by Henry James, whom Maud suspected of using her as a model for American girls abroad.[68] Julia and Maud encountered Robert Browning at a dinner party; Maud described him as a ridiculous sixty-five-year-old dandy, with a waxed mustache, a monocle, and an epicurean air. At the dinner table, he bragged that he knew the specialties of the house and would help her choose the best *plats.* She was more impressed by the Pre-Raphaelites and the opening of the Grosvenor Gallery. "The aesthetic movement was at its height, and the 'shorthaired women and long-haired men,' familiar figures at all the great . . . public fetes, waited to see the entrance one of the 'beauties,' as people wait to see Royalty pass." They went to the opening reception of the Royal Academy, where Maud's escort for the evening, fatefully, was a young Scottish artist named John Elliott.[69]

Julia and Maud kept up a terrific pace and covered the map of Europe: Holland, Belgium, Germany, Switzerland, Italy, and France. In Geneva they attended a conference organized by Josephine Butler to protest the lowering of the age of consent in England. They visited museums, galleries, cathedrals, monuments, exhibitions, art schools, and studios. In Rome, they stayed in the vast and magnificent Palazzo Odescalchi, the home of Louisa, and were escorted by her handsome son, Francis Crawford. There Maud began to study painting with an Italian landscape artist. But the lessons had to stop in February 1878 when she came down with Roman fever, a form of malaria to which tourists were susceptible. Henry James wrote about it in *Daisy Miller*, published the following summer, in which an American girl in Rome is exposed to the fever and dies; it is possible that he had been studying Maud in London. Edith Wharton's short story "Roman Fever" (1934) makes it a metaphor for illicit sexuality. The fever is momentous for these heroines, and it turned out to be so for Maud as well. In its aftermath, she found the most creative, and interesting, if the most elusive, unconventional, and intransigent, of the Howe daughters' husbands.

To recuperate, the Howes spent May at the Hotel Brufani in Perugia, where Maud again met John Elliott, her Royal Academy escort. Accompanied by a close older friend, Edward Shakerly Kemp, he was returning to England after studying in Rome. Three years younger than Maud, orphaned and penniless, Jack Elliott was a handsome, probably bisexual aesthete who loved the theatre, flowers, furniture, interior décor, and fashion. Maud was smitten. She described him to Laura as "a graceful beautiful creature, like a Donatello . . . He has wonderful deep hazel eyes and massive black wavy hair, a big beautiful mouth just in the shape of a Cupids bow, filled with white teeth."[70] Jack was smitten, too. He decided to stay on the Continent, and he wound up traveling with them, helpfully attentive to Julia and a great companion for both the Howes. In Quimper, he designed a lace cap for Julia, based on the Breton costume, with a peak and flowing side panels, which would become a much-remarked signature item in her lecture wardrobe and portraits.

After a year, the other daughters thought Maud and Mama had done enough gallivanting; it was time to come back and take care of them. Flossy and Laura, dealing with growing families on limited funds, were envious of Maud's monopoly of their mother and the pleasures she was enjoying; Julia Romana was more caustic about "our troubadour Ma" and "the Empress Maud." The Empress or the Duchess became family shorthand for Maud.[71] The sisters also developed a jocular but negative vocabulary for Howe's hectic travel: gadding about, flapping her wings, hoppings and leppings. Addressing their resentment, describing her own dependent circumstances, and pointing out Flossy's poverty, Maud wrote candidly to Laura explaining why they were staying on:

> *About our coming home, or rather our* not *coming home. I am sorry that you and Flossy are so much troubled about it. But I think mama must have told you, that she made the decision, without any pressure on my part . . . She is very anxious to go to Egypt and she would have gone this winter I think, had it not been for my illness—you know*

> *how quickly she adapts herself to new surroundings—she has enjoyed everything as fully as much, and I sometimes think* more *than I have. Her energy and enthusiasm are unlimited. We should come home in the autumn—well, what then—mama would not have wished to leave Boston, and yet how would we have lived there, on the little that we have to live on. . . . Julia's doors, or rather her husband's, have never been open to me, and poor dear Floss cannot give me the hospitality she would like to—what remains then—a couple of rooms over the club, and in Boston, which of all places in the world, I detest—rather a gloomy prospect.*[72]

The second year of their trip took them to the Middle East, most of it new territory for Julia. From Italy and France they headed to Egypt, meeting princesses in Cairo, cruising up the Nile to celebrate the New Year of 1879, and heading on to Jerusalem, Bethlehem, Jaffa, Cyprus, and Athens. When they returned to Boston in July 1879, Maud had acquired a life-changing knowledge of art, had formed a desire to gain recognition for American art among the classics of the world, and had met the man she would marry. Julia was $3,500 in debt.

1

"The Corner," home of Samuel Ward at the corner of Bond Street and Broadway.

2

Eliza Cutler Francis, "Auntie Francis."

3

Julia during her honeymoon.

4

Samuel Gridley Howe, 1857.

5

Laura Bridgman as a young girl; bust by Sophia Peabody.

6

The Perkins Institute for the Blind, South Boston.

Dr. Howe teaching Laura Bridgman drawing, 1889.

8

Laura Bridgman, 1845.

9

Green Peace, from a photo taken in 1875.

10

Annie Ward Maillard.

11

Louisa Ward Crawford, from miniature by Annie Hall.

12

The "Hotel Rambouillet"; Cliff House, Newport, R.I.; summer of 1852. *Left to right:* Thomas G. Appleton, John G. Coster, Julia Ward Howe, Fanny Appleton Longfellow, Henry Wadsworth Longfellow, and Augusta Freeman, who had been Julia's friend in Rome.

13

Walt Whitman, July 1854, engraving by Samuel Hollyer, frontispiece of first edition of *Leaves of Grass*.

14

John Brown, 1856.

15

Senator Charles Sumner, 1859.

16

The Howe children, 1869. *Left to right:* Julia Romana, Maud (in plaid dress), Harry, Flossy, and Laura.

Michael Anagnos.

17

18

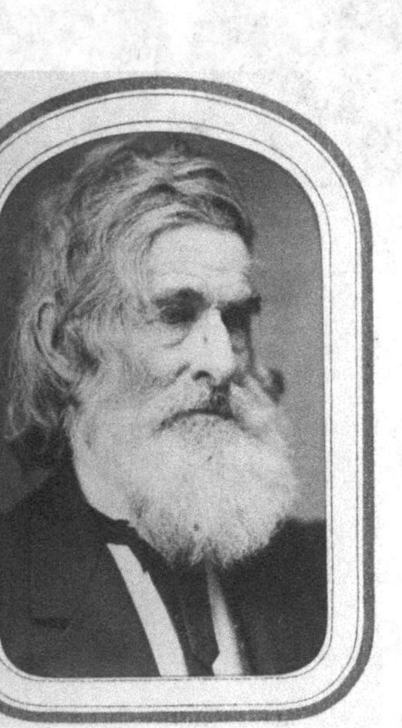

Chev, photograph by A. Marshall, 1870.

19

Julia Romana Howe Anagnos.

20

Mary A. Livermore.

21

John Elliott, by José Villegas Cordero.

Julia with her great-grandson, Henry Shaw. Her namesake grand-daughter Julia Ward Howe Richards Shaw is on her left, and her daughter Laura Richards on the right.

22

23

Julia in embroidered jacket and Breton lace cap, photograph by J.E. Purdy, 1902.

24

Julia elected to the American Academy of Arts and Letters, 1908, wearing two of her favorite rings.

Chapter Ten

THE WOMAN'S DEPARTMENT

In July 1879, Julia came home to the United States, reinvigorated by her long stay abroad and ready to take full advantage of her independence and her new ideas about women's place in the world. She was now head of the family, and her most pressing task was to see her children properly established. She would also have to resist their urging that she slow down. She had begun committing herself to women's causes before Chev's death; as she turned sixty, she moved more and more into leadership positions. The most dramatic illustration was her decision to head the Woman's Department for the New Orleans Cotton Centennial in 1884. In that job, she discovered skills in organizing and managing that she had never had a chance to develop before. The two decades of her sixties and seventies were her golden years, culminating in another trip abroad, this one triumphant in unexpected ways.

On their return from Europe in the summer of 1879, Julia and Maud went to Oak Glen, their summer house in Portsmouth, Rhode Island, twenty-five miles from Newport and close to her friends in the Town and Country Club. Reluctant to let the summer months go by without self-improvement, she had started this club in 1871. It brought writers and scientists vacationing in Newport together to listen to each other's talks on astronomy, botany, marine biology, medicine, natural history, and literature. Mark Twain gave a reading, and Dr. Silas Weir Mitchell, who later became a controversial specialist on neurotic women, lectured on snake poison. They also found time to be silly: Fanny Fern read an essay on rhinoscopy; a Harvard professor delivered a Greek version of "The Man in the Moon," part of a series of recitations from Mother Goose in seven languages; and Julia presented the "Parlor Macbeth," in which she posed as Lady Macbeth telling the story of the whole Macbeth family, including the three witchy Misses Macbeth. Between performances, she gave a number of talks and sermons, leading up to a fall lecture tour. On one whistle stop, her trunk was lost, and she had to improvise her speech and borrow an all-important black silk dress from the hostess. After that mishap, she always traveled with her lecture, lace cap, and clean collar in a lightweight palm-leaf knapsack from Santo Domingo.

As Maud had predicted, at summer's end her mother wanted to be back in Boston, although two rooms at a boardinghouse called Benedict Chambers, on Beacon Hill, were all she could afford. When she fell on the marble steps at Perkins while visiting Julia Romana and tore the ligaments in her knee, Benedict Chambers was no longer manageable; and Sam Ward, now a prosperous lobbyist and speculator in railroad stock, stepped in with his accustomed largesse. He first moved Julia and Maud into a furnished house at 129 Mount Vernon Street, a neighborhood they knew well. Throughout the winter, she was still on crutches (she would reinjure her knee periodically for years), so Maud did the legwork to search for a suitable house to buy; she had become a shrewd judge of real estate and neighborhoods, having moved so many times with her parents. Finally, in April 1880 Uncle Sam installed them at 241 Beacon Street. They brought in the stored furniture from Green Peace, including Julia's Chickering piano and a large portrait of Maud. And Sam sent them extravagant gifts such as a diamond-and-sapphire necklace for Maud, and shipments of wine for Julia—clarets, sherry, champagne,

Moselle, and vermouth, "a tonic for young women, and an appetizer for young men and a sort of universal cocktail ante-prandial."[1] The years of temperance were over.

With such incentives, Howe was inspired to entertain lavishly. Twelve Zuni chiefs in full regalia came for lunch, but their moccasins, headbands, and kilts were eclipsed by her celebrity guest of the year: Oscar Wilde. Sam was sponsoring Wilde's American lecture tour, and wrote to Maud, "His makeup is very extraordinary, long black hair hanging to his shoulders, brown eyes, a huge white face like the pale moon . . . a white waistcoat, black coat and knee breeches, black silk stockings and shoes with buckles. Until he speaks you think him uncanny as a vampire."[2] How enticing! Maud and Julia could not resist. When Wilde came to Boston to lecture at Harvard, they invited him to lunch; "delightful, simple and sincere and very clever," Julia noted.[3] Wilde was a frequent guest thereafter. A dinner party in his honor followed, and Wilde's entrance, according to a child witness, was memorable. Julia clapped her hands for silence, and he slowly descended the staircase in the famous shoes and stockings, plus green velvet knee breeches, holding a lily.[4] In the summer Wilde came to Oak Glen, and was "a rarely entertaining guest . . . [who] told endless stories of Swinburne, Whistler, and other celebrities of the day," but Julia and Maud were temporarily thrown by the presence of his valet, Davenport. "It was one thing to entertain the Aesthete, another to put up the gentleman's gentleman."[5] They recovered enough to make Wilde a round cake with a lemon peel and angelica sunflower in the middle.

In the winter of 1882–83, Harry, now a professor of metallurgy at MIT, and his wife, Fannie, came to live with them, paying for their share of expenses. Louisa's handsome blue-eyed son Francis Marion Crawford, called Marion, who had joined them on Mount Vernon Street, joined them on Beacon Street, too. A multitalented wandering minstrel (he sang Schubert lieder and played the guitar) and a student prince, Marion had studied Sanskrit at the University of Rome, Harvard, and

Allahabad in India, where he also edited a newspaper. Louisa was worried that he would never be able to earn a living, and sent him to Boston hoping to train his baritone voice for opera. The family asked George Henschel, the conductor of the Boston Symphony Orchestra, to teach him; but Henschel concluded that Marion "would never be able to sing in perfect tune."[6] Sam then suggested he might become a writer, and start with his experiences in India. He lobbied energetically for Marion in New York, introducing him to editors and publishers; and Marion's first novel, *Mr. Isaacs: A Tale of Modern India*, was a popular success in 1882, followed in 1883 by *Dr. Claudius*, with an affectionate portrait of Uncle Sam as Mr. Bellingham.

In Boston, Marion quickly became the scandalous "protégé"—i.e., toy boy—of the imperious and seductive Isabella Stewart Gardner—"Mrs. Jack." He was overweight and bibulous when he met her, but became "thin as a rail with temperance and exercise" under her guidance and gave her lessons on Dante in her private sitting room. Gossiping to William Dean Howells, Henry James wrote that the only excitement in the "social desolation of Boston" was "Mrs. Jack Gardner's flirtation with F. Marion Crawford, the American novelist of the future."[7] In 1883, Mrs. Jack proposed taking Marion, Julia, and Maud on an all-expenses-paid trip to Japan, without her husband. At the last minute, Marion decided not to go and slipped away to England, to Julia's great relief. "He has his reasons for wishing to keep very quiet about his movements," she wrote to Maud. "I am very thankful that he has decided as he has. Cannot say more on paper. Mum is the word."[8] According to family members, Mrs. Jack was devastated, and Maud had to spend several days comforting her.[9] When she finally left for her Asian tour, her husband went with her. The Howes remained friendly with Mrs. Jack, although Julia thought the notorious Sargent portrait with its deep décolleté had "great artistic merits and great faults of taste . . . The attitude is inexplicable and strikes many people as objectionable."[10]

The lives of illustrious and accomplished women were much on her mind. In spring 1882 she was writing a biographical memoir of Maria Mitchell for a book on famous women, and editing Maud's essay on her own life for the same volume.[11] "I think I am eminent for undertaking ten times more than I can do, and doing about one-tenth of it," she protested.[12] In April she began a biography of Margaret Fuller, rewarding herself for her daily stint by reading a little Greek and an Italian novel. She finished the book over the summer at Oak Glen. Fuller's story had been told in 1851 by James Freeman Clarke, William Henry Channing, and Emerson. Yet their great memoir, Howe argued, was "already set in a past light by the progress of men and of things," and "it is through the growing interest felt in Margaret and her work that a demand seems to have arisen for a later word about her, which cannot hope to be better or wiser than the words already made public, but which may borrow from them the inspiration for a new study and presentment." That growing interest came from the rise of the women's suffrage movement, with Fuller one of its greatest heroines. Moreover, Howe used Fuller's life story to explore her own education, philosophy, and politics in an oblique (auto)biography.[13] In some respects, Howe tones down her own rebellion in contrast to Fuller. She defends the strict demands of Fuller's autocratic father and qualifies her own passionate girlhood response to George Sand. "When Margaret wrote of her, the woman was at the zenith of her power, and the intoxication of her influence was so great that a calm judgment concerning it was difficult." In maturity, Fuller would have tempered her enthusiasm: "much as she loved genius, that of George Sand could not blind her to the falls and falsities that marred her work." Howe is critical of some of Fuller's choices, but overall reveres her intelligence, her aspirations, and her humility. Above all, she presents Fuller as the model for the emancipated future: "as a woman who believed in women, her word is still an evangel of hope and inspiration to her sex."[14]

Maud was writing, too, giving in to "the inevitable family calling of literature."[15] In addition to her essay on her mother, she wrote a clever Newport society column for the *Boston Transcript.* She also used local gossip in her first novel, *A Newport Aquarelle*, published anonymously in 1883. Laura was delighted with it, but warned her that "your pen is over-sharp, my dearest child, just like your little naughtily two-edged tongue and you should not talk so about Boston if you mean to live there."[16] In Maud's opinion, though, she was doomed to play second fiddle to one relative or another; cousin Marion was expected to become the family novelist and got the support of Uncle Sam and the New York contingent. "He looked the whole bunch of us over," she wrote, "as a stock raiser looks over his thoroughbreds, and picked Marion for the winner . . . He put his money on Marion."[17] No matter; having tried her hand as a painter of china, a landscape artist, and an actress, Maud decided that fiction suited her best. Her second novel, the *San Rosario Ranch* (1884), was a romance set in California, drawing on her visit to Aunt Annie and Uncle Do's San Geronimo Ranch.

Under a clutch of pen names and pet names, Julia was juggling her different personae in letters to her sisters, her brother, and her favorite daughter, Laura. She was Old Bird, O.B., Old B., and Betsy Trig, to Sam and Annie; Ma, Mar, Mother, Mammy, Mus Wus, Ma-Cats, and Gramma Gray to Laura, who was variously called Wolly, dear little sweetheart, my sweetest lollipop, Pidge, dear little conscience, and très chère. She was juggling her public roles as well. At the end of 1883, she served as president of the women's department of the Merchants and Mechanics Fair in Boston. During the winter she campaigned on behalf of the suffragists' petition for three new bills: giving mothers and fathers equal rights in making decisions about their children, guaranteeing widows half of the husband's estate after his death, and allowing husbands and wives to make economic contracts independent of each other.

Her speeches on these questions show how much more radical she had become since Chev's death, and how much her marriage had taught her about the legal double standard faced by women in the nineteenth century. "Even women of fortune possessed nothing individually after their marriage. The ring which promised to endow them with all the bridegroom's earthly goods, really endowed him all that belonged to them, even to the clothes that they wore. Their children were not their own. The father could dispose of them as he might think fit."[18] She had even come around to Elizabeth Cady Stanton's view of male legal culpability for soliciting prostitutes.

As the literary and philosophical Mrs. Howe, she regularly attended cultural events in Boston; Matthew Arnold lectured on Emerson, very poorly, in Julia's opinion: "Arnold does not in the least understand Emerson, I think. He has a positive, square-jawed English mind . . . His elocution is pitiable, and when, after his lecture, Wendell Phillips stepped forward and said a few graceful words of farewell to him, it was like the Rose complimenting the Cabbage."[19] She found time to read, but after her brother Sam died abroad (he had once again lost all his money, and fled to England to evade his creditors), fiction seemed both sentimental and shocking. "I think novels is humbug," she wrote to Laura. "They don't leave you anything but a sort of bad taste."[20]

In order to reinvent herself, Julia needed to move away from her familiar milieu and longtime comfort zone. When she was unexpectedly invited in October 1884 to become the head of the Woman's Department for the New Orleans Cotton Centennial, she seized the opportunity. Chev would never have allowed her to accept such an invitation, and the idea of a winter in the warm South, all expenses paid, was very appealing. Having discovered the comforts of female companionship, she arranged to take her support group with her, accepting the offer with the proviso that Ednah Cheney and Henrietta Wolcott, who had assisted her at the Boston fair, come along as her lieutenants. Maud came too as the chief of the Literary Department, and Maud's good friend Isabel Greeley joined the team as Julia's secretary and assistant. It was her first effort at leadership outside of Massachusetts, and it provided her with an education in realpolitik and an introduction to the strains and limitations of sisterhood.

Her appointment had raised great indignation and resentment

among the women of New Orleans, who felt insulted that a Yankee, an abolitionist, and worst of all, the author of the despicable anti-Confederate "Battle Hymn of the Republic" had been chosen for the honor. They were further miffed that she was bringing her own staff, rather than hiring highly qualified—and needy—Louisiana ladies for these prominent positions. Even before Howe got to the city, there was resentment of her entitled behavior, and she had to win the women over. Her antagonists were progressive women, not the stuffy Boston Brahmins she had faced at home or the antisuffragists she had met on the road.

Catharine Cole, a journalist for the daily New Orleans *Picayune* (her real name was Martha Reinhard Smallwood Field), was the sharpest and most persistent local critic. Thirty-six years younger than Howe, a tough and clever veteran of urban journalism, and a widow from a working-class background, Cole was also an advocate of women's rights. But the ladylike Howe, and her elegantly dressed daughter, were irresistible targets for her stinging observations and acerbic opinions. From the beginning, she made fun of Howe's "rather dull and prosy books," her dignified "Bostonness" style, and her snooty attitude. "Ah, well, we live in the hope that our Southern women will not be looked upon as such 'ninnies' at the next centennial celebration" was an opening salvo, and her sniping did not let up for the whole of Howe's residence.[21] Cole's boss Eliza Nicholson was one of the few women to be proprietor, publisher, and editor of a major urban newspaper, and she was a formidable figure in New Orleans. She had hired Dorothea Dix to write a column and was a great supporter of women journalists, but she was no fan of Howe. Still, the *Picayune*'s campaign against Howe and her team made good copy and good sales, and gave the Woman's Department a lot of coverage.

While the Southern ladies managed to keep up a gracious front, and welcome the Howes courteously to the Crescent City, behind the scenes there was envy, mistrust, gossip, and laughter at the Northern invaders. The Centennial opened on December 16, 1884, and the Boston contingent arrived by chartered steamer on the Mississippi, to be greeted by dignitaries and two military bands, plus the Mexican Band—the Mexican exhibit at the fair was the largest of all, and they had sent the Eighth Cavalry Regimental Band, which included a saxophonist and a clarinetist. When the fair ended, many of the Mexican musicians stayed on in New Orleans, where they had a huge influence on brass bands and early jazz. They would become a colorful staple of all public events at the Centennial, but Julia and Maud must have become weary of their music.

The women's party landed near the fairgrounds and marched to the Main Building, to hear a welcoming telegram from President Chester A. Arthur. Howe was dismayed to find that the building was a mess; the roof leaked, and legislative funds to renovate it had not been delivered. She rallied the troops, reminding them that "women have sometimes built churches with no better instruments than thimbles and teapots!"[22] Nevertheless, hustling to raise the money was challenging and stressful. She arranged a series of entertainments, beginning with her lecture on "Polite Society," given at Werlein Hall to a large and definitely polite audience; then a soiree Creole, then a "grand musical matinee" on February 8 at the French Opera House, with benefit performances by several singers and musicians, and of course the Mexican Band, which raised $2000. This entailed diplomatic skills. "The difficulty of persuading the different artists to sing, of pacifying their separate agents in the matter of place on the programme and size of the letters in which names were advertised, of bringing harmony out of all the petty rivalries and cabals between the different members of the troupe, required a patience worthy of a better cause."[23]

As her daughters wrote, Howe was developing "faculties hitherto dormant . . . far removed from her life habit of intellectual labor. She had moved into a new apartment in the house of life, one nearer the earth and not quite so near the stars."[24] Julia and Maud had literally moved into a new apartment, a boardinghouse downtown, rather than a luxury hotel. While Maud persuaded state delegations to contribute books by women writers, Julia's experience as the mother of a large family came into play as she balanced the rivalries of different regions, placated offended groups, and negotiated with the sensitive problems of race and religion. The Texans complained that their designated gallery was too small, and moved downstairs to a larger space; the Colored Ladies Exposition Association wanted their work to be shown in the Woman's Department rather than the Colored Department; the Woman's Christian Temperance Union wanted to hand out cups of ice water. Everyone complained about the shortage of women's toilets. Running the Woman's Department, she declared, was like "having a big Nursery to administer."[25]

Slowly, her determination, commitment, indefatigability, personal charm, good manners, and, as always, appearance, won over even the *Picayune.* If visitors expected her to be "a stout, tall, stern, masculine looking woman, the idealized nightmare of suffrage," they would be surprised and pleased to meet "a small, eminently womanish and gentle, motherly old lady, always dressed in black, and with snow-white hair and the superb, if somewhat old-fashioned, manners of a duchess."[26] When the Woman's Department opened formally on March 3, 1885, the initial response was favorable. Julia had organized a series of twenty-four Saturday lunchtime talks, free to the public, and ranging from women writers in Japanese literature to Arctic explorations. Visitors admired the exhibits of women's work from every state; women's inventions ranging from a pie lifter, to a traveling commode in a dressing case; needlework; and "beautiful work made by aged women."[27]

Smoldering hostility towards Howe and her Yankee entourage flared at the end of March when she incautiously sent a letter to the New England Woman's Club about her sorry experiences in New Orleans. They promptly published it in the *Woman's Journal*, and the *Picayune* snatched it up and reprinted it on Easter Sunday. No twenty-first-century hacker exposing an email correspondence could have done her more harm. She said that New Orleans was a gutter, that the promised funding had disappeared, and that she had to "grind and grind" to get things done. Catharine Cole pounced on every phrase: "Polite philandering with one side of the mouth and incessant complaint, reproach, or accusal with the other, made a very ugly visage, certainly not the visage of one of those whom the president of the Woman's Department would term a 'woman's woman.'"[28] Impressively, Julia did not run away but carried on with remarkable grace. No one had ever insulted her so directly and venomously; she had been protected by New England chivalry and class privilege. Nevertheless, recognizing that the success of the Woman's Department depended on her ability to get along with the local women, she stifled her anger and continued to attend tea parties, lectures, and official events with a smile. Admiring audiences were drawn to hear famous women speakers, including temperance leader Frances Willard, radical suffragist Susan B. Anthony, and wealthy newspaper magnate Miriam Leslie, who had legally changed her name to Frank Leslie after her husband's death, and managed his flagship *Frank Leslie's Illustrated Weekly*.

Maud, much ridiculed for her partying and fancy dresses, had nonetheless done a good job with the literary section. On Woman's Day, May 30, she spoke at a celebration of the Exposition, presenting the women's book collection to the Southern Art Union library. Julia presided, sitting on an incongruous leopard-skin cushion in an armchair made out of the "enormous horns of Texas oxen." "She presides at everything & has done it so long that her air, manner, smile & language are actually threadbare," Grace King wrote spitefully to her sister May.[29] Maud's speech was better accepted, although it started off badly. When she had been invited to join her mother in New Orleans, she recalled, "It seemed so absurd a thing to expect me to leave my home, my friends, my work." When she arrived, she went on, "I hated the work. I hated New Orleans. I hated most of all the Exposition and said a dozen times, 'I wish the Exposition was dead; I wish that it had never been born.'"

Then, finally, she had heard Major Burke speak of his hopes for the Exposition: "My enthusiasm was roused," she said, "and my heart was really in my work."[30] Only Maud could get away with such an artless confession.

At the end of May, Maud went home, but Julia stayed on despite feeling ill from the heat, the tension, and the exhaustion of carrying out her responsibilities. Once back in shady Oak Glen in July, she wrote to Laura to say, "How hot New Orleans was before I left it, you cannot know, nor how sick I was once upon a time, or how I came upon iced champagne and recovered myself, and became strong again. Ever since I came home, I have slaved at my report of the Woman's Department . . . Putting a pen into an ink stand, and taking it out again, scribble, scribble, nibble, nibble . . . And go to bed between whiles."[31] For the next several months, she scribbled, nibbled, and lectured, getting more than two hundred dollars for a tour in Iowa alone.

She and Maud were living in New York when she heard at the end of February 1886 that Julia Romana had typhoid. Julia rushed back to Boston, where she was relieved to find her daughter improving. She reassured Maud that "there is nothing dangerous in Julia's condition, and I can be away for two or three days without any risk or inconvenience to her."[32] After a board meeting of the New England Woman's Club, she returned to New York. On March 9, an emergency telegram summoned her back to South Boston. She arrived barely in time to see her daughter die, two days short of her forty-second birthday, on March 10, 1886.

Julia tormented herself with the thought that she had neglected Julia Romana. "My heart agonizes again with the question 'could dear Julie have been saved?' Oh! The dreadful pain of uncertainty about this. I can bear everything else. God help me from thinking that all was not done that might have been done."[33] Julia Romana had not been on easy terms with her mother and siblings, although after her death they reproached themselves for appreciating her too little. Shy, awkward in company, studious, sensitive, and selflessly benevolent, she was also stubborn, hot-tempered, sharp-tongued, and edgy. Some Howe biographers have suggested that she had a mental illness. In 1859, her parents thought she was having a breakdown from overwork. Before her marriage, she had certainly had bouts of depression, and in the summer after Chev's death, she was unable to sleep or return to her home; Julia called a doctor, who diagnosed hysteria, a catchall term that had unreliable and gendered meanings in the nineteenth century. None of these details is certain evidence of mental illness. What is clear about Julia Romana is the extraordinary degree to which she both emulated and competed with her parents. Like Chev, she was devoted to the care of the blind and to serving as "the patron saint of the Perkins Institution," in Maud's phrase.[34] Like Julia, she was a poet; her book *Stray Chords* was published in 1883. Like her mother as well, she was passionate about philosophy and had started a Metaphysical Club where thinkers could share discussions; she ruled it, her mother wrote, "with a staff of lilies."[35] Julia Romana was also an enthusiastic participant in Bronson Alcott's Concord School of Philosophy, funded by his daughter Louisa, and host to the Transcendental great and good. Howe herself had lectured there in 1881. In *Philosophiae Quaestor* (1884), Julia Romana both paid tribute to the school and satirized its sages, posing as "a dumb Dante" unable to understand everything she heard. On the other hand, she shared very few interests with her sisters, and could be very snippy about them in her letters; they also knew that she had been Chev's favorite, "the first born, the star child, the nearest to his great heart of all his children."[36]

Julia's dreams of her oldest daughter were guilty and remorseful for months. In June she dreamed of a conversation with Julia Romana speaking to her through the sitting room clock. "Dearest Dudie, why can I not feel that you are near me?" she asked the spirit, who replied, "because you do not care about it."[37] Another dream in August had Julia Romana complaining that her family did not talk about her very often.[38] In November, she saw Julia Romana again, and asked, "oh, darling, why don't you come oftener?" to which the ghost gave no clear reply but seemed more cheerful.[39] In her deep mourning, Laura wrote to Annie Mailliard, "Mama is very beautiful. Her hair is quite snow-white now, the black bonnet and veil showing the perfect features as if carved in ivory."[40] Gradually, Julia's unconscious projections of a reproachful Julia Romana subsided.

Her wishes for Maud to marry came true at last. At thirty-two, Maud finally decided to relinquish girlhood. Jack Elliott was not perfect: he had no profession and no income, and her sisters might not approve of him, but he was persistent and she loved him. "You will be surprised and I fear a good deal troubled," Maud wrote to Laura, "to learn that Jack has come out again, bent on marrying me, and seems likely to carry his point this time. I am sorry that you can't be glad, so please don't bother to write me anything about it for you couldn't write from your heart and I should feel the effort you would make to say something kind. Only wait until you see him and don't burden your heart or Harry's against him. He isn't a little black beast, he is a true-hearted creature, the only man who has ever really loved the best me. I am full of peace and hope, and the black gulf seems to be all shut over and gone."[41] Julia had always liked him, and was genuinely glad. Boston society, in the person of Jack Gardner, saw the match as a comedown. "I am disgusted, because he hasn't a copper," wrote Mr. Jack. "He is an Englishman, a painter, and has lived most of his life in Rome . . . He hopes to get work—house decoration if nothing better offers."[42] On February 7, 1887, Maud and Jack married at 241 Beacon Street with James Freeman Clarke officiating. They had designed an arty altar of laurel and palms, and she wore a sophisticated satin gown and a tulle veil. It was a pretty wedding, according to Mr. Jack, and Maud received many presents, although "neither so numerous or so handsome as they ought to have been, nothing like what they would've been if she had been or married rich."[43] They went to New York for a short honeymoon, and soon moved to Chicago, where she became an expert on American art and a fixture of high society. She also made frequent visits to Boston and Newport.

With Maud more or less settled, Julia launched into a new round of lecturing and preaching. She led prayer services at the Home for Intemperate Women in Boston. She read the "Battle Hymn" at Longfellow's memorial service at the Boston Museum. There she had to meet Lowell and Norton, although the nasty review for which she blamed them still rankled; she had "long felt an unkindness for the disrespect with which they treated or allowed to be treated my *Later Lyrics* in the *North American Review*." With the feminist perspective of the women's movement, however, she speculated that their disrespect was less personal than patriarchal. "Lowell has never had any opinion of women as poets," she thoughtfully added. "He once told me so."[44]

Another return to the past came in December 1887 when she presided over a celebration of Laura Bridgman's fiftieth year at Perkins. There were songs, flowers, and a Christmas tree decorated with gifts, including a gold bracelet and a music box. Laura was much moved by the attention. At the end of the festivities, however, Michael Anagnos made an unexpected announcement: Perkins was teaching two new deaf-blind girls, nine-year-old Edith Thomas and seven-year-old Helen Keller. He had discovered Helen Keller earlier that year, when her parents (who had read Dickens's account of Laura Bridgman in *American Notes*) wrote to him asking for a teacher for their gifted but untamed daughter at their Alabama home. Like Chev in the 1830s, Anagnos, who had just turned fifty, was ambitious and craving an opportunity to make his own mark. He had long been hoping to find a Laura Bridgman of his own, and he sent his top Perkins student, Annie Sullivan, to Alabama as her teacher. When he went there to meet Helen in March 1888, he realized that she had already surpassed Laura in intelligence, quickness of mind, beauty, and charm. In May 1888, Keller and Sullivan came to Perkins for six months of training.

The much-anticipated meeting of Laura and her eager young successor, however, was a tragicomic disaster. As an elderly woman, Laura Bridgman was obsessive about cleanliness and skittish about being touched. Keller thought she was "like a statue I had once felt in a garden, she was so motionless, and her hands were so cool, like flowers that have grown in shady places."[45] Laura scolded little Helen about her rough way of playing; then, trying to kiss Laura good-bye, Helen accidentally tromped on her toes.

Laura died at Perkins the following year. Her eulogists tended to focus on Chev's achievement, not hers. At her funeral, her minister spoke of Chev as "one of those knights errant of the middle ages, possessed of all their chivalry, setting himself down before some castle whose triply-barred gate refused him entrance, and then laying siege until the gate was forced and the imprisoned captive released."[46] The image confuses the captive and the castle, and attributes the whole triumph to the knight's assault, ignoring the girl's own struggle to overcome her handicaps. It was a perfect epitaph for Chev, if not for Laura. In any case, from then on, Michael Anagnos and Annie Sullivan would be the chivalrous heroes, and Helen Keller the beautiful emancipated princess.

The Howes were uneasy with the new Perkins regime. Maud went to Michael Anagnos's annual reception in 1893 and was not impressed by his "main attraction," Helen Keller and her teacher, Annie Sullivan. "I think Anagnos has made a mistake in choosing Miss Sullivan for her teacher. Miss S. is well prepared in one way, having herself been educated at the Perkins Institution and having known Laura Bridgman and become familiar with Papa's methods, but she has not the right feeling, remembering the beautiful modesty of Laura's behavior, compared to the almost hoydenish ways of this child. Helen recited some verses . . . The loneliest sound I have ever heard, like waves breaking on the coast of some lonely desert island."[47] Maud and Flossy defended their father's legacy in their biography *Laura Bridgman: Dr. Howe's Famous Pupil and What He Taught Her* (1903).

Julia thought the fuss over Helen Keller and Annie Sullivan was exaggerated, but she had let go of the Perkins legend. She had started reading again—daring young women poets such as Louise Guiney, whose feminist "Tarpeia" she found puzzling. She went to a lecture on the "new poetry" and found it very interesting except that the speaker "overpraised Walt Whitman, as some of us thought." And she was on the move. In 1889 she visited Kansas and saw the land Chev had bought before the war, in Grasshopper, Lawrence, and Burlington. An old Kansas farmer told her that "Grasshopper is a fine place and that eighty acres of our land are splendid farming land"; but the taxes were high, so she sold it. In Topeka, legislators came to her talk, and one suggested she might run for the US Senate.[48] She went cross-country by Pullman, lecturing from Chicago to St. Paul, to Spokane, Walla Walla, Tacoma, Seattle, and Portland, arriving in San Francisco on May 5. On Decoration Day she was the guest of honor at the Grand Opera House, where the whole audience stood to sing the "Battle Hymn" and "the lady cornetist came in with a good blast." She also went to visit Annie in California, and was entranced by the Mailliard ranch and the orange poppies on the lawn. "The middle west seems to me nowhere now that I have seen the real west," she enthused.[49]

At the end of May, Maud and Laura organized a gala festival for their mother's seventieth birthday, inviting friends and dignitaries including Oliver Wendell Holmes, James Russell Lowell, Mrs. Jack, and Edward Everett Hale, who "left too soon to do anything."[50] This party was the first of what Valarie Ziegler calls the "public rituals of veneration" from the 1890s until her death. Her birthday became an annual commemorative event. The New England Woman's Club hosted a lavish luncheon; the Boston Authors Club commissioned a volume of poems for her eightieth birthday; on her ninetieth birthday, a speaker compared the elevator installed at Beacon Street by her children to a "heavenly chariot lifting her to the regions above."[51]

Although Maud and Jack lived in Chicago, Flossy and her children in Scotch Plains, New Jersey, and Laura with her large family in Maine beginning in 1876, the daughters were determined to take over Chev's role as Julia's supervisor. The granddaughters too kept track of her travels and tried to persuade her to stay home. In 1890, Laura's daughter

Rosalind Richards moved to Boston to help her grandmother, but also to keep an eye on her activities. "Grandmama went to Philadelphia today; but is coming back tomorrow," she reported to Laura. "Why, of course!" Laura replied, "Just stepping across the street to Philadelphia! What could be more simple?"[52] Maud kept up her exhortations from a distance. "I beg of you, for all our sake, and your own, not to keep up the racket which everyday since I left you have carried on. In six weeks you went once to Washington, three times to New York, once to New Haven . . . Is there nothing worthwhile in life but the platform and the public? . . . I don't want you to hold your hands in your lap, but neither can I endure your constant and exhausting wanderings."[53] They nagged, complained, remonstrated, pleaded; but Julia would not be stopped and could fight back sharply when they pushed too hard. "The past year, which is so much deplored by some of you," she wrote to Laura, "has been to me unusually rich in instruction and in satisfaction, and I cannot say that I find any occasion to regret any of its' [*sic*] outings . . . I must make a stand for freedom to do the work which, humanly speaking, I cannot hope to do very much longer. I have said my word, and so, let us kiss and be friends, and say no more about it."[54]

Behind this defiant front, Julia felt discouraged for much of the 1890s. She thought her writing life was over. Although in 1895 she published a collection of essays, *Is Polite Society Polite?*, the sales were disappointingly low. "I cannot comfort myself as I once could," she wrote to Laura, "by thinking that I am above the level of the general public. Clearly my writings don't interest them." Laura wanted to publish a collection of her poems, but Julia could not imagine "another dead book."[55] By the close of the decade, both of her sisters had died: Annie in April 1895, Louisa in October 1897 in Rome, where she was buried in the Protestant Cemetery.

Julia was still feeling posthumous and passé in December 1897, when Maud and Jack persuaded her to spend the winter with them in Rome at the beautiful Palazzo Rusticucci overlooking St. Peter's Square.

The visit started badly: "The first day of this winter, which God help me to live through! Dearest Maud is all kindness and devotion to me, and so is Jack, but I have Rome *en grippe.* Nothing in it pleases me."[56] Her despondency hung on for a time, but the *Atlantic Monthly* had requested her memoirs, and she was attempting to write them despite her depression: "I fear that my 'Reminiscences' will be very disappointing to the world in general, if it ever troubles itself to read them. I feel quite sure that it has neglected some good writing of mine in verse and prose. I cannot help anticipating for this book the same neglect and this discourages me somewhat."[57]

Once she had established a work schedule, however, she could not stay depressed for long. The house was magnificent, tiled in red, white, and black geometrical designs, and the *grand salon* had a sixteenth-century carved wooden ceiling and pale green doors. Marion Crawford had loaned the Elliotts furniture; and Jack had turned to gardening, partly to procrastinate and avoid work on his endlessly deferred commission to paint a mural, *The Triumph of Time*, for the Boston Public Library.[58] Red, white, and yellow roses, plus urns of azaleas, honeysuckle, chrysanthemums, and geraniums bloomed on the terrace. They saw Duse perform in several plays including D'Annunzio's *Primavera* ("a rotten piece," in Maud's view), and went to receptions, luncheons, tea parties, dinners, galleries, drives, and concerts.[59] Julia perked up and organized a "small and select" women's literary club of Romans and Anglo-American expatriates. She bought a little diamond ring set in black enamel and thought about buying a small ruby-and-diamond ring as well.[60]

Yet as she was writing her reminiscences, Rome was full of memories and echoes of her past, and haunted by the specters of her youth. Jack had hung passion-flower vines along the walls, which reminded her of Horace Binney Wallace and her poems. Her dreams were unusually rich and reflective. In January, she had "a singular dream, very distinct. I thought that my death was very near, although I was not ill. People seem to be expecting it. I found my watch badly injured and thought, 'it is not worthwhile to repair it, as I shall have no further use for it.' "[61] In March, she dreamed that her father "came in and said to me that he wished to speak to Miss Julia alone. I trembled, as I so often did, lest I was about to receive some well merited rebuke. He said that he wished my sister and me to stay at home more."[62]

In the midst of these visitations, Julia found herself returned to youth in another way. Jack Elliott, working from photographs and his imagination, painted a "strange, half allegorical portrait" of her in the 1850s, in which she holds a water lily.[63] In Rome, he began designing her clothes. Julia had always loved clothes and jewels, and Louisa had sent her elaborate dresses from Paris in the 1840s and 1850s. But Jack Elliott created a style for her that brought out her beauty as she grew older: distinctive, layered, elegant striped or patterned silk dresses, topped with embroidered jackets, and finished with magnificent lace collars. He banished black dresses; under his guidance she wore green and lilac, and a beautiful white cashmere dress, "made something like the Pope's robe."[64]

In her pretty, artistic dresses, Julia was a surprising social and aesthetic star. All spring the artists in Rome were clamoring for her services as a model. She sat for a portrait by Jose de Villegas, the leader of the Spanish art colony, who had mentored Jack; and a bust by Hendrik Andersen, a strikingly handsome young sculptor, who had been born in Norway, grew up in Newport, and had settled in Rome.[65] Indeed, to Maud's delight, her elderly mother was sought after as a sitter. "People talked so much about her appearance" that her niece Daisy Chanler told her, "I am always prepared for fresh surprises from you, but I had not expected this *succès de beauté*."[66]

After Julia had returned to Boston, Maud told her great friend Henry James, a regular guest at the Palazzo, about her mother's second blossoming. As James recorded the conversation, he had been chatting with Maud on the flowered terrace "of her charming place near St. Peter's . . . with *such* a view," when she told him about Julia's "coming out at the end of her long, arduous life, and having a wonderful unexpected final moment—at 78!—of being thought *the* most picturesque, striking, lovely old (wrinkled and *marked*) 'Holbein,' etc. that ever was. 'All the artists raving about her.'" James wrote it down in his notebook as the germ of a short story about a "little old ugly, or plain (unappreciated) woman, after dull, small life, in 'aesthetic,' perceptive, 'European' 'air.'"[67] He published the resulting story, "The Beldonald Holbein," in *Harper's Magazine* in October 1901; in it, the exquisitely preserved Lady Beldonald is chagrined when her poor and plain companion becomes the toast of discriminating London. While Julia was neither unappreciated nor plain, acclamation in her late seventies as a princess hidden in the palace was a triumph.

Reminiscences came out in 1899. It concluded with Julia's summary of her life's successes:

> *It was a great distinction for me when the foremost philanthropist of the age chose me for his wife . . . I have sat at the feet of the masters of literature, art, and science, and have been graciously admitted into their fellowship . . . I have written one poem which, although composed in the stress and strain of the Civil War, is now sung South and North by the champions of a free government . . . Lastly and chiefly, I have had the honor of pleading for the slave when he was a slave, of helping to initiate the woman's movement in many States of the Union, and of standing with the illustrious champions of justice and freedom, for woman suffrage, when to do so was a thankless office, inviting public ridicule and private avoidance.*[68]

Chapter Eleven

THE ELEVENTH HOUR

As the twentieth century began, Julia had become a national treasure. She was still committed to all her long-standing causes, but she was also drawn to protesting new forms of injustice. To her anxious and protective children, she seemed even more errant and intractable than before. To the American public, she seemed to symbolize the triumphant spirit of a nation that had survived a terrible test.

Born just three days after Queen Victoria, Howe had always had a mischievous connection to her; on her honeymoon, she had written a parody of "God Save the Queen" for the ladies cabin. In old age, she came more and more to resemble Victoria. In formal photographs they look very much alike in their black gowns and lace caps, "nearly always askew," as one biographer notes.[1] Jack Elliott helped Howe create her more modern regal image, making her "a lovely coronet" out of gold braid for parties.[2] American journalists increasingly compared Howe to the monarch, one of them boasting after her eightieth birthday gala that "when Vic celebrated her 80th birthday . . . she got no ovation equal to that given this octogenarian."[3] When Victoria died in January 1901, though, Howe felt "quite overcome" and wrote an obituary for the *Woman's Journal.*

As the new century began, she was combining the traditional role of an old-fashioned Boston matriarch with an iron determination to live on her own terms. John Jay Chapman, who knew her in her old age, perceived her as a woman "of unfailing gaiety," the "pet of her numerous children," and "the Mother Superior of the latest generation of nonconformist philanthropy in Boston."[4] Her self-image was closer to the Mother Superior than to the queen, although she did not take either very seriously. She often wore the white cashmere "Pope's dress" Jack had designed for her in Italy to lectures and meetings, and dreamed of an interview with a female Pope, a majestic alter ago: "I asked on leaving whether I might kiss her hand. She said 'you may kiss my hand.' I found it fat and far from beautiful. As I left her, me thought that her countenance relaxed, and she looked like a tired old woman."[5] No one who saw Julia in these last years, however, described her as looking tired. The gaiety Chapman saw was partly her genuine love of fun, and partly an act of will. An elderly relative had told her that when she quailed at the prospect of a strenuous task, she must do it immediately; and she followed that stern precept, mastering her fatigue with stubborn self-discipline. She joked, but did not complain, about old age; the social expectations that old ladies would be wrinkled, white-haired, and bent made it easier for her to accept aging. Certainly none of the women her age she knew were looking any better or any younger.

Children, grandchildren, and great-grandchildren still took a lot of her time. Laura and Henry Richards had seven children, Flossy and David Hall had five, and they all came to Oak Glen for long visits. Maud and Jack Elliott were childless, as were Harry Howe and his wife, Fannie. Julia confided to Annie some years earlier that she thought Fannie lacked "the education which motherhood, or barring this, the habit of self-denial gives."[6] She got on well with Fannie, but they were never close. Harry was by far the wealthiest of the children (he built a summer home in Bedford Hills, a copy of Lawton's Valley), and she thought that his distinguished and prosperous scientific career gave Fannie a privileged, even pampered, life. As the only son, moreover, Harry was free from the intense emotional bonds connecting her to her daughters; he sent her a generous monthly check in her last years instead. She was immensely proud of his academic achievements, medals, speeches, honorary degrees, and prizes. In a metallurgical parallel to Chev's Order of Saint Saviour, Harry had been to Russia to receive the cross of the Order of Saint Stanislaus from the czar. "Dearest boy," she wrote to him, ". . . If your father were only here, to share our great rejoicing!"[7]

All the daughters had bequests from Charles Sumner, as well as from their father and Uncle Sam. Laura, Flossy, and Maud all became professional writers. Laura wrote or edited ninety-five books for children and adults, including the story "Captain January" (1902), which was made into one of Shirley Temple's most popular movies in 1936. Flossy had become a suffragist as well as a journalist, but in 1909, Julia was worried about her financial hardships: "Flossy has struggled most bravely with poverty," she wrote in her journal, but "has been happy, adoring her excellent, but irritable and despondent husband."[8] After David Hall died, Flossy did better supporting herself and her family. Maud was a productive, hustling journalist, with a Remington typewriter and a keen marketing sense. Julia adored "Zacko," her pet name for Jack Elliott; Maud seemed happy with him and promoted him tirelessly, but Julia worried that with "no child to draw her into the future," Maud would take it hardest when her mother died.[9] And Julia Romana continued to haunt her: "My heart still aches with the thought that I might have done better by her, as by the others."[10] Of Chev, and their thirty-three years together, she thought very little. On their anniversary most years, she would reflect on their marriage and regret that she had not understood how to establish a working marital contract with him. But she did not linger in the past.

Behaving like an old lady with an ebony cane and a white wicker wheelchair, moreover, was not at all to her taste. As recorded in her journal, almost every morning began with headache and depression, which she overcame by uplifting self-talk. Despite vertigo, sore eyes, severe cough, grippe, bronchitis, toothache, knee pains, a lump in her right breast (the doctor thought it was cancerous but could be treated with medicine; it eventually went away), "brain fog," and tonsillitis, she was always toiling on a "screed," for her huge schedule of readings, lectures, sermons, meetings, articles, and celebrations. She insisted on making her own bed every day, took a cold bath every morning, and took two long walks a day. Maud had set up an elaborate finicky routine for her, including twice-daily knee massages. "I hate to be rubbed!" Julia moaned, and by the 1900s, she had trimmed the program down, especially the healthful dietary restrictions.[11] It would be plum cake and mince pie to the end, and she would playfully compete with her grandchildren for the tastiest desserts. The daughters insisted on a half-hour nap at noon, but she detested it, resisted it, and checked her watch for the end of the wasted minutes. She took pride in writing an article on gambling in under an hour, at the urgent request of a newspaper. In 1900, she took a long, solitary midwestern lecture tour from January to May, with stops in Minneapolis, Madison, and Duluth, and was taxed by the effort but sustained by her humor. She was still forgetting where she put the keys to her moneybag, and once prayed to St. Anthony of Padua that, if he would help her, she "would take pains to find out who he was."[12] (The keys turned up right away, but St. Anthony was not invoked on further occasions.)

Her support for women's suffrage remained strong, but her vision of women's future was more visionary than legislative; the "new woman world," she wrote, was "like the rising up from the sea of a new continent."[13] In 1908, she had a utopian "vision of the world regenerated by the combined labor and love of Men and Women," in which they stood "side-by-side, shoulder to shoulder, a calm lofty and indomitable purpose lighting every face with a glory not of this earth."[14] In her imaginings of a radiant future of sexual equality, Howe shared characteristics with socialist feminists like Eleanor Marx, Olive Schreiner, and Charlotte Perkins Gilman, rather than the single-minded campaigners for the vote. She also kept up her advocacy for racial equality, and at a benefit for the Tuskegee Institute she met a number of the black leaders of the coming generation, Paul Dunbar and his wife, Alice Dunbar-Nelson; W. E. B. DuBois; and Booker T. Washington. With the Boston black activist Josephine St. Pierre Ruffin, she supported the racial integration of women's clubs and spoke out against lynching. Hate mail addressed to "Mrs. Howe, Negro Sympathizer, Boston" was delivered to her home. On December 1, 1900, she dreamed that she was telling Chev, "with the old feeling of reluctance, that I was going away for a lecture." Indeed she was going away, moving further and further away from the role he had imposed on her.

Modern technology delighted her. She took readily to the long-distance telephone, to driving with her sons-in-law in fast cars, and to her grandson Hal Richards's motorcycle. Maud and Laura had an electric elevator installed at Beacon Street, which she adored. "Watching her ascent," her daughters wrote, "clad in white, a smile on her lips, her hand waving farewell, one could only think of 'the chariot of Israel' . . ."[15] She loved her phonograph, and listened almost every evening to operas, Handel, Beethoven, and Chopin, repeating the music at her piano; although she tried to listen to modern music, she disliked even Tchaikovsky. She expanded her reading, although her literary taste and style had been formed in her youth. Studying the plays of D'Annunzio, attending a lecture on Whitman and the "new poetry" (she found Whitman overrated), or hearing W. B. Yeats speak on the revival of letters in Ireland did not inspire her to envision a new world of literature any more than the friendship of Oscar Wilde had made her an aesthete. Realism knocked when she had a visit from a "bumptious but very candid and genuine" young author named Upton Sinclair, "who admires my Battle Hymn and wants to write a three-volume novel about our Civil War."[16]

Celebrity was beginning to exact its twentieth-century toll. People pestered her for blurbs and recommendations, personal poems, and money for higher education or funeral expenses. They wanted advice;

they wanted to exploit her; they wanted her to sign photographs and scraps of cloth used for autograph quilts. A Mrs. Eugenia H. Allison, from New Decatur, Alabama, wanted her views on "The Literary Tendencies and Forces of Our Age." Mrs. Anna C. Bird of East Walpole, Massachusetts, sought her opinion of "Charlotte Brontë and Jane Austen." Mr. R. Bache of Washington, DC, wanted to publish an essay of his own under her name. A malodorous Reverend George Vaughan came to the house and bragged about his eminence until she gave him a dollar to get rid of him. One Tennessee woman wanted Howe to pay for her musical education; another wrote mysteriously to order "Secret Confessions of a Priest," enclosing forty cents' worth of stamps. And they all wanted her to speak at their tea parties, club events, and flower shows, dance at the firemen's ball, dine at the banquet of the Shoe and Leather Trade, join the Paint and Oils Association at their annual dinner. "I do verily believe," Laura grumbled, "that people of this sort would persist in their efforts if they knew that Mammy would be in her coffin the next day. They would say, 'Oh, if that is the case, we must have her last appearance!' "[17] Maud was fighting her every step of the way, preventing her from going to a meeting of the Authors Club, pleading "so piteously . . . not to go to give a lecture that I could not deny her," imploring her with tears not to go to church and face drafts and exposures, or sending a telegram forbidding her to go to damp Oak Glen.[18]

Meanwhile, she became involved with new social issues: the abolition of the death penalty, the protection of Italian immigrants, Indian affairs, the Pennsylvania coal miners' strike. With regard to the rebellion of the Armenians against the Turks, she backed the Armenians, or rather, opposed the Turks. During one crisis in 1903, she supported American intervention in the conflict: "Our own warship is where it should be. I would to God that we might hear the thunder of its guns."[19] Four thousand Armenian Americans turned out to cheer her in a Faneuil Hall rally in 1904. She went to hear Jane Addams talk about her experiments with settlement houses, and to a women's club lecture on anti-Semitism. In November 1904, she went to a meeting of the Council of Jewish Women and they asked her to recite the "Battle Hymn," making her nervous: "I had feared that the last verse might trouble them, but it did not."[20] In June 1904, when she received her first honorary degree, from Tufts University, the students gave her the college yell twice. That same month, she wrote in her journal: "In the night I dreamed of one whose memory has entered deeply into my life. Though I tried to recite before him my Flag poem and then my Battle hymn, in both broke down. Strange this recurrence of a figure not seen with mortal vision in many years!"[21] Why should these events trigger memories of Horace Binney Wallace? Perhaps she longed to show him how far she had come.

Tribute followed tribute. On her eighty-sixth birthday in 1905, the Boston Authors Club commissioned a volume of sixty quatrains in her honor and hosted a festival of readings modeled on the Welsh Eisteddfodd. She responded with mock self-deprecation:

Why, bless you, I ain't nothing or nobody, nor much,
If you look in your directory, you'll find a thousand such;
I walk upon the level ground, I breathe upon the air,
I study at a table, and reflect upon a chair.

I wrote a pretty book one time, then I wrote a play,
And a friend who went to see it said she fainted right away.
Then I got up high to speculate upon the Universe,
And folks who heard me found themselves no better and no worse.

Yes, I've had a lot of birthdays and I'm growing very old,
That's why they make so much of me, if once the truth were told.
And I love the shade in summer, and in winter love the sun,
And I'm just learning how to live, my wisdom's just begun.[22]

Age brought less welcome surprises. Michael Anagnos died on July 7, 1906, and in mid-August she learned from his executors that he had been married and divorced in Greece before the Howes met him, and had left behind a son named Polychronos. She kept the news to herself; certainly it is not mentioned in her daughters' biography, which stresses her grief over his death. Perhaps the comment in her journal that she was "much troubled in the effort to compose a poem" for his memorial service suggests her efforts to preserve his standing as the perfect son-in-law.[23] Dreams of men other than Chev, in August and September, may have been her way of processing the information about Michael. She dreamed that she was engaged to Edward Twisleton, her English friend from the 1850s, but "suddenly remembered that dear Chev was still living." In another dream, a "King Edward" wearing a black-and-gold medieval gown kissed her hand. In the last of the dreams, Edwin Booth came to call and the children sent him away, to her dismay.[24]

In January 1908, she had the satisfaction of seeing her standing as poet recognized when she was the first woman elected to the American Academy of Arts and Letters. (The second woman was not chosen until 1930.) Yet, rather endearingly, she never got over her fears of being forgotten or put "out of the running," or the pain of the bad review of *Later Lyrics*. As late as 1907, she worried that her article for a magazine would be rejected. At Longfellow's centennial service in Cambridge, she was hurt that no one asked her to read a poem. In 1909, in the same month that she received an honorary doctorate from Brown, she was upset because she was not invited to speak at the Margaret Fuller Centenary, and came home with her poem to Margaret still in her pocket, although she "was probably the only person present who had ever heard one or more of Margaret's monologues, miscalled 'Conversations.'"[25] She woke up at 4:00 a.m. one morning, brooding again about Robert Browning's "great rudeness to me in a London party. I said to myself, 'I need not reproach myself about the poem I wrote as my feeling in writing it was one of genuine affection and homage.' Browning was deeply offended at my description of his lodgings: 'the chairs were queer and rotten,' but it had been exactly my own experience in Rome in *expensive* lodgings, in 1843, and was merely a feature of my word picture. Still, the experience is a very painful one, quite unexpected."[26]

On her ninetieth birthday, her friends and family gathered at Beacon Street to honor her. A journalist from *Munsey's Magazine* described her as "the grand old woman of America" and admired the way she looked in her "picturesque and becoming Norman hat." He spoke to one of her many grandchildren, "who admitted that there were no geniuses among them, but no imbeciles or degenerates either."[27]

In her last months she was still writing poetry, and fighting with Maud to let her go to read her works: a poem called "The Capitol" for the American Academy of Arts and Letters in DC; a centenary poem on James Freeman Clarke; a poem on Abraham Lincoln to be read at Symphony Hall, Boston; and a final collection of her verse, *At Sunset.* She was still revising, too, following one of her mottoes: "Never print a poem or a speech until it has been delivered; always give the eleventh hour its chance!"[28]

Her last public speech was at the end of May 1910, when she went to plead on behalf of pure milk legislation at the Boston State House. "Her presence, the presence of the old Sybil, mother, grandmother, great-grandmother, was extraordinarily romantic," Maud eulogized. "It lifted the whole occasion out of the realm of the commonplace into that of the poetic."[29] Her private end was not quite so poetic. In June she had a bad fall carrying her chamber pot to the bathroom, broke a rib, and needed a private nurse, an imposition she endured until the end of the summer, when she demanded that the nurse be dismissed. Maud had to give in. In her "Notes on the Last Summer of JWH's Life," she explained that the "last fiery flash of the cold gray eyes and the red hot temper, completely cowed and quelled the old daughters!" But she also understood Julia's "last stand for freedom" as the natural result of her lifelong battle for independence. "I think she was balked so much in her youth, first by her own father . . . then by Papa, that her first ideal of happiness was to be let alone, and allowed to have one's own way."[30]

In October 1910, Julia roused herself somewhat grumpily to go to Northampton and accept a third honorary degree, from Smith College. To Maud, the ceremony was another romantic apotheosis and picture opportunity. "A curving gallery was filled with white-clad girls, some two thousand of them," she wrote. "As she entered, they rose like a flock of doves, and with them the whole audience." As Howe came forward to get her degree, they sang the "Battle Hymn" again. Asked by a Boston paper for a motto for the women of America, she declared "Up to Date!"—a succinct and unsentimental epitaph for a woman who lived for the present and the future.[31]

Julia's serene death of pneumonia a week later provided many sentimental tableaux, but it had long been expected; all her children except Harry were at her bedside. She was buried with Chev and Sammy at Mount Auburn Cemetery, but even on her tombstone her male relations got top billing. The inscription reads

JULIA WARD HOWE
DAUGHTER OF
SAMUEL WARD
WIFE OF
SAMUEL GRIDLEY HOWE

At the memorial service held by the city of Boston on January 8, 1911, any hint of Julia's playing a subsidiary role to her husband was excised. Mayor Fitzgerald set the tone of the evening when he called her "a representative character" who "typifies and stands for the nineteenth century." The young wife who had once felt excluded by Boston society had become the queen of the city. As John Jay Chapman wrote, "Of course everybody in Boston knew her. One couldn't help knowing her. The policemen knew her; the school-children sang her 'Battle-Hymn of the Republic'; the statesmen, scholars, scientists, and publicists for a generation regarded her as one of their cherished institutions and as a pillar of the crumbling world."[32] All of the speakers tacitly acknowledged her preeminence. William H. Lewis, a graduate of Harvard Law School, the first black United States District Attorney, and a celebrated spokesman for civil rights, drew on familiar metaphors when he elevated her above Chev: "Fifty years she reigned over us, queen of all our hearts" with her "Prince Consort, Dr. Samuel Gridley Howe . . . I find but one parallel to two such lives in all history, that of which Tennyson sings in the *Idylls of the King*,—Victoria and Albert the Good."[33]

Chev had become the prince consort to Julia's queen, and his reputation continued to decline. As early as 1917, the *Boston Transcript* lamented that "it is rather a pity, that the brilliancy of Mrs. Howe's achievements in her great age, and her 'Battle Hymn of the Republic,' have given off such a blaze of glory around her name that that of her husband is rather lost in the dazzle."[34] A reader agreed that Mrs. Howe's name, of course, would always be held in "sweet remembrance," but it was "sad to observe that the name of the noble character who, in his middle age, wooed and wedded her . . . should have begun to be dropped out of the cyclopedias, as has been noticed to be the case."[35] Writing a book about Newport in 1944, Maud reflected on the way history had treated her parents. "Nothing is so strange to me as the fact that today, when every school child can repeat 'The Battle Hymn of the Republic,' and hardly a day passes without some reference to my mother in radio or press,—my father, whose towering personality dwarfed all the rest of the family, is forgotten."[36] In the 1940s Julia was even named one of the "Wonder Women of History," a series published in every issue of the Wonder Woman comic books.

She is remembered today chiefly as the author of one great poem, but that is more than most poets achieve. In 1908, President Theodore Roosevelt, one of Julia's friends and admirers, proposed that the "Battle Hymn" should be declared the national anthem, but the idea was defeated. Southerners thought the lyrics were too bloodthirsty, calling for their half of the nation to be trampled and crushed in a Northern holy war. And despite the tolerant response of the Jewish women in New Orleans, a Jewish citizen, Jacob B. Ascher, protested in a letter to the *New York Times* against the poem's religious imagery: "The American Nation and Army are not all Christians. In both bodies there are many who prefer a different religion to what Christ taught; and there are many who have no religion at all."[37] In 1931, the unsingable "Star-Spangled Banner" became the American national anthem.

Over time, however, the "Battle Hymn" became an unofficial national anthem, and also an international anthem for times of heroic challenge, mourning, sacrifice, and faith. It was sung at the funeral of Winston Churchill in 1965 and after the assassination of John F. Kennedy. It was performed at the funerals of Robert Kennedy, Richard Nixon, and Ronald Reagan. It was quoted by Martin Luther King Jr. in his last sermon in Memphis in 1968. After September 11, 2001, it was performed at memorial concerts around the world.

Howe's image too was transformed in the twentieth century. In 1978, she had come to seem like a relic of the dusty Victorian past. The book dealer and scholar Madeleine B. Stern disparaged the idea that critics had once praised Howe as "the most notable woman of letters" of her age. "It is more accurate," she opined, "to regard her as 'the Dearest Old Lady in America.'"[38] But at exactly that moment, the wheel of history was turning. In the 1950s, Howe's granddaughter and executor Rosalind Richards donated the Howe family's huge archive of correspondence and journals to the Houghton Library at Harvard; they revealed the disappointment, frustration, anger, and rebellion behind Howe's motherly mask. Louise Tharp looked at them in 1956 when she published her book about Howe, her sisters, and her brother Sam. Then in 1979, the historian Deborah Pickman Clifford published the first biography based on the archive, *Mine Eyes Have Seen the Glory.* The academic scholars Mary H. Grant, Gary Williams, and Valarie Ziegler came to Harvard to do indispensable research on Howe's life, ideas, and writing. In the twenty-first century, she is a new woman.

Julia began her life as a damsel imprisoned in an enchanted castle and ended it as an international icon. As a young woman, she had been a diva, flattered but excluded from any real knowledge of the world. As a young wife, she had painfully come to the realization that her husband could not be the partner she had dreamed of, no matter how many times she sacrificed her wishes to his command. As a mother, she slowly revised her concept of maternity and questioned its centrality to a woman's life. For the first half of her life, she was a bystander to history, silenced or speaking with a soft and timid voice. During the Civil War, Julia understood that she was also fighting a domestic and personal civil war. Using her power struggles with her husband as lessons, she stepped out to claim her own voice and her own power, as a spokeswoman for women's rights and then for the disempowered everywhere. She never became the great poet or playwright she had longed to be; she knew she would not live to see women enfranchised; she never achieved the level of feminine self-denial and scorn of material things that society still demands from its female saints. But as she wrote at the end, "I do not desire ecstatic, disembodied sainthood . . . I would be human, and American, and a woman."[39] She won her civil wars, and she earned her place in American history.

ABBREVIATIONS

AW: Annie Ward.

AWM: Annie Ward Mailliard.

Chapman: John Jay Chapman, "Doctor Howe," *Learning and Other Essays* (New York: Moffatt, Yard and Company, 1910).

Clifford: Deborah Pickman Clifford, *Mine Eyes Have Seen the Glory: A Biography of Julia Ward Howe* (Boston: Little, Brown and Company, 1979).

Donald: David Herbert Donald, *Charles Sumner* (New York: Da Capo Press, 1996).

Donald, *Coming*: David Herbert Donald, *Charles Sumner and the Coming of the Civil War* (Napierville, IL: Sourcebooks, 2009).

Eleventh Hour: Maud Howe Elliott, *The Eleventh Hour in the Life of Julia Ward Howe* (Boston: Little, Brown and Company, 1911).

Elliott and Hall, *Laura Bridgman*: Maud Howe Elliott and Florence Howe Hall, *Laura Bridgman: Dr. Howe's Famous Pupil and What He Taught Her* (Boston: Little, Brown and Company, 1904).

Gale: Robert L. Gale, *Thomas Crawford: American Sculptor* (Pittsburgh: University of Pittsburgh Press, 1964).

Gitter: Elizabeth Gitter, *The Imprisoned Guest* (New York: Picador, 2001).

Grant: Mary H. Grant, *Private Woman, Public Person: An Account of the Life of Julia Ward Howe from 1818–9 to 1868* (Brooklyn, NY: Carlson Publishing Company, 1994).

Grinnell: Nancy Whipple Grinnell, *Carrying the Torch: Maud Howe Elliott and the American Renaissance* (Hanover and London: University Press of New England, 2014).

Grodzins: Dean Grodzins, *American Heretic: Theodore Parker and Transcendentalism* (Chapel Hill: University of North Carolina Press, 2002).

Hatvary: George Egon Hatvary, *Horace Binney Wallace* (Boston: Twayne Publishers, 1977).

Hermaphrodite: Julia Ward Howe, *The Hermaphrodite*, edited and with an introduction by Gary Williams (Lincoln and London: University of Nebraska Press, 2004).

Howe: Laura E. Richards, ed., *Letters and Journals of Samuel Gridley Howe*. 2 vols. (Boston: Dana Estes & Company, 1906).

Hungry Heart: Gary Williams, *Hungry Heart: The Literary Emergence of Julia Ward Howe* (Amherst: University of Massachusetts Press, 1999).

Journal: JWH, Journal 1863–1910. MS Am 2119 (1107), Houghton Library, Harvard University. Typescript at Maine Historical Society, and partly digitized at www.juliawardhowe.org/genealogy/journals/index.htm.

JWH: Julia Ward Howe.

LHR: Laura Howe Richards.

ABBREVIATIONS

LOC: Library of Congress.

Longfellow, *Letters*: Andrew Hilen, ed., *The Letters of Henry Wadsworth Longfellow*. 6 vols. (Cambridge: Harvard University Press, 1967–1983).

LW: Louisa Ward.

LWC: Louise Ward Crawford.

MHE: Maud Howe Elliott.

MS Am 2119: Howe Family Papers 1819–1910, Houghton Library, Harvard University.

Philosophies of Sex: Renée Bergland and Gary Williams, eds., *Philosophies of Sex: Critical Essays on the Hermaphrodite* (Columbus: Ohio State University Press, 2012).

Rem.: Julia Ward Howe, *Reminiscences, 1819–1899* (Boston and New York: Houghton Mifflin Co., 1899).

Renehan: Edward J. Renehan Jr., *The Secret Six* (Columbia, SC: University of South Carolina Press, 1997).

Reynolds: David S. Reynolds, *Walt Whitman's America: A Cultural Biography* (New York: Vintage, 1996).

Reynolds, *John Brown*: David S. Reynolds, *John Brown, Abolitionist* (New York: Vintage, 2006).

Richards and Elliott, *JWH*: Laura E. Richards and Maud Howe Elliott, with assistance by Florence Howe Hall, *Julia Ward Howe, 1819–1910*. 2 vols. (Boston and New York: Houghton Mifflin, 1916).

Richards, *SGH*: Laura E. Richards, *Samuel Gridley Howe* (New York: D. Appleton & Company, 1935).

Schwartz: Harold Schwartz, *Samuel Gridley Howe: Social Reformer 1801–1876* (Cambridge: Harvard University Press, 1956).

ABBREVIATIONS

SGH: Samuel Gridley Howe.

Stepping Westward: Laura E. Richards, *Stepping Westward* (New York and London: D. Appleton & Company, 1931).

SW: Samuel Ward.

Tharp: Louise Hall Tharp, *Three Saints and a Sinner* (Boston: Little, Brown and Company, 1956).

Three Generations: Maud Howe Elliott, *Three Generations* (Boston: Little, Brown and Company, 1923).

Trent: James W. Trent Jr., *The Manliest Man: Samuel G. Howe and the Contours of Nineteenth-Century American Reform* (Amherst and Boston: University of Massachusetts Press, 2012).

Two Noble Lives: Laura E. Richards, *Two Noble Lives: Samuel Gridley Howe, Julia Ward Howe* (Boston: Dana Estes & Co., 1911).

Uncle Sam Ward: Maud Howe Elliott, *Uncle Sam Ward and His Circle* (New York: MacMillan, 1938).

Venet: Wendy Hamand Venet, *A Strong-minded Woman: The Life of Mary A. Livermore* (Amherst: University of Massachusetts Press, 2005).

YHPCCL: Yellow House Papers, Colby College Library.

Ziegler: Valarie H. Ziegler, *Diva Julia: The Public Romance and Private Agony of Julia Ward Howe* (Trinity Press International, 2003).

NOTES

INTRODUCTION

1. Julia Ward Howe, *Reminiscences, 1819–1899* (Boston and New York: Houghton Mifflin Co., 1899), 273. Hereafter abbreviated as *Rem.*
2. Nicholas Butler to Maud Howe Elliott, MHE Papers, Brown University Library, June 4, 1917, box 1, folder 25. Quoted in Valarie H. Ziegler, *Diva Julia: The Public Romance and Private Agony of Julia Ward Howe* (Trinity Press International, 2003), 11. Hereafter abbreviated as Ziegler.
3. Laura E. Richards and Maud Howe Elliott, with assistance by Florence Howe Hall, *Julia Ward Howe, 1819–1910.* 2 vols. (Boston and New York: Houghton Mifflin, 1916). Hereafter abbreviated as Richards and Elliott, *JWH.*
4. John Jay Chapman, "Doctor Howe," *Learning and Other Essays* (New York: Moffatt, Yard and Company, 1910), 91. Hereafter abbreviated as Chapman.
5. Laura E. Richards, *Two Noble Lives: Samuel Gridley Howe, Julia*

Ward Howe (Boston: Dana Estes & Co., 1911). Hereafter abbreviated as *Two Noble Lives.*

6. Chapman, 120.
7. *Rem.*, 57.

CHAPTER ONE: THE PRINCESS IN THE CASTLE

1. *Rem.*, 49.
2. Ibid., 61.
3. Richards and Elliott, *JWH*, I:15.
4. Ibid., 15–16.
5. Louise Hall Tharp, *Three Saints and a Sinner* (Boston: Little, Brown and Company, 1956), 33. Hereafter abbreviated as Tharp.
6. Ibid.
7. *Rem.*, 30.
8. Tharp, 16.
9. Richards and Elliott, *JWH*, I:21.
10. *Rem.*, 18.
11. Ibid.
12. Ibid., 53.
13. Richards and Elliott, *JWH*, I:24.
14. JWH, ed., *Sex in Education: A Reply to Dr. E. H. Clarke's "Sex in Education"* (Boston: Roberts Brothers, 1874), 27–28.
15. *Rem.*, 46.
16. Richards and Elliott, *JWH*, I:29.
17. *Rem.*, 15.
18. Ibid., 57.
19. Ziegler, 18.
20. Tharp, 42. "The Literati," *Godey's Lady's Book*, 1846.
21. *Two Noble Lives*, 39–40.
22. Mary H. Grant, *Private Woman, Public Person: An Account of the*

Life of Julia Ward Howe from 1818–9 to 1868 (Brooklyn, NY: Carlson Publishing Company, 1994), 34. Hereafter abbreviated as Grant.

23. Richards and Elliott, *JWH*, I:35.
24. Maud Howe Elliott, *The Eleventh Hour in the Life of Julia Ward Howe* (Boston: Little, Brown and Company, 1911), 44. Hereafter abbreviated as *Eleventh Hour.*
25. Deborah Pickman Clifford, *Mine Eyes Have Seen the Glory: A Biography of Julia Ward Howe* (Boston: Little, Brown and Company, 1979), 27. Hereafter abbreviated as Clifford.
26. Tharp, 53.
27. Louis Legrand Noble, *The Life and Works of Thomas Cole* (Cambridge: Harvard University Press, 1964), 203.
28. See Joy Kasson, "The Voyage of Life: Thomas Cole and Romantic Disillusion," *American Quarterly* 27, March 1975, 42–56.
29. Richards and Elliott, *JWH*, I:43.
30. Ibid., 44.
31. Tharp, 56–57.
32. *Rem.*, 49.
33. Ibid., 67–68.
34. JWH, *Is Polite Society Polite? and Other Essays* (Boston and New York: Lamson, Wolfe and Co., 1895), 39.
35. JWH, "George Sand," *Atlantic Monthly* 8, November 1861, 514.
36. *Rem.*, 21.
37. Andrew Hilen, ed., *The Letters of Henry Wadsworth Longfellow* (Cambridge: Harvard University Press, 1967), II:143. Hereafter abbreviated as Longfellow, *Letters.*
38. *Rem.*, 61.
39. Ibid., 41.
40. Grant, 45.
41. Ibid.

42. Julia Ward Howe, *The Hermaphrodite*, edited and with an introduction by Gary Williams (Lincoln and London: University of Nebraska Press, 2004), 173–78. Hereafter abbreviated as *Hermaphrodite*.
43. Grant, 47.
44. Clifford, 48, and 280, n. 40.
45. Robert N. Hudspeth, ed., *Letters of Margaret Fuller* (Ithaca, NY: Cornell University Press, 1983), II:72.
46. *Rem.*, 65–66.
47. Grant, 32.
48. Ibid., 33.
49. Maud Howe Elliott, *Uncle Sam Ward and His Circle* (New York: MacMillan, 1938), 175–77, 183. Hereafter abbreviated as *Uncle Sam Ward*.
50. *Rem.*, 54.
51. Grant, 42.
52. Ibid., 51.
53. *Rem.*, 62–63.
54. Sermon, "Solitude and Religion," Howe Collection, folder 57, LOC, in Grant, 52.
55. Grant, 50.
56. Richards and Elliott, *JWH*, I:57–58.
57. Ibid., 58.
58. Clifford, 40.
59. Grant, 58.
60. *Rem.*, 81.
61. Ibid., 84.

CHAPTER TWO: THE KNIGHT-ERRANT

1. Laura E. Richards, ed., *Letters and Journals of Samuel Gridley Howe*. 2 vols. (Boston: Dana Estes & Company, 1906), I:17. Hereafter abbreviated as Howe.

2. Edward J. Renehan Jr., *The Secret Six* (Columbia, SC: University of South Carolina Press, 1997), 33. Hereafter abbreviated as Renehan.
3. Howe, I:388.
4. Ibid., 13.
5. James W. Trent Jr., *The Manliest Man: Samuel G. Howe and the Contours of Nineteenth-Century American Reform* (Amherst and Boston: University of Massachusetts Press, 2012), 1. Hereafter abbreviated as Trent.
6. Ibid., 5.
7. Howe, I:19.
8. Elizabeth Gitter, *The Imprisoned Guest* (New York: Picador, 2001), 14. Hereafter abbreviated as Gitter.
9. Howe, 25.
10. See Gary J. Bass, *Freedom's Battle: The Origins of Humanitarian Intervention* (New York: Random House, 2008), 150.
11. William St. Clair, *That Greece Might Still Be Free: The Philhellenes in the War of Independence* (Oxford: Oxford University Press, 1972), 59–60.
12. Thomas H. O'Connor, *The Athens of America: Boston, 1825–1845* (Amherst: University of Massachusetts Press, 2006), 96.
13. David Herbert Donald, *Charles Sumner* (New York: Da Capo Press, 1996), 32. Hereafter abbreviated as Donald.
14. Trent, 2.
15. Ibid., 26–27.
16. Harold Schwartz, *Samuel Gridley Howe: Social Reformer 1801–1876* (Cambridge: Harvard University Press, 1956), 9. Hereafter abbreviated as Schwartz.
17. Gitter, 16.
18. Trent, 39, and 281, n. 27.
19. Howe, I:138–39.
20. Ibid., 209.

21. Chapman, 93.
22. Howe, I:366.
23. *Two Noble Lives*, 16; Howe, I:36.
24. Franklin B. Sanborn, *Dr. S. G. Howe: The Philanthropist* (New York: Funk and Wagnalls, 1891), 79–80.
25. Laura E. Richards, *Samuel Gridley Howe* (New York: D. Appleton & Company, 1935), 48. Hereafter abbreviated as Richards, *SGH*.
26. Howe, I:385.
27. Richards, *SGH*, 389.
28. See Trent, 56–58; Schwartz, 44–48.
29. Howe, II:23.
30. Chapman, 107.
31. Howe, II:16.
32. JWH, I:32.
33. Donald, 48.
34. Ibid., 53.
35. Ibid., 37.
36. Ibid., 38.
37. Trent, 80.
38. Ibid., 121.
39. Gitter, 55–56.
40. Ibid., 46.
41. William Ingalls, MD, *A Lecture on the Subject of Phrenology* (Boston: Dutton and Wentworth, 1839), 10.
42. SGH, "Laura Bridgman," *Barnard's American Journal of Education* (December 1857): 390.
43. Mary Swift Lamson, *Life and Education of Laura Dewey Bridgman: The Deaf, Dumb, and Blind Girl* (Boston: Houghton Mifflin: 1878), 87.
44. Richards and Elliott, *JWH*, I:92.
45. Trent, 97.

46. Gitter, 4.
47. Ibid., 113.
48. Ibid., 77.
49. Photograph in Ernest Freeberg, *The Education of Laura Bridgman* (Cambridge: Harvard University Press, 2001), 216.
50. Gitter, 118, and SGH, *Tenth Annual Report of the Trustees of the Perkins Institution and Massachusetts Asylum for the Blind*, 29.
51. Gitter, 119, and SGH, *Ninth Annual Report of the Trustees of the Perkins Institution and Massachusetts Asylum for the Blind*, 37–38.
52. Maud Howe Elliott and Florence Howe Hall, *Laura Bridgman, Dr. Howe's Famous Pupil and What He Taught Her* (Boston: Little, Brown, and Company, 1904), 79.
53. Ibid., 86.
54. *New York Times* (May 18, 1883), in *Philosophies of Sex: Critical Essays on The Hermaphrodite*, ed. Renée Bergland and Gary Williams (Columbus: Ohio State University Press, 2012), 173. Hereafter abbreviated as *Philosophies of Sex*.
55. Freeberg, *The Education of Laura Bridgman*, 26.
56. Howe, I:106–107.
57. Gary Williams, *Hungry Heart: The Literary Emergence of Julia Ward Howe* (Amherst: University of Masschusetts Press, 1999), 148. Hereafter abbreviated as *Hungry Heart.*
58. Gitter, 148.
59. Howe, II:343.

CHAPTER THREE: THE HERO AND THE BELLE

1. Longfellow, *Letters*, II:383.
2. Tharp, 49–50.
3. Ibid., 88.
4. Cornelius Felton to SW, July 17, 1842, in *Uncle Sam Ward*, 353.
5. *Hungry Heart*, 222, n. 45.

6. Tharp, 89.
7. JWH to AW and LW, MS Am 2119, 1842, 392.
8. SGH to SW, in *Hungry Heart*, 201, 223, n. 49.
9. SGH to SW, MS Am 2119, February 21, 1843 (870).
10. Tharp, 91.
11. JWH to AW and LW, MS Am 2119, 1843 (394).
12. SGH to Henry Wadsworth Longfellow, MS Am 2119, April 1843 (1171).
13. SW to John Ward, February 22, 1843, in *Uncle Sam Ward*, 376.
14. *Hungry Heart*, 49.
15. Longfellow, *Letters*, II:318.
16. Tharp, 93.
17. April 7, 1843, quoted in *Hungry Heart*, 223–24, n. 50.
18. February 3, 1843, in *Uncle Sam Ward*, 372.
19. Tharp, 93.
20. Clifford, 65.
21. "Correspondence between SGH and JWH," YHPCCL, record group 20, in Ziegler, 176, n. 1.
22. *Hungry Heart*, 39.
23. SGH to SW, MS Am 2119, February 3, 1843 (1139).
24. Ziegler, 27.
25. Clifford, 62.
26. Ziegler, 28.
27. JWH to Eliza Francis, MS Am 2119, February 27, 1843 (466).
28. Richards and Elliott, *JWH*, I:79.
29. Ibid., 79–80.
30. *Rem.*, 89.
31. JWH to LW, MS Am 2119, May 12, 1843 (381).
32. *Rem.*, 91–92.
33. *Hungry Heart*, 40.
34. Ibid., 63.
35. *Rem.*, 100.

36. Ibid., 106–107.
37. Ibid., 93.
38. Richards, *SGH*, 113.
39. JWH to LW, 1843, in Clifford, 70.
40. Richards and Elliott, *JWH*, I:84.
41. *Rem.*, 96.
42. JWH Scrapbook, in Grant, 61.
43. Richards and Elliott, *JWH*, I:92–93.
44. *Rem.*, 116.
45. Judith W. Page, *Wordsworth and the Cultivation of Women* (Berkeley: University of California Press, 1994), 149.
46. Richards and Elliott, *JWH*, I:86.
47. *Hungry Heart*, 66.
48. Francis Marion Ward to LW, September 19, 1843, in Robert L. Gale, *Thomas Crawford: American Sculptor* (Pittsburgh: University of Pittsburgh Press, 1964), 207, n. 25. Hereafter cited as Gale.
49. SGH to Charles Sumner, MS Am 2119, October 9, 1843 (1189).
50. Ibid., November 8, 1843 (1190).
51. Grant, 63; *Rem.*, 123–27.
52. JWH to John Ward, December 13, 1843, in Clifford, 77.
53. *Rem.*, 131.
54. Diary, 1843, in *Hermaphrodite*, xi.
55. *Rem.*, 161.
56. Dean Grodzins, *American Heretic: Theodore Parker and Transcendentalism* (Chapel Hill: University of North Carolina Press, 2002), 387. Hereafter abbreviated as Grodzins.
57. *Rem.*, 161.
58. Ibid., 160, 162.
59. Grodzins, 399.
60. Ibid., 401.
61. SGH to Charles Sumner, MS Am 2119, March 16, 1844 (1201).

62. *Rem.*, 134.
63. Gale, 41.
64. Mark Bostridge, *Florence Nightingale* (London: Penguin, 2008), 86–87.
65. Ibid., 86.
66. Richards and Elliott, *JWH*, I:98.
67. *Rem.*, 142.
68. Richards and Elliott, *JWH*, 98.

CHAPTER FOUR: MARRIAGE AND MATERNITY

1. SGH to Charles Sumner, MS Am 2119, September 11, 1844 (920).
2. *Rem.*, 150–51.
3. Richards and Elliott, *JWH*, I:103.
4. Richards, *SGH*, 123–24.
5. Richards and Elliott, *JWH*, I:103–4.
6. May 30, 1846, in Trent, 166.
7. *Rem.*, 150; Richards and Elliott, *JWH*, I:129.
8. Richards and Elliott, *JWH*, I:106, 107.
9. Clifford, 88.
10. JWH to LWC, MS Am 2119, December 1845 (334); Richards and Elliott, *JWH*, I:113.
11. Schwartz, 148.
12. Ibid., 149.
13. *Rem.*, 175.
14. Grant, 72.
15. Clifford, 89.
16. Gitter, 154, 155.
17. Richards and Elliott, *JWH*, I:169.
18. Gitter, 160.
19. Maud Howe Elliott and Florence Howe Hall, *Laura Bridgman: Dr. Howe's Famous Pupil and What He Taught Her* (Boston: Little,

Brown and Company, 1904), 178. Hereafter abbreviated as Elliott and Hall, *Laura Bridgman*.

20. JWH to LWC, MS Am 2119, August 7, 1845 (506).
21. Ibid., December 15, 1845 (508).
22. Ibid.; Richards and Elliott, *JWH*, I:115–116.
23. JWH to LWC, MS Am 2119, January 31, 1846 (519).
24. Ibid., February 15, 1846 (520).
25. JWH to SGH, MS Am 2119, 1846 (376).
26. Phyllis Rose, *Parallel Lives: Five Victorian Marriages* (New York: Vintage, 1984), 7–9.
27. Richards and Elliott, *JWH*, I:151.
28. *Rem.*, 152.
29. Laura E. Richards, *Stepping Westward* (New York and London: D. Appleton & Company, 1931), 10. Hereafter abbreviated as *Stepping Westward*.
30. Richards, *SGH*, 182.
31. Adolph Mailliard had been a secretary to Prince Joseph Bonaparte in France and executor of his estate. Joseph built a castle in Bordentown, New Jersey, and eventually returned to France. See Henry Steele Commager, "The Story of a Magnificent Family," *New York Times Book Review*, September 30, 1956.
32. Tharp, 145.
33. SGH to Horace Mann, dated July 30, 1840, in Houghton, but Trent thinks probably 1846.
34. Richards, *SGH*, 199.
35. JWH to LWC, MS Am 2119, September 20, 1846 (526).
36. Richards, *SGH*, 180.
37. JWH Scrapbook 32, in Grant, 80.
38. Clifford, 88.
39. Richards and Elliott, *JWH*, I:122.
40. JWH to LWC, MS Am 2119, January 31, 1847 (535).
41. JWH to AWM, in Clifford, 93.

42. JWH to LWC, in Clifford, 93.
43. JWH to LWC, MS Am 2119, May 15, 1847 (537).
44. Ibid., May 17, 1847, in Clifford, 94.
45. Ibid., June 15, 1847, in Grant, 81.
46. *Rem.*, 60.
47. JWH to LWC, MS Am 2119, September 20, 1847 (533).
48. Ibid.
49. Edward Wagenknacht, ed., *Mrs. Longfellow: Selected Letters and Journals of Fanny Appleton Longfellow* (New York and London: Longman's, Green and Co., 1956), 130.
50. SGH to LWC, MS Am 2119, April 5, 1848 (1024).
51. Ibid.
52. JWH to LWC, MS Am 2119, April 18, 1848 (555).
53. *Rem.*, 131.
54. Fanny Longfellow, April 12, 1848.
55. JWH to AWM, October 12, 1848, in *Hungry Heart*, 112.
56. JWH to LWC, MS Am 2119, November 19, 1848.
57. *Rem.*, 131.
58. Renée Bergland and Gary Williams, introduction to *Philosophies of Sex: Critical Essays on the Hermaphrodite*, ed. Bergland and Williams (Columbus: Ohio State University Press, 2012). Book hereafter abbreviated as *Philosophies of Sex.*
59. *Hermaphrodite*, 3. Page numbers in parentheses in the text.
60. Gary Williams, who edited the manuscripts of *The Hermaphrodite*, is the premier critic and scholar of this difficult text. See also the essays in *Philosophies of Sex.*
61. Howe's letters give no indication of what she was reading during these childbearing years, or how she obtained books, but the 1840s were a major literary decade for English fiction. In the summer of 1848, *Jane Eyre* was such a rage in the United States that literary observers described a "Jane Eyre fever" that struck the female members of every family. Reprinted by at least six American publishers,

in the age before international copyright law, and selling for a mere twenty-five cents, about a fifth of the price of an American book, it was read by American women of all ages, classes, and races, from millgirls in Lowell to plantation heiresses in the South. On July 29, Florence Nightingale wrote to Julia, asking, "But have you read *Jane Eyre*? There are some authors of fiction, like Shakespeare, who, like sculptors, set the human form before you, perfect in every part, behind, before, on either side, not a point of view is wanting—it needs but the colouring and breath of our own actual life. . . . Now *Jane Eyre* seems to me to be real life—we know her—we have lived with her, we shall meet her again. It has all the faults of real life—but real and living it is." (Julia Ward Howe Collection, Perkins School for the Blind, Series 1, Box 1). Laura Howe read *Jane Eyre* as a girl, but Julia did not read it until 1899.

62. *Hungry Heart*, 113.
63. March 1850, in Grant, 8.

CHAPTER FIVE: ROME AGAIN, HOME AGAIN

1. Tharp, 168.
2. JWH to SGH, in Ziegler, 72.
3. JWH to MHE, in Ziegler, 185, n. 35.
4. Theodore Parker to JWH, September 2, 1850, in *Hungry Heart*, 123, 248.
5. George Egon Hatvary, *Horace Binney Wallace* (Boston: Twayne Publishers, 1977), 24. Hereafter abbreviated as Hatvary.
6. Ibid., 25.
7. JWH, *From the Oak to the Olive: A Plain Record of a Pleasant Journey* (Boston: Lee and Shepard, 1868), 66.
8. AWM to SGH, in *Hungry Heart*, 117, 245.
9. JWH to LWC, October 28, 1851, in *Hungry Heart*, 117, 245.
10. *From the Oak to the Olive*, 45.

11. *Rem.*, 204.
12. JWH to AWM, in Ziegler, 76.
13. Tharp, 173–74.
14. Ibid.
15. JWH to AWM, MS Am 2119, December 17, 1851.
16. SGH to Charles Sumner, November 1851, in Schwartz, 175.
17. Ibid., December 6, 1851, in *Hungry Heart*, 130.
18. Schwartz, 182. Harold Schwartz agreed: "The tone of its articles was exceedingly offensive. There was no depth of vulgarity and vituperation to which its writers would not descend to pillory the opposition."
19. Frederick L. Mulhauser, ed., *Correspondence of Arthur Hugh Clough* (Oxford: Clarendon Press, 1957), 2:356.
20. *Two Noble Lives*, 53.
21. Ziegler, 76.
22. JWH to AWM, in *Hungry Heart*, 250, n. 56.
23. Hatvary, 30–31.
24. Tharp, 174.
25. JWH to AWM, November 8, 1852, in Grant, 101.
26. Julia's unsent letter to Horace Binney Wallace, in the Houghton Library, is quoted in two different places, with different gaps. Hatvary, 33–34, and G. E. Hatvary, "Horace Binney Wallace: A Study in Self-Destruction," *Princeton University Library Chronicle* 25 (Winter 1964): 148–49.
27. Hatvary, 32.
28. JWH to AWM, MS Am 2119, December 8, 1853 (618).
29. JWH to LWC, MS Am 2119, February 18, 1853 (612).
30. Bill from Mme Du Wavran, Paris, MS Am 2119, January 22, 1853 (1108).
31. JWH to Auguste Comte, MS Am 2119, February 15, 1853 (613). Translation by English Showalter.
32. JWH to LWC, MS Am 2119, February 18, 1853 (612).

33. JWH to AWM, MS Am 2119, February 25, 1853 (615).
34. James T. Fields to SGH, Chapin Library of Rare Books, Williams College, May 5, 1853, in *Hungry Heart*, 252, n. 7.
35. JWH to AWM, MS Am 2119, December 8, 1853 (618).
36. Ibid.

CHAPTER SIX: *PASSION-FLOWERS*

1. JWH to AWC, MS Am 2119, December 29, 1853 (620).
2. Renée Bergland, *Maria Mitchell and the Sexing of Science* (Boston: Beacon Press, 2008), 61.
3. Richards and Elliott, *JWH*, I:105.
4. JWH to AWC, MS Am 2119, December 29, 1853 (620).
5. *Rem.*, 436.
6. Longfellow Journals, December 24, 1853, in *Hungry Heart*, 253, n. 10.
7. Ibid., December 28, 1853, in *Hungry Heart*, 253.
8. JWH to AWC, MS Am 2119, December 29, 1853 (620).
9. Richards and Elliott, *JWH*, I:140.
10. Ibid., 152.
11. See James D. Wallace, "Hawthorne and the Scribbling Women Reconsidered," *American Literature* 62 (1990): 218.
12. Letter to William D. Ticknor, 1857, *Centenary Edition of the Works of Nathaniel Hawthorne: The Letters, 1857–1864* (Columbus: Ohio State University Press, 1987), XVIII:53.
13. Elizabeth Barrett Browning to Mary Russell Mitford, June 6, 1854, in *Letters of Elizabeth Barrett Browning*, ed. Frederic G. Kenyon (London: Smith, Elder & Co, 1895), II:166.
14. *Hungry Heart*, 252.
15. Tharp, 230.
16. Joel Myerson and Daniel Shealy, eds., *The Journals of Louisa May Alcott* (Athens: University of Georgia Press, 1997), 127.

17. JWH to Edward and Ellen Twisleton, MS Am 2119, April 17, 1854, 164.
18. *Hungry Heart*, 136.
19. *Putnam's* 3, February 1854, 224.
20. *Journal of Music*, January 11, 1854, 124–25. Unsigned, attribution in *Hungry Heart*, 261, n. 3.
21. Nathaniel Parker Willis to SGH, MS Am 2119, January 10, 1854 (2339).
22. SGH to Charles Sumner, MS Am 2119, January 16, 1854 (1425); Charles Sumner to SGH, January 18, 1854, in *Hungry Heart*, 253, n. 10.
23. JWH to AWM, MS Am 2119, February 1854 (621).
24. Ziegler, 83. Valarie Ziegler was the first scholar to notice the changes in the second and third editions.
25. SGH to JWH, "Correspondence between SGH and JWH," YHPCCL, in Ziegler, 83.
26. JWH to LWC, MS Am 2119, begun July 23, 1854, continued November 4, 1854 (384).
27. JWH to AWM, MS Am 2119, February 2, 1848 (553).
28. *Hungry Heart*, 175.
29. JWH to AWM, MS Am 2119, June 19, 1854 (390).
30. Ibid.
31. Theodore Parker to William Silsbee, 1839, in Grodzins, 95.
32. Renehan, 45.
33. *Stepping Westward*, 23.
34. Maud Howe Elliott, *Three Generations* (Boston: Little, Brown and Company, 1923), 4–5. Hereafter abbreviated as *Three Generations*.
35. JWH to LWC, MS Am 2119, November 4, 1854.
36. JWH to AWM, MS Am 2119, November 8, 1854 (629).
37. Journal, November 9, 1867.

38. Clifford, 118–19.
39. Mary H. Grant, "Meeting the Hermaphrodite," in *Philosophies of Sex*, 21.
40. Ziegler, 78.
41. *Rem.*, 229.
42. *Hungry Heart*, 134, 171.
43. Cheryl Walker, *American Women Poets of the 19th Century: An Anthology* (New Brunswick, NJ: Rutgers University Press, 1992), xli.
44. David S. Reynolds, *Walt Whitman's America: A Cultural Biography* (New York: Vintage, 1996), 44–45. Hereafter abbreviated as Reynolds.
45. Ibid., 285.
46. See Charles C. Calhoun's description of Longfellow's beard in *Longfellow: A Rediscovered Life* (Boston: Beacon Press, 2004), 221–22.
47. Reynolds, 340. Reynolds says that Whitman exaggerated the failure of the first edition of *Leaves of Grass*. It may have sold a few hundred copies.
48. Ibid., 342.
49. Elliott and Hall, *Laura Bridgman*, 267.
50. JWH to AWM, MS Am 2119, December 27, 1854 (630).

CHAPTER SEVEN: THE SECRET SIX

1. Louisa May Alcott to Anna Alcott, November 6, 1856, in Harriet Reiser, *Louisa May Alcott* (New York: Macmillan, 2009), 169.
2. Gale, 172–73.
3. *Rem.*, 68.
4. Ibid., 69.
5. Schwartz, 202.
6. David Herbert Donald, *Charles Sumner and the Coming of the Civil*

War (Napierville, IL: Sourcebooks, 2009), vii. Hereafter abbreviated as Donald, *Coming*.

7. Ibid., 285; David S. Reynolds, *John Brown, Abolitionist* (New York: Vintage, 2006), 161. Latter hereafter abbreviated as Reynolds, *John Brown*.
8. C. E. Brown-Séquard, "Note on the effects produced on man by subcutaneous injections of a liquid obtained from the testicles of animals," *Lancet* (1889), 2:105–107.
9. Andrea J. Cussins, et al., "Brown-Séquard revisited: a lesson from history on the placebo effect of androgen treatment," *Medical Journal of Australia* 177, no. 11 (2002): 678–79.
10. June 24, 1858, in Donald, *Coming*, 338.
11. Donald, *Coming*, 341.
12. Edward L. Pierce, *Memoirs and Letters of Charles Sumner,* vol. 3 (Boston: Roberts Brothers, 1893), 564.
13. Renehan, 146.
14. Dorothy Mermin, *Elizabeth Barrett Browning: The Origins of a New Poetry* (Chicago: University of Chicago Press, 1989), 276, n. 9.
15. Gale, 101.
16. George Curtis, "American Literature and Reprints," *Putnam's* 50, February 1857, 219.
17. "Literary Notices," *Harper's New Monthly Magazine* 14, February 1857, 408.
18. *New York Times*, March 30, 1857.
19. Arthur Hobson Quinn, *A History of the American Drama from the Beginning to the Civil War* (New York: F. S. Crofts, 1944), 367.
20. Zoe Detsi, "Seduction, Revenge, and Suicide: Julia Ward Howe's 'Lenora: or, the World's Own,'" *New England Theater Journal* 7, 1996, 4.
21. Ednah D. Cheney, *Louisa May Alcott: Life, Letters, and Journals* (New York: Gramercy Books, 1995), 65.
22. JWH to AWM, MS Am 2119, July 13, 1857 (644).

23. Wagenknacht, *Letters of Mrs. Longfellow*, 209.
24. Richards and Elliott, *JWH*, I:203.
25. Ibid., 204–5.
26. Journal, May 1907.
27. Julia Ward Howe, *Memoir of Dr. Samuel Gridley Howe* (Boston: Albert J. Wright, 1876), 45.
28. *Rem.*, 254.
29. Renehan, 3.
30. JWH to AWM, MS Am 2119, May 26, 1857 (643).
31. Theodore Parker to JWH, July 29, 1857, in Dean Grodzins, *"Dear Chev . . . O, Julia": A Critical Edition of the Theodore Parker Letters in the Howe Papers at the Chapin Library* (Williamstown, MA: Williams College, 1983), 110–12; cited in *Hungry Heart*, 267, n. 53.
32. JWH to AWM, MS Am 2119, October 1, 1857 (646).
33. JWH to AWM, n.d., in Grant, 140.
34. Renehan, 183.
35. Richards and Elliott, *JWH*, I:172.
36. Julia Ward Howe, *A Trip to Cuba* (Boston: Ticknor and Fields, 1860), 81.
37. SGH to Theodore Parker, March 25, 1860, in Trent, 212.
38. JWH, *A Trip to Cuba*, 48, 49.
39. Trent, 212.
40. Ziegler, 92.
41. Ralph Waldo Emerson, "Courage," in Reynolds, *John Brown*, 366.
42. Tony Horwitz, *Midnight Rising: John Brown and the Raid That Started the Civil War* (New York: Henry Holt, 2011), 62.
43. *Rem.*, 114.
44. JWH to AWM, November 6, 1859, in Grant, 133.
45. Reynolds, *John Brown*, 343.
46. Ibid.
47. JWH to SGH, November 21, 1859, in Ziegler, 189, n. 99.
48. SGH to JWH, November 24, 1859, in Ziegler, 90–91.

49. JWH to AWM, December 22, 1859, in Ziegler, 189, n. 99.
50. Richards and Elliott, *JWH*, I:180.

CHAPTER EIGHT: THE CIVIL WAR

1. *Rem.*, 273–74.
2. Nathaniel Hawthorne, "Chiefly about War Matters," *Atlantic Monthly* 10, July 1862, 59. See also Richard Wallace Carr and Marie Pinak Carr, *The Willard Hotel: An Illustrated History* (Washington, DC: Dicmar Publishing, n.d.).
3. *Rem.*, 270.
4. Tharp, 242.
5. Richards and Elliott, *JWH*, I:190.
6. *Rem.*, 272.
7. Ibid., 274–75.
8. Clifford, 146–47.
9. Richards, *SGH*, 224.
10. *The Century* V, August 1887.
11. Richards and Elliott, *JWH*, I:190.
12. Reynolds, *John Brown*, 4–5.
13. Journal, May 19, 1863.
14. SGH to JWH, November 29, 1863, in Ziegler, 101.
15. Mary Loeffelholz, *From School to Salon: Reading Nineteenth-Century American Women's Poetry* (Princeton University Press, 2004), 173, 259.
16. Judith A. Roman, *Annie Adams Fields: The Spirit of Charles Street* (Bloomington: Indiana University Press, 1990), 32–34.
17. Journal, January 20, 1864.
18. Ibid., May 11, 1864.
19. Tharp, 264.
20. Richards and Elliott, *JWH*, I:216.
21. Journal, March 12, 1865.

22. Richards and Elliott, *JWH*, I:220, and Florence Howe Hall, *Memories Grave and Gay* (New York: Harper and Brothers, 1918), 27.
23. Richards and Elliott, *JWH*, I:221.
24. Journal, April 23, 1865. Valarie Ziegler says that JWH stuck to her plans and spoke at the prison, but subsequent journal entries indicate that she did not. On May 28, 1882, for example, she wrote: "I think I could preach to the prisoners as I once tried to do years ago when dear Chev found the idea so intolerable that I had to give it up."
25. Ziegler, 2.
26. Journal, April 25, 1865.
27. *Rem.*, 258.
28. Richards and Elliott, *JWH*, I:233.
29. Journal, December 31, 1865.
30. Ibid., June 5, 1865.
31. Richards and Elliott, *JWH*, I:230.
32. Ibid., 244.
33. Journal, April 22, 1865.
34. Richards and Elliott, *JWH*, I:246–48.
35. JWH, Notebook 9, MS Am 2214 (32), in Trent, 255–56.
36. SGH to Charles Sumner, June 5, 1866, in Schwartz, 281–82.
37. Richards and Elliott, *JWH*, I:259.
38. Richards, *SGH*, I:261.
39. Journal, January 24, 1867.
40. Ibid., May 1, 1867.
41. "Mrs. Howe's Later Lyrics," *North American Review* 104, April 1867, 644–45.
42. Journal, October 30, 1867.
43. Ibid., November 9, 1867.
44. Richards and Elliott, *JWH*, I:289.
45. Florence Marion Howe Hall, *Julia Ward Howe and the Woman Suffrage Movement* (Boston: Dana Estes and Company, 2009), 39.

46. SGH to JWH, MS Am 1715, vol. 4, October 2, 1868, in Trent, 252–53.

CHAPTER NINE: A NEW WORLD

1. *Rem.*, 372–73.
2. Ibid., 72–73.
3. Ibid., 379.
4. "Speech on Equal Rights," February 12, 1906, in Hall, *Julia Ward Howe and the Woman Suffrage Movement*, 224.
5. *Rem.*, 374–75.
6. "Debt to Pioneers," 1904, Julia Ward Howe Collection, Schlesinger Library, in Grant, 195.
7. See Grant, chapter 12, for an excellent analysis of Howe's conversion.
8. Richards and Elliott, *JWH*, II: 311.
9. *Three Generations*, 225.
10. New York, May 12–14, 1869, in *The Concise History of Woman Suffrage*, ed. Mary Jo and Paul Buhle (Urbana: University of Illinois Press, 1978), 259.
11. JWH, *Woman's Journal*, January 8, 1870.
12. *Rem.*, 372. Mary and her husband were Boston socialites, and JWH and Mary Ward Dorr fell out of touch in the 1870s. As Howe remembered in her old age, "we were never other than friends, but in our maturer lives our tastes and associations diverged widely. She became a spiritualist and interested herself a good deal in some of the more fashionable set. I became a convert to suffrage and worker for and with women, in a way not so acceptable to fashion. I felt her neglect somewhat and she seemed to feel that I neglected her." Journal, February 5, 1903. Mary Dorr told Laura Richards, "I have been reading your mother's old letters. They were very clever. I burned them" (*Uncle Sam Ward*, 209).

13. Richards and Elliott, *JWH*, I:381.
14. Wendy Hamand Venet, *A Strong-minded Woman: The Life of Mary A. Livermore* (Amherst: University of Massachusetts Press, 2005), 173. Hereafter abbreviated as Venet.
15. Richards and Elliott, *JWH*, I:380.
16. February 7, 1870, quoted in Clifford, 181. A Vermonter, Clifford was an expert on the suffrage campaign. See Deborah P. Clifford, "An Invasion of Strong-Minded Women: The Newspapers and the Woman Suffrage Campaign in Vermont in 1870," *Vermont History* 43 (1975): 1–19; and Marilyn S. Blackwell, "Remembering Deborah Pickman Clifford," *Vermont History* 77 (Winter/Spring 2009): 3–5.
17. *Rem.*, 390.
18. Venet, 174–75.
19. Richards and Elliott, *JWH*, I:389.
20. *Rem.*, 376.
21. "Col. Higginson on Mrs. Howe," Howe Collection, vol. 4, Schlesinger Library, in Grant, 198.
22. SGH to LHR, August 25, 1874, in Ziegler, 198, n. 2.
23. Journal, June 17, 1871.
24. *Rem.*, 328.
25. Mother's Day was celebrated in a few states in the nineteenth century; in 1912 the term was trademarked by Anna Jarvis as a commercial and sentimental holiday. In 1914, President Woodrow Wilson made it a national holiday celebrated on the second Sunday of May.
26. Charles Sumner to SGH, August 3, 1871, in Trent, 262.
27. SGH to Andrew White, August 8, 1872, White Papers, Cornell, quoted in Schwartz, 311.
28. SGH to Henry B. Blackwell, September 6, 1874, in Trent, 264.
29. "My experiences in Santo Domingo," Howe Papers at Perkins, in Schwartz, 319.

30. Tharp, 308.
31. Journal, June 29, 1872.
32. Ibid., October 6, 1872.
33. Elizabeth Barrett Browning to Sophie Eckley, MS in New York Public Library, quoted in *Dearest Isa: Robert Browning's Letters to Isabella Blagden*, ed. Edward C. McAleer (Austin: University of Texas Press, 1951), 30.
34. Journal, October 5, 1872.
35. Ibid., October 9, 1872.
36. Richards and Elliott, *JWH*, II:374.
37. Journal, October 17, 1872.
38. Ibid., December 16, 1872.
39. Kimberly Ann Hamlin, "Beyond Adam's Rib: How Darwinian evolutionary theory redefined gender and influenced American feminist thought 1870–1920," PhD diss., University of Texas at Austin, 2009, 29.
40. Hamlin, "Beyond Adam's Rib," 31. Clarke's work was published in 1873 in Boston by Houghton, Mifflin.
41. Julia Ward Howe, ed., *Sex in Education: A Reply to Dr. E. H. Clarke's "Sex in Education"* (Boston: Roberts Brothers, 1874), 18.
42. Ibid., 20.
43. Journal, March 31, 1874.
44. Francis Bird to SGH, April 1, 1874, in Schwartz, 330–31.
45. SGH to Francis Bird, August 12, 1874, in Schwartz, 331.
46. SGH to George Finlay, August 13, 1874, in Trent, 266.
47. August 18, 1874, in Clifford, 197.
48. Tharp, 312.
49. SGH, *Forty-third Annual Report of the Trustees of the Perkins Institute*, 96.
50. Journal, December 23, 1874.
51. Ibid., January 16, 1875.
52. Ibid., April 30, 1875.

53. Ibid., May 19, 1875.
54. Ibid., July 26, 1875.
55. Ibid., August 13, 1875.
56. Ibid., November 23, 1875; December 7, 1875.
57. Ibid., December 8, 1875.
58. Ibid., December 9, 1875.
59. JWH to AWM, November 6, 1859, in Tharp, 316.
60. Journal, December 9, 1875.
61. Elliott and Hall, *Laura Bridgman*, 309–10.
62. February 6, 1876, in Gitter, 270.
63. Journal, January 10, 1876.
64. Ibid., July 10, 1876.
65. Ibid., April 30, 1876.
66. Ibid., December 31, 1877.
67. *Three Generations*, 139.
68. Ibid., 140.
69. Ibid., 141.
70. Grinnell, 40.
71. Ziegler, 129.
72. MHE to LHR, May 1878, YHPCCL, Grinnell, 37–38.

CHAPTER TEN: THE WOMAN'S DEPARTMENT

1. Kathryn Allamong Jacob, *King of the Lobby: The Life and Times of Sam Ward* (Baltimore: Johns Hopkins University Press, 2010), 140.
2. Ibid., 143.
3. Journal, January 29, 1882.
4. See David M. Friedman, *Wilde in America: Oscar Wilde and the Invention of Modern Celebrity* (New York and London: W. W. Norton, 2014). This account by Alice Carrie Williams may be a confabulation, but it certainly combines all the elements of Wilde's performance in Boston.

5. Richards and Elliott, *JWH*, II:72.
6. George Henschel, *Musings and Memories of a Musician* (New York: Macmillan, 1919), 256–58.
7. Louisa Hall Tharp, *Mrs. Jack: A Biography of Isabella Stewart Gardner* (New York: Congdon & Weed, 1965), 61, 68. Hereafter abbreviated as Tharp, *Mrs. Jack*.
8. JWH to MHE, April 7, 1883, YHPCCL, Coll. 2085, Record Group 16, in Nancy Whipple Grinnell, *Carrying the Torch: Maud Howe Elliott and the American Renaissance* (Hanover and London: University Press of New England, 2014), 55. Book abbreviated hereafter as Grinnell.
9. Tharp, *Mrs. Jack*, 350–51.
10. Journal, February 10, 1888.
11. *Our Famous Women: An Authorized Record of Their Lives and Deeds* (Freeport, NY: Books for Libraries Press, 1883).
12. JWH to SW, March 28, 1883, in Richards and Elliott, *JWH*, II:83.
13. Gary Williams, "Julia Ward Howe's (Auto)biography of Margaret Fuller," www.webpages.uidaho.edu/jgw/HoweFuller.htm.
14. Julia Ward Howe, *Margaret Fuller (Marchesa Ossoli)* (Boston: Roberts Brothers, 1883), 137, 278.
15. Grinnell, 49.
16. LHR to MHE, August 1883, YHPCCL, Coll. 2085, Record Group 14, in Grinnell, 51.
17. Grinnell, 49.
18. "The change in the position of women," in Florence Howe Hall, ed., *Julia Ward Howe and the Woman Suffrage Movement* (Boston: Dana Estes and Company 1913), 141–42.
19. JWH to SW, December 15, 1883, in Richards and Elliott, *JWH*, II:87.
20. Richards and Elliott, *JWH*, II:96.
21. *Picayune*, November 23, 1884.

22. Richards and Elliott, *JWH*, II:101–102.
23. Ibid., 103.
24. Ibid., 102.
25. Journal, December 27, 1884.
26. *Picayune*, January 7, 1885.
27. I am indebted to Miki Pfeffer's splendid *Southern Ladies and Suffragists: Julia Ward Howe and Women's Rights at the 1884 New Orleans World's Fair* (University Press of Mississippi, 2014), for my description of the Exposition.
28. *Picayune*, April 5, 1885.
29. Pfeffer, *Southern Ladies*, 201.
30. *Picayune*, May 31, 1885.
31. Richards and Elliott, *JWH*, II:111–12.
32. JWH to MHE, March 5, 1886, in Ziegler, 136–37.
33. Journal, March 24, 1886.
34. Maud Howe Elliott, *This Was My Newport* (Cambridge: The Mythology Company, 1944), 93–95; Ziegler, 141.
35. *Rem.*, 440.
36. Elliott and Hall, *Laura Bridgman*, 314.
37. Journal, June 24, 1886.
38. Richards and Elliott, *JWH*, II:128–29.
39. Journal, November 26, 1886.
40. Tharp, 352.
41. Grinnell, 59.
42. John Lowell Gardner Jr. to George Gardner, Massachusetts Historical Society, Gardner Family Papers, Series 1, F2, in Grinnell, 60.
43. Grinnell, 61.
44. Journal, Thursday, March 31, 1887.
45. Gitter, 282; Helen Keller, *Midstream: My Later Life* (Garden City, NY: Doubleday Doran, 1929), 247.
46. Gitter, 283–84.

47. *Three Generations*, 228.
48. Clifford, 209.
49. Tharp, 355.
50. Richards and Elliott, *JWH*, II:150.
51. Ziegler, 156–57.
52. LHR to AWM, December 8, 1890, in Ziegler, 129.
53. MHE to JWH, July 11, 1894, YHPCCL, Coll. 20815, Record Group 15A, F3, in Grinnell, 100.
54. JWH to LHR, June 21, 1891, in Ziegler, 129.
55. Ibid., MS Am 2119, August 21, 1896 (896).
56. Journal, December 1, 1897.
57. Ibid., January 3, 1898.
58. See Grinnell, 101–102. When it was finally finished and acclaimed in March 1901, Boston was scandalized to recognize that Maud had been the model for an allegorical figure of "The Hours," who was bare-breasted and winged. Chev was the imagined model for "Father Time."
59. *Three Generations*, 284.
60. Richards and Elliott, *JWH*, II:239, 251.
61. Journal, January 17, 1898.
62. Ibid., March 31, 1898.
63. Tharp, 354.
64. *Three Generations*, 289.
65. Henry James also met Henrik Andersen at one of Maud's parties at the palazzo and became deeply attracted and attached to him. Although James was thirty years older, they corresponded until his death. James's letters were overflowing with affection and tender desire.
66. *Three Generations*, 288.
67. May 16, 1899, in Henry James, *Notebooks*; www.henryjames.org.uk /beldh/home.htm.
68. *Rem.*, 444.

CHAPTER ELEVEN: THE ELEVENTH HOUR

1. Clifford, 246.
2. Journal, January 20, 1903.
3. "Boston Warmed Up," *Philadelphia Press*, May 1899, in Ziegler, 155.
4. John Jay Chapman, "Julia Ward Howe," *Memories and Milestones* (New York: Moffatt, Yard and Company, 1915), 238, 239.
5. Journal, February 11, 1902.
6. JWH to AWM, July 30, 1883, in Ziegler, 157.
7. Richards and Elliott, *JWH*, II:283.
8. Journal, February 23, 1909.
9. Ibid., December 25, 1900.
10. Ibid., March 12, 1900.
11. Richards and Elliott, *JWH*, II:337.
12. Ibid., 275.
13. Journal, April 25, 1900.
14. Richards and Elliott, *JWH*, II:377–78.
15. Ibid., 350.
16. Journal, February 3, 1903.
17. LHR to MHE, April 23, 1908, Folder 42, Yellow House Papers, Gardiner Public Library, Gardiner, Maine, in Ziegler, 131.
18. Journal, April 17, May 15, 31, 1903.
19. Clipping, Scrapbook Five, Schlesinger Library, 1903, cited in Paul S. Boyer, "Julia Ward Howe," *Notable American Women 1607–1950* (Cambridge: Harvard University Press, 1971), II:229.
20. Journal, November 12, 1904.
21. Ibid., June 30, 1904.
22. "Mrs. Howe's Reply," Richards and Elliott, *JWH*, II:336.
23. Journal, August 31, 1906.
24. Ibid., August 14, September 14, 21, 1906.
25. Ibid., May 12, 1910.

26. Ibid., July 9, 1909.
27. Nathan Haskell Dole, "Julia Ward Howe and Her Talented Family," *Muncy's Magazine* XLII, February 1910, 613, 619.
28. *Eleventh Hour*, 6.
29. Ibid., 27–28.
30. Maud Howe Elliott, "Notes on the Last Summer of JWH's Life," Record Group 18, YHPCCL, in Ziegler, 156.
31. *Eleventh Hour*, 7.
32. Chapman, "Julia Ward Howe," 240.
33. William H. Lewis, "Address," *Memorial Exercises in Honor of Julia Ward Howe* (Boston: City of Boston Printing Department, 1911), 23–24.
34. "The Listener," *Boston Transcript*, August 11, 1917.
35. [S. E. Lane], *Boston Transcript*, September 12, 1917.
36. Maud Howe Elliott, *This Was My Newport*, 64. Chev did get some attention in popular culture. In 1952, Hedda Hopper reported that Darryl Zanuck was planning a movie about his Greek adventures (Trent, 4). It was never made, but on July 15, 1956, Kevin McCarthy played Chev in an episode of the TV series *Telephone Time*. Beverly Washburn was Laura Bridgman.
37. *New York Times*, August 15, 1908.
38. Wendy Dasler Johnson, "Julia Ward Howe," *Encyclopedia of American Poets: The 19th Century*, ed. Eric L. Haralson (Chicago and London: Fitzroy Dearborn Publishers, 1998), 222.
39. Richards and Elliott, *JWH*, II:383.

ACKNOWLEDGMENTS

The Howe Family Archive at the Houghton Library of Harvard University is the starting point for researching Julia Ward Howe. My thanks to Rachel Howarth and Susan Halpert at the Houghton Library, and Michelle Gachette at the Lamont Library, who made special arrangements for me to read the Howe letters and other manuscripts at the University Archives reading room in the Pusey Library. James Capobianco searched the Howe archives at Harvard for essays by JWH. Michelle Wright, Chamisa Redmond, Kenneth Johnson, and Jasminn Winters helped me obtain materials at the Library of Congress. Thanks also to Molly Sothert-Maurer and Phuong Nguyen at the Samuel P. Hays Research Library at the Perkins School for the Blind. At the Maine Historical Society in Portland, Tiffany Link and Sofia Yalouris helped me with the Yellow House Papers, the family archives of Laura Howe Richards, which are now deposited there.

I owe a huge debt of gratitude to the Howe scholars who excavated these archives and blazed the trails before me—Mary H. Grant, Valarie Ziegler, and especially Gary Williams, whom I met in London at the very beginning of this project. Miki Pfeffer has been a fountain of information about Howe's time in New Orleans, and a Howe enthusiast and supporter in every way. Kate Stickley, a descendant of Julia Ward Howe through her daughter Florence Howe Hall, has created an indispensable online site to make Howe's writings accessible, and to digitize her journals. Helene Foley of Barnard College shared her work on productions of *Hippolytus* before it was published, and Marion Miller supplied information on nineteenth-century Boston residences.

Three wonderful literary agents have backed this biography from the inception. Elaine Markson in New York, whose warmth, friendship, and savvy sustained me for thirty years, brought it to Simon & Schuster. The urbane and erudite Derek Johns, at A.P. Watt in London, was especially enthusiastic about Chev and the philhellenes, and gave me wise counsel about telling the story of both the Howes. After Elaine's retirement, Geri Thoma graciously stepped in to advise, represent, and cheer me in the final stages of the book.

It has been a pleasure to work with the team at Simon & Schuster. Alice Mayhew has brought her legendary editorial expertise to presenting Julia's story. Stuart Roberts has helped me negotiate the process of publication with patience, clarity, and efficiency. Jessica Chin has been a lifesaving copyeditor.

And as always, my husband, English Showalter, has been travel companion, research partner, translator, editor, computer expert, and much, much more. English actually enjoys spending time in literary archives, deciphering illegible handwriting, and sorting through unidentified photographs. I have been blessed to have married him.

PHOTO CREDITS

1. "The Corner," home of Samuel Ward at the corner of Bond Street and Broadway (from *Julia Ward Howe 1819–1910*, vol. I).
2. Eliza Cutler Francis, "Auntie Francis" (The Yellow House Papers: The Laura E. Richards Collection, Gardiner Library Association and Maine Historical Society, Coll. 2085, RG34, F8).
3. Julia during her honeymoon (The Yellow House Papers: The Laura E. Richards Collection, Gardiner Library Association and Maine Historical Society, Coll. 2085, RG10, F6).
4. Samuel Gridley Howe, 1857. Courtesy of Perkins School for the Blind Archives.
5. Laura Bridgman as a young girl; bust by Sophia Peabody. Courtesy of Perkins School for the Blind Archives.
6. The Perkins Institution for the Blind, South Boston. Courtesy of Perkins School for the Blind Archives.
7. Chev teaching Laura Bridgman. Wikimedia Commons.
8. Laura Bridgman, 1845. Courtesy of Perkins School for the Blind Archives.
9. Green Peace (from *Julia Ward Howe 1819–1910*, vol. I).
10. Annie Ward Maillard (The Yellow House Papers: The Laura E. Richards Collection, Gardiner Library Association and Maine Historical Society, Coll. 2085, RG10, F9).

11. Louisa Ward Crawford, from miniature by Annie Hall (The Yellow House Papers: The Laura E. Richards Collection, Gardiner Library Association and Maine Historical Society, Coll. 2085, RG10, F6).
12. The "Hotel Rambouillet"; Cliff House, Newport, R.I.; summer of 1852. Left to right: Thomas G. Appleton, John G. Coster, Julia Ward Howe, Fanny Appleton Longfellow, Henry Wadsworth Longfellow, and Augusta Freeman, who had been Julia's friend in Rome. Courtesy of Perkins School for the Blind Archives.
13. Walt Whitman, July 1854, engraving by Samuel Hollyer, frontispiece of first edition of *Leaves of Grass*. Library of Congress, 07143u.
14. John Brown, 1856. Library of Congress, 3c06337u.
15. Charles Sumner. Library of Congress, 26559u.
16. The Howe children, 1869. From left to right: Julia Romana, Maud (in plaid dress), Harry, Flossy, and Laura (The Yellow House Papers: The Laura E. Richards Collection, Gardiner Library Association and Maine Historical Society, Coll. 2085, RG34, F5).
17. Michael Anagnos. Courtesy of Perkins School for the Blind Archives.
18. Chev, photographed by A. Marshall, 1870. Courtesy of Perkins School for the Blind Archives.
19. Julia Romana Howe Anagnos (The Yellow House Papers: The Laura E. Richards Collection, Gardiner Library Association and Maine Historical Society, Coll. 2085, RG34, F5).
20. Mary A. Livermore. Library of Congress, LC-USz62-73255.
21. John Elliott, by José Villegas Cordero. Wikimedia Commons.
22. Julia with Henry Shaw, granddaughter and daughter. The Yellow House Papers: The Laura E. Richards Collection, Gardiner Library Association and Maine Historical Society, Coll., 2085, RG34 F7.
23. Julia in embroidered jacket and Breton lace cap, photograph by J. E. Purdy, 1902. Library of Congress, LC-US Z62-46364.
24. Julia elected to American Academy of Arts and Letters, 1908, wearing two of her favorite rings. Library of Congress, LC-USZ62-53518.

INDEX

INDEX

INDEX

INDEX

INDEX

INDEX

INDEX

INDEX

INDEX

INDEX

INDEX

INDEX

ABOUT THE AUTHOR

Elaine Showalter is Professor Emerita of English and Avalon Professor of the Humanities at Princeton University. She is the author of nine books, most recently *A Jury of Her Peers; American Women Writers from Anne Bradstreet to Annie Proulx*, which was awarded the Truman Capote Prize for Literary Criticism. Showalter has written widely for such diverse publications as the *Guardian*, the *Times Literary Supplement*, *London Review of Books*, the *Washington Post*, *Los Angeles Times*, *Tate Etc.*, *Vogue*, and *People*. She has been a judge for the National Book Awards (US), the National Magazine Fiction Awards (US), and the Orange Prize for Women's Fiction (UK); and chaired the Man Booker International Fiction Prize in 2009. She is a Fellow of the Royal Society of Literature in London, where she has been a frequent speaker on radio and television.

She lives in Washington, D.C., and London with her husband, English Showalter. They have two children, Vinca LaFleur and Michael Showalter, and four grandchildren.